MARRIAGE

REVISED EDITION

Earl Lomon Koos

Florida State University

HENRY HOLT AND COMPANY   NEW YORK

To S. G. K.

Copyright © 1953, 1957
By Henry Holt and Company, Inc.
Library of Congress Card Catalog No.: 57-5723
25018-0217
Printed in the United States of America

Preface
to the Revised Edition

THIS REVISED EDITION is written primarily for the student who makes his first—and possibly only—excursion into that portion of the academic world which devotes itself to matters concerning marriage and the family. There is no intent in these pages to provide an elaborate treatise upon the family as an institution, nor to discuss its variations from one culture to another. Neither is there any intent to indicate that every marriage in the twentieth century is automatically confronted with a variety of problems which almost defy solution—for such is not the case. There is, rather, the intent to offer the student a textbook which will focus upon the opportunities and responsibilities—and only incidentally upon the problems—that are afforded those who marry in our society. This is *not* to say that the student is asked to view the study of marriage as a course in "sweetness and light"; he is asked, rather, to attempt a continuing *objective* view of what is necessarily a highly *subjective* phenomenon.

This edition is in many respects quite different from its predecessor. There is a more complete divorcement from the Ernest Grove's writing upon which the first edition drew in part, and more material is included in those sections which deal with the individual prior to his entering the dating and courtship stages of his life. The attempt is made, however, to distill from contemporary research such findings as will aid the student in building an adequate philosophy regarding marriage—by which we mean one which will permit him to capitalize upon its possibilities. To this end we have deliberately kept from repeating a multitude of research findings of vital concern to the professional worker, but of little interest to the student whose focus is not upon the science but rather upon the art of living in marriage.

The attempt, again, is to provide a highly "readable" book, for there seems no valid reason for a textbook in this area to be pedantic and stilted. To this end illustrations from case records and histories are included from a variety of sources.

The student who uses this textbook will not be an "authority" on marriage and family living when he has completed his course, and such is not the purpose of the book. It is hoped, however, that he will have been provoked to a sense of inquiry that will lead to a continuing search for reality in marriage, for that is the purpose in writing it.

E. L. K.

Tallahassee, Florida

February 1, 1957

A Note
to the Instructor

IN WRITING THIS book a number of points were kept in mind which should be known to the instructor using it as a text.

First: this book attempts to exploit no one point of view, nor to confine the student to one approach. It is neither exclusively Freudian nor excessively sociological. In consequence, it deliberately avoids an exhaustive discussion in many areas where such might be expected. It also avoids, insofar as possible, material which is more directly related to a course in *The Family*. It hopes, in so doing, to allow the instructor freedom to approach the subject matter as his predilections may dictate.

Second: it makes every effort to provide "points of entrance and exit," rather than to close the door on discussion. Few things, it appears, are more frustrating to students in the course in marriage than to be told that there are no alternative points of view.

Third: it has deliberately kept footnotes and technical presentations to a minimum, for the student's sake, but provides an expanded bibliography to which the inquisitive or advanced student can be referred.

Finally: it has made liberal use of quotations which serve to illustrate the points being made, but most of these have been chosen so that they may serve as *foci* for student discussion—and not a few as suggestions for socio-drama.

Contents

Why Study Marriage?

FIFTY YEARS AGO the young person approaching marriage and family experience found no college textbooks and no courses available on that subject. Today there are numerous textbooks, and such courses are standard offerings in colleges. The subject is also included in many high school programs, and countless informal lecture and discussion groups are held in communities of all sizes. Something must have happened to create this new emphasis and widespread interest. One of the answers to the question *Why Study Marriage?* is to be found in the changes that have been (and are) occurring in our society. An understanding of these will provide something of a framework for the discussions of marriage and family living which are to follow.

OUR CHANGING SOCIETY

The changes which have occurred in recent decades in American society are many and varied. Here we can consider only a few of the most important, and those which have a direct bearing upon how marriage and family life will be carried on.[1]

[1] For a thorough discussion of the statistical aspects of these changes, see Ogburn and Nimkoff, *Technology and the Changing Family.*

Industrialization

One of the very important changes in our society is that involving the way in which people get a living. An increasing portion of the families in our population lives by *earning* a living in industry or commerce rather than by *making* a living through agricultural pursuits.[2] The verbs used in the last sentence are important, since they indicate a fundamental difference in several aspects of life today as contrasted with that in the past.[3] The family which made its living off the land had some sense of security, in that it used the food it raised or bartered it for other necessities. In contrast, the family which earns a living is directly dependent upon the successful functioning of industry; if the pace of industry slackens, unemployment can result and the family may suffer. Students of this generation are too young to have experienced at first hand the effects of the depression of the 1930's, but for some years thousands of men who were willing and anxious to support their families were without a regular means of employment and were dependent upon some form of "made work" or upon outright grants of food, clothing, and shelter if they and their dependents were to survive.[4]

The family which made its living off the land tended to do so as an interrelated group. Life was a coordinated and integrated venture under these circumstances, and was very much family-centered. When the living is earned, it is usually one member of the family who goes outside the home and into the factory or market place, and his economic activities as a wage earner are therefore remote—if not completely divorced—from the home activities. Children, in the latter instance, drain rather than contribute to the family income; they are, as a result, something of an *economic liability* rather than an *economic asset*.

[2] We are indebted to Lawrence K. Frank for the important distinction between these two as discussed in his *Society as the Patient*.

[3] These differences are most sharply drawn between the agrarian and the industrial ways of life, but are also to be found in the increasingly different patterns of the older methods of industry as contrasted with those of recent years.

[4] For a study of important aspects of a depression, see Komarovsky's *The Unemployed Man and His Family*.

If our involved economic system is to function, it can do so only by producing quantities of goods. These goods must be sold, and to sell them considerable pressure (through one or another medium of advertising) must be exerted upon potential customers. In the case of goods used by the family, this pressure is created through developing a sense of need for new products or at least for new versions of the old. Consequently, the appeal to the family to discard the old and buy the new, or to add to its equipment items that formerly were unknown or at least not considered necessities, is great. The pressures are sometimes very subtle; one has only to study the advertisements in magazines devoted to the interests of homemakers to realize the truth of this statement. To say that the family has more money today and can therefore afford these items is only partially correct, for their cost tends to increase as fast as does the earning power of the average family.

One correlate of this effect upon married life is the extent to which married women now work outside the home.[5] There are other reasons for the wife's working outside the home, as we shall see, but very often there is a frank admission that the plane of living desired in the home could not be attained if the husband's income were not supplemented. This is true both for the young couple beginning married life and for those who have already partially reared their children. Two quotations from recent interviews illustrate this.

I'm not particularly happy to be working now that I'm married. It's not what I'd really like to do, or what I originally planned to do. But there are so many things we need that we won't be able to afford for a long time unless I do work. . . . I'm only going to work, though, until we get them, and then I'll stop and have my children.

I feel my place is at home with the children, but we can't get along as we want to unless I do work. . . . We have to get the children through high school and on their own, and we can't do it with prices the way they are today and the things we have to have,

[5] Current Bureau of the Census reports estimate that one-fourth of all married women worked outside the home in 1954.

unless I work, too. Neither my husband or I like the idea of my working, but what else can we do?

A more subtle but no less real impact of industrialization upon married life lies in its effect upon the wage-earning member(s).[6] The modern factory most often places an emphasis upon the worker's performing a relatively mechanical task over and over again. Such limited tasks rarely provide the worker with much satisfaction in his job, and little (other than money) is gained from the work experience. Just how this carries over into the human relationships of married living is not yet fully understood, but there is some evidence from case materials that it does have an effect. For example,

> When I come home at night [from the Ford assembly plant] I'm just about dragged out. It isn't just the amount of work I do, it's the grind of doing the same thing over and over again all of the time. I only make about twelve motions on each part I work on, but I do it from start to finish all day long. . . . I know I'm cranky a lot of the time with Bart and the kids just because I hate to face another day of doing it all over again. . . . It's a way to get a living, though, so how can I kick?

The unrewarding nature of modern industrial work contrasts, at least in some degree, with the highly individual and constantly changing tasks of the family which made its living. In the latter case, there was not only a sense of personal accomplishment, but a sharing in certain tasks—both of which made some contribution to family interaction. The unrewarding nature of factory work is, of course, tempered somewhat by the increased leisure time available; this will be considered in some detail in a later chapter.

It should be noted in this connection that families living on farms are not entirely exempt from the effects we have noted. Increasingly, the farm becomes an "agricultural factory" upon which one or two specialized crops are raised, largely with the use of machinery. The tendency, then, is to produce a crop and to

---

6 Some of these effects are concisely stated in Biesanz and Biesanz, *Modern Society*, Ch. 21.

planted the hand labor of the homemaker. The old kitche[n]
[h]as been replaced by a gleaming gadget (gas or electric[)]
[i]s replete with controls; the modern counterpart of the ol[d]
[washin]g machine is an automatic laundry which washes, rinses
[a]n dries the clothes—all for the pushing of a few buttons
[?] technical advances make homemaking an easier—an[d]
[plea]surer—task, but they also impose a greater burden upo[n]
[?]ly. The capital investment necessary for a "modern" hom[e]
[c]entury ago was small compared with that today. The [contem]
[p]orary household finds itself having to expend a con[siderable]
[?] portion of its income for the equipment it must have[.]
[T?]e of living is higher, to be sure, but at some added cost[.]
[?]d financial burden imposed by modern home technology [is especia]
[l]ly great for the newly married couple, since many items
[cons]idered "necessities" were either unknown or luxuries to [earlier gene]
[?]rations. This is described by a middle-class mother in [the follow]
[?]ing words:

[Whe]n we set up housekeeping, we needed very few things, and [they]
[di]dn't cost a great deal. Now my daughter is about to marry, [and wh]
[a]t they think they *must* have is frightening. They think they [can't po]
[?]ssibly get along without a vacuum cleaner, an electric stove, [a deep]
[?]r-refrigerator, a mixer, and a television set. They're going [to want]
[?] to have all of these things right from the start. . . . When [I thi]
[n]k about it, though, they do seem to have to have a lot of [t]
[?]hings we never knew about until we'd been married for [?]
[b]ut it is bound to make things more difficult—my daughter [wants ch]
[?]ildren but she's going to have to work a while until they [get some]
[?] of these things paid for.

[This c]hapter will set forth in some detail a few of the very [real dif]
[fi]culties which may be encountered as a result of this [gener]
[a]l change; for the moment we can accept it as part of [the changin]
[g] scene in which marriage occurs today.

[Migrati?]on

[Societies] differ from each other, and every society changes [fr]
[o]m one point in time to another. In some, the change

depend upon its sale for the cash with which to live. Increasing numbers of farm families fail to raise their own foodstuffs. As a result they are as dependent upon the pay check as are their urban neighbors. The opportunity and need for shared activities by the farm family in getting a living is therefore lessened. In the words of a young farm wife in Western Texas:

> My mother loaded hay, helped milk, fed the chickens, and did a lot of things with my father in making the farm go. . . . Now, Eugene and I live on the same farm, and I don't go near the barns. We don't even have a chicken on the place—we just raise wheat and soybeans. Our food all comes from town; I don't do any of the canning and preserving my mother did. . . . It isn't anything like it was when I was a child here.

While this young wife's statement may indicate an extreme situation, it does show the direction in which modern farm life is moving. It does not, unfortunately, show the extent to which farm as well as city people are exposed to the pressures already referred to.

Urbanization

In recent decades, and as an accompaniment of industrialization, there has been a pronounced growth in the proportion of the population living in and adjacent to cities. Today, more than half of the population of our country lives in urban places.[7] The impact of urban conditions upon married life has as yet had insufficient study, but some effects are readily apparent. Urban life tends, first of all, to diffuse the interests of the individual family members. The husband's work necessarily gives him one set of friendships and associations, the wife's another. When there are growing children, still other patterns of association are introduced. The family of the past found much of its interaction and many of its pleasures inside the home. The family of today,

[7] In 1950, more than 60 percent of the population was considered by the U. S. Bureau of the Census to be urban-dwelling, as contrasted with less than one-half that percentage one hundred years ago.

edspecially in the city, finds the interests of its members more specialized (and often commercialized), and tends to depend less upon the home and more upon outside associations for the satisfaction of its interests.

With this diffusion of interests has come an increasing anonymity in urban life. Death, illness, and other crises brought the old-time family many offers of help from neighbors; today the tendency in urban life is to depend upon one's own resources or to resort to professional assistance. It is not unusual, in fact, for urban dwellers not to know all the families living in the same block, and residents in apartments often admit that they do not know the people who live in the same building. All these suggest that the family is forced to depend upon its own resources, with the loss of the values that are present in those face-to-face relationships such as characterized rural living.

Mobility

Industrialization has had an important effect upon American family life in that it has caused large numbers of people to move from the country or village to the city, from city to city, and even from one region to another—as new jobs have become available.[8] Such shifts present the family with problems not characteristic of more stable populations. Removal from the home community makes contacts with relatives more difficult to maintain, and the feeling of "family-belonging" is likely to be lessened. Friendships are broken (or at least rendered less personal), and new ones must be established; associations with the church, the school, and other organizations must be broken and formed anew. The result, frequently, is to create tensions and frustrations for one or more of the family members.

Equally important, if the move is from one region of the country to another, is the need to exchange one set of traditions,

[8] Exact figures for this migration are not available, but the rapid growth of many states, and of communities within states so far exceeds any natural increase (an excess of births over deaths) that it is self-evident.

---

behavior patterns, and values for anothe
northern family which moves to the deep
way of life quite different from the old, and
confused by the change. This is well illus
quotation.

> We lived in a city in the North before
> husband's company sent him here to be
> their new plant, and it was a real step up
> likes his work, but we've had a terrib
> expected to do a lot of things we aren't
> the things we used to do are frowned o
> like to do just aren't available here, ei
> different, and there's very little in the
> cultural activities. People just think and
> John and I have had to depend mostly
> here, and we didn't do that as much
> we had no children who had to make

The effects of changing from one r
to be even more important where th
rural area and now must live in a
need to change is not only from one
the same time to adapt to new ways

Technological Change

This term is ordinarily applied
activities and suggests the introd
techniques in the factory. The hon
in equipment and techniques in
small machines been introduced
homemaking, but also many of
over by commercial interests. On
which foods are now available in
little activity in the kitchen. Fro
minutes of simple preparation,
addition of water (and which
"just right")—these are examp

---

has su
stove
which
washin
and ev

These
possibly
the fam
a half
contemp
siderable
The plan
The adde
is especia
now cons
past gene
the follow

Whe
they di
and wh
can't p
a freeze
in debt
you thir
these—t
years. B
wants ch
have all

A later
practical di
technologic
the changin

Secularizati

Societies
somewhat fr

is rapid and great; in others, it is slow and small. In the discussion to this point we have indicated that the changes are both rapid and great in our own society. Social change is not confined, however, to the material aspects of life. It also involves the ways of thinking and associating of people, both as individuals and as groups. This has been especially true in our own society, and there are profound implications for marriage and family life. The term "secularization" as used here implies the tendency of a society's members to accept change and to forego the controls which are characteristic of very stable and tradition-controlled societies.[9] In our society changes associated with this process of secularization have occurred, and these need to be kept in mind. All are inter-related and constitute parts of a very complex process.

Changes in control by religion. Statisticians report that more people belong to and attend church now than ever before. Even if this is true, the influence of religion in controlling human behavior has changed, if not lessened. No longer is "the devil breathing down your neck" the means of controlling human behavior that it once was. The threat of hell-fire-and-damnation has, for many religious groups, been replaced by a milder set of suggestions of "proper" forms of behavior. For example, smoking and dancing, once anathema to many denominations and con-sidered "first-class tickets to hell," are no longer considered the concern of most religious groups. Divorce, similarly, is accepted by many denominations which not so long ago were violently opposed to it.

Dependence upon the supernatural, through the medium of religious groups, for definitive patterns of behavior has therefore lessened for both the individual and the family in a large portion of our society.

Changes in control by public opinion. The opinion of one's fellow men regarding behavior is always important to some degree. Recent decades, however, have witnessed a lessening of

[9] For a detailed discussion of this point, see Howard Becker, "Interpreting Family Life in Context," in Becker and Hill, *Family, Marriage, and Parenthood.*

the control once exerted by "what the neighbors will think." As people are able to move in larger circles through use of the automobile, as their contacts with others are less limited to a particular neighborhood, there is less reason to be concerned with what other people will think. There is, in turn, greater freedom to act as an individual, with more dependence upon one's own judgment. This can be illustrated from an interview with the father of an eighteen-year-old.

> When I was a boy and had my first dates, it was with a girl in the neighborhood, of course. My parents knew hers, and everybody in the neighborhood knew both of us. We went to the movies or a band concert, and we were constantly in view of people whose opinions were important to us. You might almost say they held us in line. . . . Today my son takes the car and in ten minutes is away from anybody who knows him. We may not know the girl he is out with, or her parents, and there is no one where they go whose opinion about his behavior is important to him. He's strictly on his own.

Being "on his own" is by no means confined to a situation such as the one just described. This independence increasingly characterizes life in our society; the importance of the individual's own judgment replaces the importance of the group's thinking in determining behavior.

Changes in control by the family. The family as a multi-generation group (in which the attitudes and opinions of all generations and many degrees of relationship were important and integrated) has increasingly been replaced by a parent-and-child-only family (the family of procreation). As a result, the larger family no longer exerts the influence it once did in matters of mate selection, in the establishing of the home, and in the conduct of the affairs of the married couple. More and more the responsibility rests with married couples themselves, and the intrusion of advice from "the relatives" is often taken as an affront rather than as a help in the managing of marital affairs.

Science and human behavior. In the past few decades the horizons of scientific knowledge regarding human needs and behavior have been pushed back at a rapid rate. How the child comes to be a mature person, what the individual needs for the optimum of personal development, and the causes of personality failure have all been the subject of intensive study. As a result, great emphasis is placed upon the individual's being permitted to live and act in accord with his own drives and wishes. The "modern" mother exercises less control over her child, and he is allowed, if not urged, to express himself fully. This emphasis upon personal freedom extends into all levels of adulthood. While it is not yet characteristic of all groups in our society, the tendency is to emphasize "rational" behavior. Stated in other words, the growing emphasis in our society is upon the individual's being free to direct and be responsible for his own behavior, rather than to be subject to control by the family, the neighborhood, and other groups of which he is a member.

While these changes in the control of behavior have been un-even, in that they have occurred and are occurring at different rates in different parts of the country and among different groups, the total effect is one of significance. Norman Cousins has described what is happening in these words:

> The suspicion grows that the direct need that exists between men is deeply felt but only rarely observed in our time. Except for a disaster or other emergency, there is very little outlet in man for the natural longing of a human being to share fully and freely. *We have become masters of the impersonal and inanimate.* Our energy and even our emotions have gone into *things*; the things serve us but they come between us, changing the relationship of man to man. And the things take on an authority that men accept without protest.
>
> The impersonality is epidemic. It is almost as though we feared direct contact, almost as though the soul of man had become septic.
>
> If a man becomes ill, he hardly hangs up his hat in the doctor's office before he is placed before a whole battery of machines and testing devices. The traveled road is not between the mind of the diagnostician and the heart of the patient, but between the clinic and the laboratory. . . . If a man submits himself for a job, he is seen not as a personality but as a fit subject for various tests which presumably have more to do with ascertaining his worth than the human responses which may figure largely in the work he is called upon to do.

If a man builds a house, he no longer participates in a wonderful joint enterprise with neighbors but in a juggling contest with figures, and he may not see his neighbors from one year to the next. The house itself may be shiny and functional, but not a thing is known about the people who made it.

If a man wishes to help needy people he generally does it not on a man-to-man basis but through an agency; and his contribution becomes a statistic rather than a strand in a lifeline thrown out to a recognizable being.[10]

THE CHANGING PURPOSE OF MARRIAGE

The establishing of a family in earlier decades had very "practical" aspects. The individual married not only because it was expected, but also because of the very practical problems related to getting a living. The individual who did not marry was looked upon with suspicion, and the terms "old maid" and "bachelor" were applied with some scorn. The married couple had children for very *practical* economic reasons; on the farm the child very early had a place in the activities directed toward getting the living, and in the city he was something of an insurance policy against want when his parents could no longer work for themselves. There was undoubtedly companionship, and even love, in the marriage of the past, but the practical reasons were equally if sometimes not more important.

In recent years, as the character of our society has changed, these practical reasons for marrying have in good measure been relegated to a minor position. No longer is the unmarried woman looked upon with quite the same degree of scorn—in fact, the term "old maid" is no longer used so widely. Children are no longer an economic asset. Increasingly, "love" (however defined) becomes the motivating force which leads two people to marry, and affection for the child as an individual becomes the reason for bringing him into the world. Under these circumstances the family

10 From Norman Cousins' editorial, *The Saturday Review*, October 29, 1955. Used by permission of Mr. Cousins.

is an affection-bound group, rather than primarily an economic group, and its interaction takes on a new and quite different meaning.

THE IMPORTANCE OF THESE CHANGES

No one of the changes already noted is all-important in its challenge to the family. Collectively, however, they present a serious challenge to the couple entering the marriage relationship. When the individual married in earlier times, his path was fairly well set for him, both by his family and by the larger society in which he lived. He grew up in a community in which he was known and whose members exerted face-to-face influences upon him. Ordinarily, in childhood and adulthood he lived in the same community in which he had been born. His work may or may not have been satisfying, but it lacked some of the pressures suggested. Choosing a mate was not too complicated a process, for he married in part for the practical reasons mentioned, and these very often overshadowed any major concern about whether or not love was the central aspect of the relationship. Also, his family very likely had an important part in the choosing of his mate. Whether or not the marriage functioned smoothly was also not of primary importance, for the expectations of marriage were essentially practical, and the individual "put up with a bad bargain," if this was necessary, because it was expected and because there was no great emphasis upon divorce.

Today, in sharp contrast, the responsibility for mate selection rests very largely upon the individuals concerned, and many parents have at best only an advisory role. If the marriage is to succeed, that is, to afford the individuals the satisfactions they expect from it, the responsibility for this success rests squarely upon the shoulders of the participants. If it does not meet their needs, divorce is a relatively easy means of ending the union, and there is little stigma attached to the failure of the couple "to make a go of marriage." How many children the couple will have need no longer be a matter of biological chance (except for members of certain religious groups), but can be planned ahead.

At the same time, youth coming to maturity in the mid-twentieth century find their world essentially casual about marriage. The movies, the radio, television, the short story, and the novel all impute a casualness to the business of choosing a mate and succeeding in marriage. If one believes the average short story or movie scenario, choosing a mate or living together in marriage is something of an Arabian Nights fantasy. Boy meets girl, they look deeply into each other's eyes, they are struck dumb with love, they marry and—presumably—live happily ever after. And if they don't—well, a divorce can always be had.

The result is likely to be confusion for many individuals. Some marriages do end in divorce; others are forced to seek the help of counselors in order to continue; still others simply exist—without happiness for the individuals involved. It is safe to say that those who understand their own personality needs, who recognize what they need and can give in marriage, who realize the importance of considered mate selection, and who understand ahead of time what successful living in marriage will demand of them are less likely to have their marriages end in divorce, to need the help of an outsider, or to live out their lives in an unhappy relationship.

A POSITIVE ATTITUDE TOWARD MARRIAGE

The reader is cautioned against thinking that the changes and conditions discussed above necessarily make marriage an uncertain venture in our time. If the rising divorce rate is to be taken as evidence, then the marriages of today are more likely to fail than were those of earlier generations. It must be remembered, however, that most often the marriage which fails is the one into which the participants have stumbled blindly and without previous consideration of its opportunities and responsibilities—it is the marriage in which the participants have not faced the realities of their own and their mate's personality needs—it is the marriage in which there has been no will to make the relationship succeed.

This is not to say that the possession of college credits in a preparation-for-marriage course is *ipso facto* evidence that the individual will succeed in his marriage. It is to say that the student who is alerted to the responsibilities, the demands, and the opportunities in the marriage relation, and who is helped to see objectively what it is that he must give to marriage if it is to meet his and his mate's needs and expectations, stands a very good chance of realizing the satisfactions and the enriching experience that marriage can give. It is to this end that textbooks are written, that courses are given, and that students are encouraged to study the subject. It is, in other words, one major answer to the question with which this chapter began.

SUMMARY

Marriage in mid-twentieth century is quite different from that in past generations. The social order has changed, in that industrialization, urbanization, mobility, secularization, and so on, have all lessened the controls exerted by the larger society. Those who will marry, therefore, have a greater responsibility for their own decisions and actions.

At the same time there is a greater understanding of the psychological and social needs of the individual in marriage, and of what a person must bring to marriage if it is to succeed. The purpose of the succeeding chapters is to help the student to an understanding of this *relationship* into which he or she will enter when marriage takes place.

READINGS AND TOPICS FOR REPORTS

1. Read Karl Jungk's *Tomorrow Is Already Here* and discuss the ways in which the characteristics of our society as depicted in that book appear to affect modern marriage and family life.
2. Read James West's *Plainville, USA* and contrast the conditions of life in that community with those in the community from which

you come. How do these differ in relation to their effect upon family living and marriage?

3. Read a novel of family life written in 1910 and one written in 1950. Contrast the ways in which the "social environment" appears to have affected the lives of the two families.

4. Describe fully and analyze an American subculture such as the Amish in Lancaster County, Pennsylvania, and show how it is differentiated from your own.

5. Using representatives from rural areas and from large cities in your class, have a panel discussion indicating the very practical ways in which life is different for young married couples in the two types.

ADVANCED READINGS

Becker, Howard, "Processes of Secularization," *British Sociological Review*, 24:138 ff., 266 ff. (1932).

Redfield, Robert, *The Folk Culture of Yucatan*.

2

Marriage and the State

In our society marriage is a *civil contract* between the two parties and is subject to regulation and registration by the state. Marriage may also be subject to regulation and registration by a religious body—as in the case of the Roman Catholic Church, which regards marriage as a sacrament, that is, "as a visible sign instituted by Christ to confer grace or Divine Life upon those who are worthy to receive it." Protestants vary in their position, but in general hold the marriage to have religious significance—that is, they deny the sacramental character of marriage but consider it "a good and holy ordinance of God." In this chapter we are concerned only with marriage as a relationship regulated by the state.

The concept of states' rights, which was basic in the founding of our nation, included the state's right to set the requirements for both marriage and divorce. These requirements varied from state to state; they were—and are—in actual disagreement in some cases. Despite the changing attitudes toward marriage and the changing emphasis upon it, as outlined in the preceding chapter, the states continue to exert certain controls over those who wish to marry as well as those who wish to terminate a marriage. These controls are gradually being extended in some areas and modified in others, but in general they have not been changed greatly since they were first established.

THE REGULATION OF MARRIAGE CONTRACTS

A number of reasons exist for the state's setting requirements for those who desire to marry. The state, which fundamentally is the organization of the citizens for the guarding of the public welfare, has an interest in the family because of the functions ordinarily assigned to and assumed by it. The family continues to be the primary economic unit; it is the sanctioned group for the bearing and rearing of future members of society; it is the unit through which property is inherited; it is an important agency for indoctrinating the young with the values of the society; and it is still a major unit through which social controls are exercised. Since all these are vital to the public welfare, the regulation of marriage (as a safeguard for family life) is deemed a reasonable function of the state. It is impossible, however, to say that all the controls exerted are solely for the good of society as a whole; as we shall see, most of the regulations also have a humanitarian concern for the individual's welfare.

Age

Every state imposes certain restrictions regarding the minimum age at which individuals may marry (see Table 1). For those who marry without parental consent this is usually twenty-one years for males (forty-four states), and eighteen years for females (thirty six states). Where the parents' consent can be had, the minimum age for both sexes is somewhat lower (see Figure 1).

The reasons for such control are fairly obvious. The establishing of a family usually means the setting up of a new economic unit—if those who marry are too young to assume financial responsibilities, their families or other groups must assume them. The establishing of a new family means that the emotional respon-

TABLE 1. Some Legal Requirements for Marriage in the United States

State	Minimum Age Permitted[a]		Blood Test Required	Waiting Period Required[b]
	Male	Female		
Alabama	17	14	*	
Arizona	18	16		
Arkansas	18	16		*
California	18	16	*	
Colorado	16	16	*	
Connecticut	16	16	*	*
Delaware	18	16		
Florida	18	16	*	*
Georgia	17	14		*
Idaho	14	12	*	
Illinois	18	16	*	
Indiana	18	16	*	
Iowa	16	14	*	
Kansas	18	16		*
Kentucky	16	14	*	*
Louisiana	18	16		*
Maine	16	16	*	*
Maryland	18	16		*
Massachusetts	18	16	*	*
Michigan	18	16	*	*
Minnesota	18	16		*
Mississippi	14	12		*
Missouri	15	15	*	*
Montana	18	16		
Nebraska	18	16		
Nevada	18	16		
New Hampshire	14	13	*	*
New Jersey	14	12	*	*
New Mexico	18	16		
New York	16	14	*	*
North Carolina	16	16	*	*
North Dakota	18	15	*	
Ohio	18	16	*	*
Oklahoma	18	15	*	
Oregon	18	15	*	*
Pennsylvania	16	16	*	*
Rhode Island	18	16	*	*
South Carolina	18	14		*
South Dakota	18	15	*	
Tennessee	16	16	*	*
Texas	16	14		
Utah	16	14	*	
Vermont	18	16	*	*
Virginia	18	16	*	
Washington	14	12		*
West Virginia	18	16	*	*
Wisconsin	18	15	*	
Wyoming	18	16	*	

[a] With or without parental consent.
[b] Some states specify no waiting period, but the time required for the blood test serves as an equivalent.

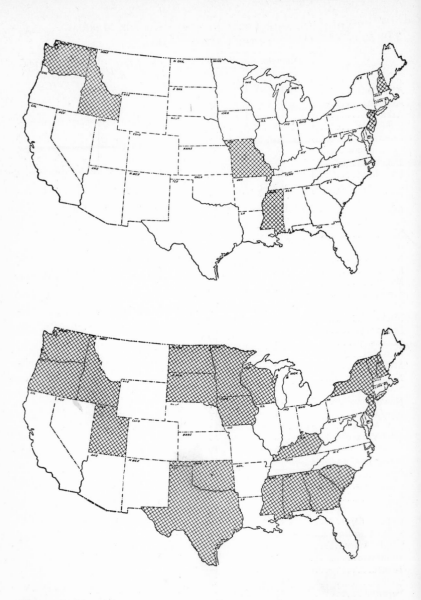

Figure 1. Youthful marriage is permitted in some states. The upper map shows the states in which boys *under 16 years of age may* marry with parental consent. The lower map shows the states in which girls of similar age may marry with parental consent. (The minimum in any state is 14 years for boys; 12 for girls.)

sibilities involved in living together in marriage must be shouldered —if those who marry are too young to have emotional maturity, there is increased chance that these responsibilities cannot be met. The establishing of a family very often results in an early pregnancy —if those who marry are too young, they may not be able to fulfill their physical and psychological obligations to the child. (The incidence of maternal and infant deaths, for example, is very high among girls who become mothers in their sixteenth year as compared with those who bear a first child in their twentieth year.)[1]

Interracial Marriage

Historically, certain races have been considered by dominant groups to be inferior to their own race. In our Western states the Chinese and Japanese have often been regarded as inferior; in the South the Negro has similarly been given an inferior status. The historical, economic, and social reasons for these attitudes are too well known to need elaboration here. Their result is important, however, in that many states prohibit the marriages of individuals from different races (see Figure 2). The intent, of course, is to preserve the "blood purity" of the dominant race, but there are other practical values in such legislation (whether originally intended or not), as we shall see in a later chapter.

Mental Disease and Feeble-mindedness

All states have legislation prohibiting a marriage in which one or both of the intended partners suffers from a mental disease, or is feeble-minded. In the former case, the regulation arises from the fact that marriage is a legal contract and people who are mentally ill are legally incapable of entering into contracts. For the feeble-minded, it is an attempt to prevent the procreation of mentally defective children. It must be admitted that in both cases these regulations are largely a matter of announced principle rather than

---

[1] It must be admitted that this increase in such deaths is due to two factors which are not easily separated. Many such births take place under very unfavorable circumstances, but equally important is the fact that very young mothers are often not biologically ready for the processes associated with pregnancy and natality.

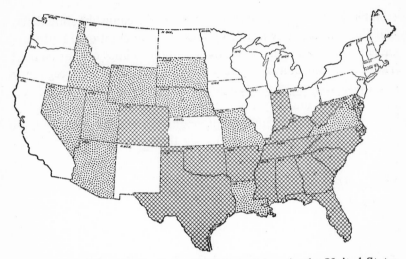

Figure 2. The prohibition of racial intermarriage in the United States.
Negro-white intermarriage is prohibited in the states indicated by cross
hatching; Negro-white *and* Mongolian-white intermarriage is prohibited in the states indicated by dotted shading.

active regulation. Few of the authorities who issue licenses to marry
make any real attempt to determine the sanity or mental competence of the individuals who apply for marriage licenses—in fact,
most of them appear to be quite casual about the whole matter.
It is also obvious that few, if any, of the individuals who apply for
a license to marry would admit their defects or deficiencies.

Degree of Relationship

In all states there is a prohibition of marriage between close
blood relatives, although the states differ markedly in their
definitions. Parent-child, grandparent-grandchild, brother-sister,
aunt-nephew, and uncle-niece marriages are regarded as in-
cestuous, and are, therefore, prohibited.[2] In more than one half
the states the marriage of first cousins is prohibited, and a few even
prohibit the marriage of second cousins.

2 Such prohibitions, where they deal with distant relationships have their basis less
in biological fact than in folklore.

These prohibitions have their basis in the incest taboos, which are found in all societies. They have, however, a practical biological aspect. Because close relatives tend to have similar genetic traits, their inbreeding is likely to perpetuate an undesirable hereditary trait. Highly desirable hereditary traits would also be perpetuated, but it is probable that these laws (which have been in existence since a time when little was known of inheritance patterns) were originally intended to protect the incest taboos rather than to encourage outbreeding. One evidence of this is in the fact that some prohibitions extend beyond any possible blood relationship.

Venereal Disease

The most recent restriction upon those who would marry involves the presence of venereal disease in one or both parties to the contract. Prior to 1935 only a few states had required an examination for venereal disease, and these for the male only. In 1935 Connecticut passed a law requiring both males and females to have a "blood test." Since that time thirty-two states have adopted the requirement of an examination for both parties, and two others (Texas and Louisiana) require an examination of the male only. Twenty-two states require a laboratory examination for syphilis only, and eight for both syphilis and gonorrhea.

The intent in such legislation is twofold. First, it is obviously for the detection of (and incidentally, to prevent the spread of) the venereal diseases among the adult population. Second, it has a long-range objective, in that it is one means of helping to prevent the far-reaching effects of later stages of syphilis (which can cause certain types of mental illness and other physical diseases) and, in the case of gonorrhea, it is of some assistance in preventing certain types of blindness in the newborn and of alerting individuals to the possibility of sterility. All these, of course, are measures in the interest of the public health.

Impetuous Marriage

The states have shown an increasing concern with the problem of hasty marriages. More than three fourths of the states have passed legislation which demands a period of time to elapse between the application for a license and the actual marriage. In twenty-two states the law requires a waiting period of from one to five days after application; in a few there is a specified period of time before the license can be used after it has been issued. In some there is no legal specification of a waiting period, but the law requiring an examination for venereal disease automatically delays the marriage because of the time required for a laboratory test. In most states these provisions can be set aside by certain public officials where undue hardship can be shown were the marriage to be postponed.

The waiting period serves, as did the banns of earlier times (still required in Roman Catholic parishes and locally by a few Protestant groups) to prevent marriages which "are proposed in haste to be repented at leisure." Such proposals are often made upon the briefest acquaintance or when one or both parties are intoxicated. That legislation designed to prevent hasty and ill-advised marriages is effective is seen in the fact that in every state a number of applicants fail to return for their licenses at the expiration of the waiting period.

The Method of Control

As was indicated, the actual method by which the state controls marriage is through the issuing of a license. In each community, specific officials are designated whose responsibility it is to issue and record licenses. The application for a license to marry does not constitute marriage, however; this step must be followed by a ceremony performed by one of several designated public officials or by a clergyman of recognized standing. The marriage becomes a matter of legal record only upon the report by that person of his action, and failure to file such a report has upon occasion caused confusion and legal difficulties in a few instances.

Twenty-one states, however, recognize the common-law marriage, in which no license has been issued and no ceremony performed, but in which the man and woman have lived together as husband and wife—usually for a period of seven years. Such marriages have been forbidden by the Roman Catholic Church since the middle of the sixteenth century and were abolished in England in 1753. They were recognized in our own country because of frontier conditions in which there were no designated authorities and no clergy available, and have been continued largely through inertia on the part of the legislatures. When such "marriages" have continued for the required period of time, the union has full validity in the law, both for the couple and their offspring. These "marriages" are rare today, and usually occur among the lower-income groups.

LEGAL EXPECTATIONS OF MARRIAGE

Every state has certain concepts of the responsibilities of the couple who marry. These are not necessarily set down in the law in so many words, but they are so firmly fixed in the beliefs and the behavior patterns of the people that laws are enacted to assure their acceptance—or to allow legal relief or redress if they are violated.[3]

Cohabitation

The couple who marry are expected by society to live together. If one partner refuses to abide by this expectation, the "innocent" partner is permitted by law to seek redress—through legal separation or divorce.[4] The place in which they shall live together is

---

[3] These expectations appear to be inherent in the thinking of all states even though there is no recourse to divorce provided in some states. New York State, for example, appears to expect the couple to fulfill these expectations, but will view only a violation of the "sexual fidelity" expectation as a reason for divorce.

[4] See discussion of differences between divorce and separation which follows later in the chapter.

ordinarily considered to be that selected by the husband, although the wife is legally entitled to a voice in that selection where health factors are involved or where there is a reasonable question of the suitability of the location chosen by the husband.

Sexual Access

The couple who marry are expected by society to live together in the traditional sense of "man and wife." If one or the other refuses sexual relations, this act is considered by the courts to be a form of desertion, and redress through legal separation or divorce may be had by the injured party.

Sexual Fidelity

Inherent in the Christian tradition, and carried into the law of all states, is the prescription that the husband and wife shall be sexually faithful to each other. In only one state is sexual *infidelity* the *only* cause for divorce, but the courts of all states will grant either a divorce or separation if one partner can be shown to have been sexually unfaithful to the other.

Conjugal Kindness

Marriage is considered by the states to be a relationship in which each partner gives emotional and physical support to the other—if in no other way than by abstaining from physical and mental abuse. Conjugal kindness, then, is the expectation which is violated by cruelty, violence, indignities, or other abuse. Only six states do not specifically list cruelty as grounds for terminating a marriage by divorce, and these allow separation for this reason. In actual practice, violation of the conjugal-kindness expectation is very broadly interpreted by many courts, especially in those states with a liberal attitude toward divorce. The "silly" reasons sometimes given for seeking a divorce and reported in the daily press—for example, the plaintiff's report that her husband's red hair "drove her crazy" and hence constituted cruelty—are usually accepted under this category.

Role Expectations

Traditional in our society is the idea that the husband will be the breadwinner and the wife the homemaker. Traditional, too, is the state's expectation that these roles will be accepted and performed. As we shall see in a later chapter, these roles are being modified today in that husband and wife sometimes share one or both in varying degree. Where the husband *refuses* to support his wife or she to perform her duties as homemaker, the courts will most often interpret such behavior as adequate grounds for the termination of the marriage in one way or another.

For each of these expectations there is wide variation in interpretation and execution by the courts. Whether or not they are formally listed in the law is not important, for judges necessarily have relative freedom in interpreting the written law as it applies to the termination of a marriage. The following section will indicate the ways in which the courts offer redress to the "injured" person.

THE TERMINATION OF MARRIAGE

We have noted that all states recognize that not every marriage will succeed, and for a variety of reasons. There are important variations, however, in the ways in which a couple may be relieved of the obligations or expectations just discussed.

Annulment

One way in which marriage is terminated is through annulment. In such cases the court in effect declares that the marriage *has never legally existed* and the individuals concerned are therefore not held to the legal expectations just discussed. An annulment is granted for conditions which existed *at the time of or before the wedding*—not for any condition arising after the wedding. It is intended as a legal protection where there has been deception as to age or previous marital status, where the innocent partner has not been told of an existing pregnancy, where sterility is known but not admitted, where the wedding has been performed while the innocent party was intoxicated, and so on.

Since annulment declares a marriage null and void, property and inheritance rights do not follow the usual pattern. The states have established special safeguards where undue hardship would result from an annulment, but there is no uniform policy in such cases, and their discussion is beyond the scope of the present chapter.[5]

Separation

A second way in which the state terminates a marriage is through legal separation. Many separations are informal, that is, they are simply private agreements which have no legal sanction and can be revoked or changed at any time. Legal separations, in contrast, are duly entered in a court of record, and the stipulations and agreements arrived at must be adhered to unless the permission of the court is given for a change. Any property involved is disposed of or assigned by contract in such cases, and the couple are no longer permitted to live together. Neither are they free to remarry. There are great variations among the states in the procedures and provisions relating to legal separation, and their discussion is not pertinent to our subject matter.[6]

Divorce

The third way in which the state terminates a marriage is through divorce. Here the court in effect states that the marriage *has*

[5] The student is referred to the laws of his own state as currently interpreted for a further discussion of this point.

[6] It is suggested that any detailed discussion of this point be carried on with a local lawyer as a resource person. Not only do the laws differ from state to state, but the interpretations of the laws vary from court to court in terms of the judge's own philosophy. For example, in one community known to the writer, lawyers will do almost anything within reason to keep their separation cases from being heard by one judge because of the peculiar way in which he interprets the law.

existed but no longer exists. The individuals are freed from the expectations of cohabitation, sexual access, and sexual fidelity, and are free to remarry. The husband may be required, however, to continue the support of his wife through payment of alimony even though he remarries. No uniformity exists among the states as to the grounds upon which a divorce may be secured, nor is there uniformity in the provisions for alimony or property settlements. Table 2 shows the wide variation in the allowable grounds for divorce. New York, for example, recognizes only adultery, while some states recognize as many as ten different grounds. As recently as 1948, one state (South Carolina) did not permit divorce for any reason; it now allows divorce for adultery, physical cruelty, desertion, and drunkenness.

The legal philosophy regarding the termination of a marriage by divorce demands that the innocent party must bring the action and must prove through legal evidence that the other party is guilty. No collusion can be admitted, and, in theory, the innocent party can admit to no wrong in the relationship. In actual practice, many divorce hearings are a farce; the judge may be fully aware that both parties desire the divorce, the grounds upon which the suit is filed may be fictitious, and the evidence may be manufactured out of whole cloth. This is one of the areas in American jurisprudence where laws and court procedures lag seriously behind the needs of the society which they are intended to serve.

The personal aspects of divorce are a quite different dimension of the whole problem of terminating marriage. These will be considered in a later chapter. This brief discussion is intended only to indicate in general the ways in which the state exerts a control over the continuation of marriage.[7]

---

[7] For thorough discussions of the several legal aspects of the problem of divorce, the reader is referred to the several pertinent issues of *Law and Contemporary Problems.* See especially the issues: Summer, 1944; Winter, 1953.

TABLE 2.   GROUNDS FOR DIVORCE IN THE UNITED STATES

Grounds[a]	Number of States
Adultery	48
Desertion	45
Cruelty	42
Alcoholism	40
Impotency	34
Felony Conviction	31
Neglect to Provide	29
Mental Illness	27
Separation	17
Imprisonment	17
Pregnancy at Marriage	14
Bigamy	14
Indignities	10
Violence	10
Drug Addiction	8
Misrepresentation in Marriage Contract	8
Infamous Crime	7
Relationship Within Prohibited Degree	4
Previous Felony	3
Loathsome Disease	2

[a] Each state has numerous qualifications which apply in specific instances. For details regarding the grounds in any one state, see The Council of State Governments: *The Book of the States, 1954-55.*

SUMMARY

The importance of the family as an economic and social unit in our society requires that the state exert certain controls both at the inception of family life and when it is to be terminated through socially acceptable means. To this end, requirements regarding minimum age, interracial marriage, mental status, degree of relationship allowed, the presence of venereal disease, and haste in marriage have been established. While these vary sharply from state to state, their underlying purpose is the protection of the individual and of the common welfare.

The state has certain expectations of marriage (cohabitation, sexual access, sexual fidelity, conjugal kindness, and certain role performances). Where these expectations are not met, the innocent party has a right to apply to the state for termination of the marriage. This termination may take the form of annulment, separation, or divorce. Each of these is designed to meet certain needs, and each varies widely from state to state.

READINGS AND TOPICS FOR REPORTS

1. Invite the judge who presides over marital discord cases in your community to meet with the class and discuss the legal aspects of both marriage and divorce with him.
2. Study the marriage license statistics of your community for the past five years. What proportion of the marriages have been among individuals so young as to require parental consent? What proportion of the licenses issued have never been used? Is there any evidence that your community is used to an exceptional degree by people from other communities as a "Gretna Green"? If so, what are the reasons for such use?
3. Invite a Protestant minister and a Roman Catholic priest to appear before the class to present the basic stand of Protestantism and Roman Catholicism regarding divorce.
4. By constructing a spot map of the location of residence of all couples who secured divorces in your community in the past several years, determine whether divorce is (1) relatively rare among the poorest members of the community, (2) relatively rare among certain ethnic and nationality groups, and (3) relatively confined to the urban population.
5. Many judges believe that alimony should not be granted. (Alimony is not to be confused with payments for the care of children.) Submit as a class a simple set of questions to the judges of your state who handle divorce cases to ascertain differences of opinion in this matter.
6. Compare the divorce legislation of your own state (by studying the pertinent statutes) and compare it with the proposed uniform divorce law (which may be obtained from the Clerk of the United States

Senate, Washington, D.C. In what significant ways does your state's legal stipulation differ from that of the proposed law.

ADVANCED READINGS

Law and Contemporary Problems (all issues pertaining to the problems related to divorce legislation).

Vernier, Chester G., *American Family Laws*, Vols. 1-5.

3

Physical Qualifications for Marriage

IT IS PROBABLY quite usual for those who intend to marry to speculate on the possible consequences of joining their germ plasms—although not in those words. This may be a superficial speculation, to be sure: "Will our children have my nose? Will they be short like me or tall like John?" Whether superficial or not, we have the right—and the responsibility—to be concerned about the possible consequences of bringing two people with differing physical characteristics together in marriage.

UNFAVORABLE CHARACTERISTICS

Each cell in the body contains chromosomes which are really chains of small units called genes. One set of chromosomes is contributed to the child by the father, an equivalent set by the mother. This joining occurs when the sperm fertilizes the ovum. Each gene determines one or more body characteristics, and each such characteristic is either dominant or recessive. If dominant, it means that in combining with the gene of the opposite sex, its characteristic will always occur. Thus, the gene determining black hair, when combined with the gene determining blond hair, will always cause the individual to have black hair.[1] If the genes of husband and wife were identical, all offspring would of course be carbon copies of their parents and would be identical. The only chance for the latter to occur is in the case of identical twins, and these are alike because they have developed from one ovum fertilized by one sperm (see Chapter 12).

The concern of the individual who expects to marry is primarily with possible defects of a serious nature. If the male child will inherit a tendency toward baldness, it is of little concern—for many baldheaded men have made their mark in the world. If, in contrast, the child's chances of inheriting a strong tendency toward—or a real—defect that will handicap him through life, it is a matter of importance, and it should be given serious consideration.

It would help greatly if the geneticists were able to offer concrete evidence with which to evaluate the contributions each prospective parent will make to his offspring. This is impossible, for other factors enter the picture. Three generations of fathers in one family may have died of tuberculosis, but this is no proof that tuberculosis will be inherited by the great-grandson. All three may have had contacts from which they received the infection—all three may have lived in an environment which offered fruitful ground for the tubercle bacillus. The harsh (and at the same time comforting) fact is that inheritance can seldom be shown to be clear-cut; it apparently most often contributes only a weakness in the organs or a susceptibility to a disease rather than the disease itself.[2]

This is obviously not a definitive answer to the question of what can be inherited, but it can be of help, particularly when coupled

---

[1] This is an oversimplification, but adequate for our discussion. For a more complete treatment of the subject see Edith L. Potter, *Fundamentals of Human Reproduction*. For a fascinating and nontechnical discussion of the whole matter of human heredity, see Amram Scheinfeld's *The New You and Heredity*.

[2] There are, however, a few diseases which are definitely transmitted *via* the genes.

with certain rational considerations. The individual needs to consider as objectively as possible the chance of "black" genes[3] being
present in the hereditary past of the prospective mate as in one's
own past. Two wrongs never make a right; neither do two recessive
(and therefore hidden) characteristics of the same kind make a
good heritage for the next generation. Such objective considerations are not easy when one is in love, but blindness and obtuseness
are hardly requisites for intelligent mate selection. If, to use an
extreme example, one falls in love with a girl whose family history
"features" Huntington's chorea (one of the most terrible of all
known "black" genes), which is dominant and causes complete
disintegration of the neuromuscular system,[4] he has every reason
to retreat from such an alliance. But this may be easier to say than
to do. "Love conquers all," in some cases, and the couple may feel
the need to put their need for each other above all else. In this
case, as Scheinfeld puts it,

> If children are not important to you, the situation can resolve
> itself easily. But if having children is a primary objective, you may
> have to weigh the "black" gene [those responsible for some harmful
> or detrimental condition] odds against your affections—even to the
> point, where the risk is menacing, of considering marriage to some-
> one else. However, in only a small proportion of cases (among them,
> sometimes, those involving first cousins) need such a predicament
> arise. Generally, where the risk is not too great, you are justified in
> being swayed by the advantageous prospects of the marriage.[5]

Such a decision, of course, requires the couple's acceptance of
contraception as a fundamental part of their behavior in marriage
—and rigid adherence to its demands.

The persistence in a family's history of a condition such as
diabetes or cancer—which suggests some ill-defined hereditary
weakness—need not prevent marriage but should serve to alert the
couple to constant vigilance after marriage. This leads to a further
consideration—What physical disabilities now present will the

---

[3] This is Scheinfeld's general term for those genes which are known to transmit the
dangerous or undesirable inheritable characteristics.
[4] *Cf.* Scheinfeld's *The New You and Heredity*, pp. 154 ff.
[5] *Ibid.*, p. 221.

prospective partners be willing to accept in each other? The traditional marriage ritual requires the husband and wife to cherish
each other "in sickness and in health . . . until death do us part."
It is, however, one thing to see the girl of one's dreams as "deli-
cate" and in need of constant loving care; it may be something
quite different to face a life together with her inabilities preventing
normal activities. This is well illustrated in the following quotations
from an interview.

> I was intrigued with her being frail and not able to do a good
> many things before we were married . . . . Oh, her condition is
> genuine enough—it's what they call a "rheumatic heart"—but it
> wasn't as bad then as it is now. . . . I do love her, but I'm not sure
> that we should have married. She can't help but be demanding, and
> after I've been away all day at work, I hate to come home and start
> all over again. We can't live a normal life—we don't do any of the
> things other people do—we just exist. Life is too limited this way for
> either of us. If I had foreseen the kind of slavery we'd each be living
> in, I think I would never have allowed myself to go on when I began
> to fall in love with her.

To marry in health and then have one's partner suffer from acute
or chronic illness is an eventuality everyone must be prepared to
face; to marry with illness already present, and with its future
effects unpredictable, is something quite different. While it is true
that marriage can be successful under these circumstances, it is
also true that such success requires an exceptional quality of
devotion. Where continued poor health appears to be the lot of
one or the other, the prospective mates need especially to evaluate
their emotional satisfaction in and love for each other. It is
obviously far better, under circumstances where there is any such
question, to refrain from an alliance than to spend the later years
regretting the conditions under which the marriage continues.

The Rhesus (Rh) Factor and Mate Selection

Much publicity has been given to the Rh factor (so called because
it was first found in Rhesus monkeys) as a cause of infant deaths.[6]

---

[6] As a cause of infant mortality, the Rh-factor is relatively unimportant. Its discussion here is warranted, however, for its importance as a personal matter in the
lives of husbands and wives.

Since the factor is directly related to inheritance, it is of some interest to us here. The Rh factor does not prevent pregnancy, nor is it related to sterility. Under certain circumstances, however, the result of its presence is a disease called *fetal erythroblastosis*, in which red blood cells are destroyed and the child is either stillborn or dies shortly after birth.[7]

There is still much to be learned about the Rh factor, and what is known is far too complicated to be given in detail here. This discussion will give the student a general idea of the way in which the Rh factor affects pregnancy; it is sufficient for all practical purposes.[8]

If the individual has the Rh factor in his blood, he is termed an Rh-positive. If he does not, he is Rh-negative. This factor is a dominant, that is, its presence in one parent will always cause it to be present in the offspring (see Figure 3). He can be Rh-negative only if both parents are Rh-negative.[9] In the total white population about 85 percent of all individuals are Rh-positive, but these can have either two Rh-positive genes or one Rh-positive and one Rh-negative gene, depending upon the characteristics of their parents.[10]

Most authorities believe that the greatest difficulty in this connection is in the group of pregnancies where the father is Rh-positive (but with one gene Rh-positive and the other Rh-negative), the mother is Rh-negative, and the child Rh-positive.[11] This combination occurs, however, in less than 10 percent of all pregnancies. *If* blood cells from the fetus find their way into the blood stream of the mother (and since there is no direct connection

---

[7] Erythroblastosis is often considered by laymen to be the cause of spontaneous abortion (the spontaneous delivery of the foetus before it is fully developed), but obstetrical authorities tend increasingly to reject this theory.

[8] A full and highly technical discussion of the Rh-factor can be had in Edith L. Potter's *Rh: Its Relation to Congenital Hemolytic Disease.*

[9] *Ibid.*, pp. 65 ff.

[10] *Ibid.*, pp. 86 ff.

[11] It should be kept in mind that with the number of combinations possible, as shown in Figure 3, this 50 percent of the pregnancies resulting from these genetic patterns in the parents will be a very small percentage of all pregnancies.

Figure 3. Schematic representation of the inheritance of the Rh factor.

Father	Mother		
	Rh-positive		
	Homozygous— both genes Rh-positive	Heterozygous— only one gene Rh-positive	Rh-negative both genes Rh-negative
Rh-positive Homozygous— both genes are Rh-positive	All offspring Rh-positive	All offspring Rh-positive	All offspring Rh-positive
Heterozygous— only one gene is Rh-positive	All offspring Rh-positive	75 percent of off-spring Rh-positive; 25 percent Rh-negative	**50 percent of off-spring Rh-posi-tive*** 50 percent of off-spring Rh-negative
Rh-negative— both genes Rh-negative	All offspring Rh-positive	75 percent of off-spring Rh-posi-tive; 25 percent Rh-negative	All offspring Rh-negative

* See Footnote 11, page 37.

between the two blood streams,[12] this is accidental, her system will immediately begin to produce substances which destroy such cells.[13] *If* these substances (called antibodies) find their way back (again, accidentally) into the blood stream of the fetus, they will destroy its Rh-positive cells, and the fetus will either die *in utero* or shortly after birth. But the *if*'s are important here. Only *if* the fetus is Rh-positive and its mother Rh-negative, only *if* the child's Rh-positive blood gets into the mother's Rh-negative blood, only *if* a sufficient concentration of antibodies is formed in the mother's blood, and only *if* these find their way back into the fetal blood

[12] See Chapter 12.
[13] The mother's system can also produce these substances—quite apart from pregnancy—if she is Rh-negative and has been given a transfusion of Rh-positive blood.

stream—only in these circumstances is the fetus vulnerable to erythroblastosis.[14]

The chance of a couple's dissimilarity in the Rh-factor affecting their offspring is therefore not nearly as important as publicity or hear-say would indicate. (Also, the newborn child can now be treated, one way being to transfuse Rh-negative blood into its system.) If the couple have questions in this connection, they can easily have blood typings done, and any competent obstetrician, after receiving their histories, will be able to advise on the prospects of having successful pregnancies.

THE PREMARITAL PHYSICAL EXAMINATION

The idea that the prospective husband and wife should have premarital physical examinations has had increasing acceptance in recent years. The acceptance of such an idea is relatively easy, since in so many states some physical evaluation is mandatory. Such an examination is not required until a few days before marriage, however, and is concerned only with the presence of the spirochete (the organism causing syphilis) in the blood. This examination has little value in determining the physical fitness of the prospective mates.

The complete physical examination has a number of functions. First, if carried out in detail, it will serve to inform the woman of a number of conditions which may inhibit her adjustment in marriage. The physician will be able to alert her to possible difficulties in her initial sexual experiences—for example, the presence of an abnormal hymen; he will be able to indicate the need for adjustments of the uterus as it relates to other organs—which, if not corrected, can make conception difficult. He will also be able to forecast her ability to bear children by determining the topography of the pelvic basin. If he is thorough in his examination, he will

---

[14] Erythroblastosis is relatively rare in first pregnancies even though genetic conditions are favorable, probably because the mother's blood has as yet not developed sufficient antibodies to affect the foetus. Subsequent pregnancies are more likely to be affected.

also give her notice of heart or other conditions which may later cause difficulty. (In the last, of course, this is no different from any routine health examination.) Second, the man will not only be alerted to conditions which may affect his general health, but a thorough examination of the genital tract (perhaps even including an evaluation of the sperm content) will indicate possible difficulties. Third, the physical examination affords both man and woman an opportunity to have questions regarding sexual relations answered under quite impersonal circumstances. Whether this is done in a joint conference after the physical examinations or individually is not important, but most couples do have some questions (and some misinterpretation) which need to be aired. Finally, the premarital physical examination affords the couple a chance to learn more about contraception—if it is to be used in marriage.[15]

To be effective, the physical examination should not be postponed until a few days or weeks before marriage. By that time, the couple's emotional involvement has progressed to the point where breaking off the relationship (in those infrequent cases where an anomaly or illness is uncovered) seems almost an impossibility, and the social stigma of such a break militates against it. If, in contrast, the individuals have had thorough physical examinations earlier in courtship, and a significant condition has been discovered, there is time for remedial action—or for adjustment to the new situation where it cannot be remedied. An example of the positive value of such an examination is seen in the following quotation.

> We had no idea anything was wrong with either of us, and saw Dr. —— only because our minister had advised it in a course he gave at the church to our young people's club. . . . The doctor found that I have what he called an "infant's uterus," and told us afterward that I will probably never be able to have a child. I knew all along that

15 A matter of medical ethics is involved in this latter function of the premarital examination. Many physicians are unwilling to prescribe contraceptive methods prior to the marriage of the couple; the physician's attitude on this point should therefore be determined at the inception of the interview.

something wasn't right there, but there wasn't any reason to see a doctor. . . . Now we've had to face the truth—that what we wanted most in life we can't have—at least not unless we adopt them. . . . It's awful to know this, but at least we've been able to talk it over and make our decision. . . . We're going to be married, and will adopt our children.

SUMMARY

The frequency or statistical importance of defects which may be transmitted to offspring in marriage is relatively small. Because of the importance of the questions which couples may raise regarding their own genetic characteristics, however, the whole matter assumes a relatively important place in the whole discussion of preparation for marriage. Important as inheritable characteristics may be in the exceptional case, the couple may well consider marriage if due attention is paid to the prevention of conception.

Of greatest concern to young couples today is the possibility that they are unsuited for mating as regards the Rh factor. This factor has in recent years received considerable publicity, some of it unfounded, and much of it unwarranted. As we have seen in the preceding discussion, the chance of the Rh factor's affecting the offspring in a given marriage can be determined within reasonable limits. We have also seen that the frequency of the resulting blood condition (erythroblastosis) is not great.

The complete physical examination, when given by a competent physician and in the early stages of serious courtship, serves not only to reassure the couple regarding defects which *might* be inherited in a given marriage, but also affords the couple the opportunity to understand more thoroughly the nature of their future sexual relations and to aid them in planning for such child-spacing measures as they believe indicated at the start of marriage.

READINGS AND TOPICS FOR REPORTS

1. Using a standard college textbook on genetics, list the conditions which you would include under Scheinfeld's heading "black genes";

compare your list with those of other members of the class, and discuss the reasons for the differences in the makeup of the several lists.

2. Mary's grandmother, mother, and two of three maternal aunts have all been operated upon for cancer of the reproductive organs. After an examination of the literature, discuss the arguments *pro* and *con* for Mary's marrying (in so far as this factor is concerned). Outline, in view of this history, the steps that Mary and her husband should take after marriage *if* they marry in spite of the presence in her family of this disease.

3. Do the same with John's problem, which differs in that the illness is diabetes, and that his great-grandfather, grandfather, and father have all suffered from the disease. (Note: the literature on diabetes is quite different from that on cancer in this respect.)

ADVANCED READINGS

Gilbert, Margaret S., *Biography of the Unborn.*
Scheinfeld, Amram, *Women and Men.*
——, *The New You and Heredity.*

4

The Psychological Qualifications for Marriage

IN CHAPTER 1 it was noted that the marriage relationship is increasingly one in which individuals attempt to meet their own needs and expectations rather than fulfill the expectations of outsiders. The responsibility for success is largely that of the persons involved. Consequently, a successful marriage must be based not only upon an understanding of what each partner is, but also upon how each developed to his present adult status. The need then arises for an eclectic approach—that is, for one which synthesizes the beliefs of the several behavioral disciplines—for it is extremely doubtful that any one of the behavioral sciences has either all or the final explanations of why human beings behave as they do. The followers of Freud would confine the explanations of human development and behavior to the principles of dynamic psychology;[1] the sociologist would explain them in terms of group relationships;[2] the cultural anthropologist would

[1] Cf., for example, J. C. Flügel, *The Psychoanalytic Study of the Family*.
[2] Cf., for example, James H. S. Bossard, *Parent and Child*.

load his explanations with an emphasis upon the culture's pre- and pro-scriptions of behavior,[3] and so on. All of these sciences are still pushing back the frontiers of knowledge about man, and the day has not yet arrived when any but the die-hard disciple can confine his explanations to a narrowly limited point of view.

In this and in the following chapters we shall examine the developmental processes of the individual while he is in his family of *orientation* (see Figure 4).[4] The emphasis in the chapters dealing with situations after the ceremony will be upon the individual in his family of *procreation*. In the present chapter, concern is with the individual as infant, child, and adolescent—each of which will be discussed in turn.

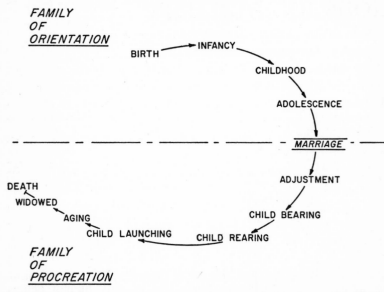

Figure 4. The stages in the life cycle of the individual as related to his position in the family of orientation and of procreation. Experience in the former prepares him for the experiences he will have in the latter.

[3] *Cf.*, for example, Margaret Mead, *Coming of Age in Samoa.*

[4] This is not to suggest that the human personality is fixed and unchangeable by the time marriage occurs, but that the greater development takes place in the more plastic period of early life.

THE DEVELOPMENT OF THE INDIVIDUAL

The old statement that "the child is father of the man" can very well be translated into "what we are as children determines what we will become as adults." This is not to say that environment in later years has no effect upon our behavior as adults, but rather to emphasize the importance of the early experiences of the individual as they affect his later relationships.

Broadly speaking, the individual lives in three "worlds." Each of these has very special characteristics; each has special functions in aiding the individual to become an adult. The first, the "family world," is an affection-centered group sanctioned by society, and constituting (in his first years) almost the total environment of the child. It is in this group, and especially through contacts with his mother, that the infant normally gains most of his satisfaction and experience. The second, the "peer world," is that group consisting of his equals, in which he plays, studies, and works and which constantly changes as he grows and associates with first one group and then another. The third, the "institutional world," consists of those associations (church, school, clubs, and so on) which are usually manned by adults and which play special parts in the drama of his growth.

These three worlds are to some extent independent of each other in the contributions they make to the child's development. They are, in some instances, in actual conflict with each other—for example, where family and peer group have quite opposite expectations of the child and he must decide which he will attempt to meet. In general it may be said that the child's development is aided and abetted to the extent that these three worlds are integrated into a smoothly functioning whole.

Maturation and Socialization

The child undergoes two major processes as his life unfolds. One of these is essentially biological and consists of the physical development which normally occurs. The child is unable to stand alone at birth, if for no other reason than that his muscles and bones are physically unable to support him in an erect position and that his nervous system has not matured to the point where he can balance himself. The biological growth process enabling him to stand alone is termed "*maturation.*"[5]

The second necessary process is that of *socialization*, in which the individual *learns* to behave, to think, and to believe as his fellows do. Socialization obviously cannot occur if maturation is not going on at the same time. Ongoing maturation enables the child increasingly to accept socialization, and in turn, socialization encourages maturation. This reciprocal relation is seen, for example, in the small child's learning to walk. The maturing of bones, muscles, and reflexes permits the child to accept his elders' teaching him to walk, whereupon his increasing efforts to walk further strengthen his muscles and sharpen his reflexes so that he moves from toddling to walking to running with increasing skill.

The rates at which these two processes take place vary in one individual from one stage of life to another, and, more important, from one individual to another. For example, the child grows very rapidly in the first two or three years of life (attaining approximately half of his height in the first two years), and then appears to "rest" until the spurt in growth just prior to adolescence, when he enters the "gangling" stage. Similarly, one child may attain the physical signs of puberty at eleven years, while another does not reach the same point of development for another two or three years. The same differences will also be found in the times when children begin certain social relationships, as in the case of dating. These social differences will be discussed in a later section.

Emotional Development

Whether or not one subscribes to the more extreme doctrines of analytical psychology, it must be recognized that while maturation

---

[5] This process of maturing is essentially one in which the potentials of nerve, muscle, and bone are realized.

and socialization are occurring, the child is also undergoing certain emotional developments. Briefly stated, these are as follows: (1) the stage of self-love, in which the emotional interest is centered upon one's own self; (2) the stage of parent love, in which the mother—and secondarily, the father—is the center of affection; (3) the latency stage, in which the emotional interest seems diffused and ill-defined; (4) the same-sex stage, in which the individual joins clubs or gangs and has "crushes" on friends of the same sex and age; and (5) the heterosexual stage, in which the emotional interest focuses upon members of the opposite sex, and the individual is ready "to fall in love." (see Figure 5).[6] While norms are often set for the age limits of these stages, children do vary in the rate at which they progress from one to the other, as is true of maturation and socialization.

INFANCY

Some students of child behavior are concerned about influences upon the child's emotional development before birth;[7] one school of psychiatric thought places great emphasis upon the shock of birth (the "birth trauma") as it is presumed to influence emotional development.[8] For our purposes, however, we may leave such concerns to the specialists and begin with the newborn infant. It is recognized that the very young child's concerns are elemental and are related primarily to his own comfort—to his being warm, well fed, and comfortable. There is considerable clinical evidence that the infant who is cuddled, fed in a personal fashion, and in general given tender care will thrive; in contrast, the infant who is neglected or treated impersonally tends to suffer in a variety of ways.[9]

[6] The student will recognize the reality of these stages (from his observations of his own past "interest stages" and of children younger than himself) even though he may reject the psychoanalytic explanation of how and why they occur.

[7] *Cf.*, for example, Lester Sontag, "War and the Fetal-Maternal Relationships," *Marriage and Family Living*, 6 (1944), p. 3 f.

[8] *Cf.*, for example, Otto Rank, *The Trauma of Birth.*

[9] This need is so well recognized that doctors often prescribe "TLC" (tender, loving care) as part of the nursing routine during an infant's hospitalization.

INFANCY-BABYHOOD
Boy and girl interested only in themselves

EARLY CHILDHOOD
Seek companionship of other children, regardless of sex

ABOUT AGE EIGHT
Boys prefer to play with boys, girls with girls

AGES 10 to 12
Antagonism shown between sex groups

AGES 13 to 14
Girls become interested in boys, try to attract their attention; boys aloof

AGES 14 to 16
Boy group also shows interest in girls; some individuals begin to pair off.

AGES 16 to 17, ON
"Going out in couples" becomes general

Figure 5. The focus of emotions in the various stages of emotional development. (Reproduced through the courtesy of Amram Schienfeld and Harcourt, Brace and Co. from *Women and Men*.)

48

Our society—especially that part of it termed middle and upper class—places great emphasis upon certain aspects of child behavior thought to be related to emotional development. For example, whether or not breast feeding is essential to the child's "normal" emotional development is a subject of sharp debate among professionals and parents alike. Too early toilet training receives its share of criticism, as does the permitting of thumb-sucking.[10] Whether or not discipline has a thwarting effect upon the child's development is also of concern to many people.[11] What the final answers may be regarding the way the characteristics of the American culture affect emotional development cannot at this point be determined. There is no doubt, however, that what occurs in the earliest years of the child's life has a bearing on the way he is conditioned to face his later existence. If the infant receives affection and emotional support, he will soon show signs of returning affection. He appears to gain a kind of fundamental confidence in those who care for him.

CHILDHOOD

The emphasis in the preceding section on emotional development in infancy does not mean that there has been no socialization. From the time the infant begins to be conscious of others, he is undergoing the learning process. As he moves into a more active phase of life involving not only his mother and father but also his siblings and neighborhood playmates, he is confronted with numerous challenges. First, he is challenged to adjust his own behavior to the needs and demands of others. This means not only adjustment to the discipline imposed by his parents so that he can be a functioning member of the family group, but also an adjustment to the demands of the peers with whom he comes to associate. He must learn, in other words, that he is only one member of the family and that both parents and siblings have certain

[10] A whole literature (*pro* and *con*) has developed on such matters. See, for example, the files of *Child Development Abstracts*.

[11] *Cf.*, for example, Dorothy Baruch, *New Ways in Discipline*.

rights which may conflict with or take precedence over his own self-centered demands. He must learn, too, that his peers have ideas regarding who shall play with what toys at what time. These are sometimes in sharp conflict with his own ideas and he learns that he must make adjustments accordingly. Second, he has to learn that immediate demands must sometimes be postponed in favor of future needs or desires and also that one must very often deny one's own desires in order to share with others. Third, he has to develop a recognition of his own "self," that is, to see himself as he is viewed by others and to realize that others have certain expectations of that "self." He must learn to be the kind of person others expect one of his age, sex, and physical characteristics to be.

All the development called for in the preceding paragraph is socialization.[12] Socialization involves learning to adjust to the demands of his fellows and to behave in terms of their expectations, admitting their having rights, and recognizing that they have contributions to make to his well-being as he has to theirs. This learning comes about through communication, which can be symbolic as well as verbal. The small infant, for example, lacks an ability to receive communication through words, but understands the mother's caress or even the sharply spoken sound; the small boy learns that his mother's gestures indicate satisfaction or displeasure—and acts accordingly. The greater the number of situations which the child faces, the greater the need for (and chance for) communication—and hence learning. It is this aspect of family interaction which both Bossard[13] and Baber[14] have emphasized, although in a different connection. In Baber's words:

> All in all, . . . the most normal development of children is fostered when they can *grow up together*. The tired father after his day's work, no matter how hard he may try, cannot take the place of a

[12] It should be evident that socialization is a continuing process and one not confined to childhood; nevertheless, its greatest influence in developing human personality is undoubtedly in the early and more formative years.

[13] *Cf.*, James H. S. Bossard, *Parent and Child*, Ch. 4, 5, 6.

[14] Ray E. Baber, *Marriage and the Family*.

boisterous brother, nor can the mother take the place of a sister as playmate. Even nursery schools are at best poor substitutes for the noisy, interesting happenings in a family of lively children. In such an atmosphere many lessons are learned easily that come with difficulty when learned alone. Someone has said that in a large family so many "little bridges" are being crossed daily that no one has to make the big jumps to new adjustments that cause so much strain. With children stepped up through various ages, ideas are handed down as easily as outgrown garments and accepted much more readily. Taking care of younger brothers and sisters may sometimes bring protests, but that training is received cannot be denied. Differences in characteristics and interests, due to differences in age, and sex, become a matter of common knowledge and facilitate the process of adjustment in later life. Even matters of sex, in both general and specialized aspects, are more naturally learned when brothers and sisters grow up together. In short, membership in a fair-sized family of children is an education in itself, and to make up to an only child for the loss of this experience is a task calling for the best thought.[15]

It is this interaction with parents, siblings, and peers (and in the later years of childhood, with adults in the "institutional world") which gives the child his sense of values—his "right" ways of behaving. He learns to avoid those things which result in punishment and to do those which gain for him approval (status) of the groups to which he belongs. Even the very small child quickly learns to do those things which will bring his mother's approval and to avoid those which bring her displeasure. He is learning to recognize the approved or "good" ways of living and to avoid the disapproved or "bad" ways. He develops, in other words, a conscience.[16]

This does not mean that all of childhood must be "sweetness and light." The bitter aspects of life, the disappointments and frustrations, play their role in developing him into an individual who can adapt his living to the demands of others and the exigencies of daily living.

[15] *Ibid.*, p. 279 f.
[16] In other words, "an awareness by the child that his behavior would arouse the approval or disapproval of his group."

ADOLESCENCE

As the child enters his teens, the body undergoes marked changes. These changes differ in boys and girls, and it is in this period that the characteristic physical differences between the sexes are attained. Sexual maturity comes at this time, and the emotional focus becomes heterosexual.[17] Adolescence is very often described by parents as "the difficult age." It is the time when the child becomes the adult in the biological sense; it is also the period when he strives to free himself from the dependent relationship he has enjoyed in the past to find the independence of adulthood.

In some societies elaborate ways of helping the child to cross the bridge into adulthood are incorporated into the culture.[18] In our own society it is probably correct to say that most children are allowed to find their way into adulthood without much assistance from the society.[19] For a period of time, in many cases, the individual is neither child nor adult; he is at once expected to assume certain adult responsibilities and at the same time is forbidden adult privileges. He very often finds that his parents are unsympathetic to his demands for adult freedom and desire to hold him to his earlier patterns of dependence. He finds, too, that his parents live according to patterns of belief and behavior which were current in their own youth but which are untenable to him and his peers.

In this period the struggle of the adolescent is not only to free himself from the strictures of family control; in many instances he also finds himself restive under the expectations of his institutional world. It is in this period that attending Sunday school may seem "childish," that school teachers are "old meanies," that Scouting is "boring," and so on. But life is even more complicated, for the

[17] See Figure 5.

[18] Examples of these *rites de passage* are plentiful in anthropologists' descriptions of primitive tribes.

[19] High School "commencement exercises" and confirmation ceremonies are two rites of passage used to help children move toward adulthood in our culture.

adolescent has the need to be accepted as a *person* by his peers. The modes of speech and dress become important, for they are a means of identifying with the peers, and the girl, for example, "would sooner be caught dead than wearing something different" from that which her peers are wearing. Acceptance as an *adult* by others who are also striving to be *adults* is the important rule of life. That family and institutions lack "understanding" only complicates life.

The end result of all this striving, of course, is adulthood. Somehow the differences among the three worlds are adjudicated; somehow a balance is struck between the demands of parents, peers, and the institutions; somehow parents relax their controls (or have them wrested away); somehow the individual achieves independence and is ready to assume the responsibilities of maturity.

THE RESULTS OF INADEQUATE SOCIALIZATION

Until this point it has been assumed that there is a positive relation between the individual and his three worlds. It has been assumed that the end product of all this socialization will be an individual who becomes adult in a psychological and social, as well as biological, sense. But this is not always the case, for any one—or two, or all—of the three worlds may fail to contribute its part in the process of maturing the individual.

The Inadequate Home

Not every child has parents who can or will provide him with the affection and security he needs. His coming may not have been planned for or accepted, for many reasons. As many authorities have indicated, if he is not wanted, he has every chance of being rejected, that is, of being denied affection.[20] He will, therefore, have little means of learning either to give or to receive affection. If, in contrast, his parents love him too much and are

---

[20] *Cf.*, James H. S. Bossard, *The Sociology of Child Development*, p. 336 ff.

unable to release him from their strong emotional bonds as he seeks freedom in his adolescent years, they provide effective barriers against his achieving the independence characteristic of maturity. If his parents' own relationships are emotionally sterile and sexually unsatisfying, the child again is deprived of part of the whole learning experience that would result in his becoming an adult in the affectional sense.

Where parents are "good" parents (in the physical sense)— where the mother "works her fingers to the bone" for her children or the father "slaves" to provide the advantages he thinks his children should have—but where there is no time for love and play and light-hearted companionship, the child grows to adulthood without a sense of what love and companionship mean in life.[21] The result of all of these is a basic emotional impoverishment, to the end that the physical adult is unable to love or to receive love fully.

The Inadequate Peer Group

We have already indicated the importance of the peer world in the whole socialization process, both in the childhood years when it aids in developing a sense of "the other's rights," and in adolescence where there is a mutual reinforcement in the search for independence.[22] Where there are sharp differences between peers' and parents' values and behavior patterns, however, the individual may be torn between loyalty to family (based upon strong affectional ties) and need for achieving status and participation with peers. This is illustrated in a portion of a college senior's autobiographical account.

> I think my first year in college was the worst I could possibly have had. I came to college with high standards that I received mainly from mother and daddy. We have always been a "close" family, and have done most things together. . . . [My parents] don't believe in dancing and sororities. We are Baptists, and our pastor

21 It is in this sense that the family of orientation makes its greatest contribution (or the reverse) to the family of procreation.

22 *Cf.* Baber, *op. cit.*, Ch. 8.

has been with us for years and has always been strict in his interpretation of how we should act. I came to college believing that
these things were wrong, mainly because of the way my parents
believed. Here I soon found that I was an "outsider." I stayed in
my room when the freshman mixer [a dance] was held, and I didn't
go to any of the rush teas. . . . Every girl I liked pledged to a sorority,
and every boy I thought I could like went fraternity. So I was left
out, completely. I've never been so lonesome as I was that year. . . .
In my sophomore year I couldn't stand the pressure. I pledged ——,
and I've felt guilty and unhappy ever since in my relations with my
parents. They try to understand and are nice about it, and perhaps
have gotten over being hurt, but I know it makes a difference.

The reader may question the parents' right to impose their own
values upon this student. It is evident from other parts of the
autobiography that they did not *impose* them; rather, that the
student shared them without any hostility or frustration until such
time as the peer group's values came to have prime importance in
her life. The term "inadequate peer group" used to head this
section may well be interpreted in the sense of inadequate to
support the girl's earlier values. Situations such as this girl faced
are seemingly inevitable in our society (with its changing of values
from one generation to the next). The point to be made is that the
peer group was innocently effective in creating an emotional
imbalance between the girl and her parents.

The Inadequate Community

Since the family never lives entirely apart from the neighborhood
and community but is in a constantly reciprocal relation with its
many parts, we cannot ignore the contribution of the community
to the individual's socialization. In Hill's words, the socialization
of the child

> . . . is not wholly a matter of intrafamily interaction. The entire
> family is involved in a number of processes of interaction in the
> community, in the social class, in the church, and in the economic
> system, and it is as true of the family as of any other group that its
> external relations determine its [internal functioning in socializing
> the child]. The status which the child gains [or lacks] outside the

family inevitably has its repercussion within it. The boy who distinguishes himself in athletics or in his studies is thought to reflect credit upon the entire family group, and his status in the family is correspondingly enhanced. The girl who disgraces the family may likewise find her family relations endangered.[23]

What the community affords the youth in the way of aids to his socialization is therefore important. Those who grow up in an impoverished community with few opportunities for any recognition in school or community groups have little opportunity to grow in their family's estimation. Those who have such opportunities outside the home are likely to find themselves achieving increased recognition within the home, which in turn can build a higher level of emotional integration among the family members. The opposite can be true, of course, in that the community can afford so many attractive opportunities for the youth that his relations with his family are diffused. In such instances, the youth tends to lose rather than gain from his contacts with his family.

THE RESULTS OF ADEQUATE SOCIALIZATION

Socialization (in the inclusive sense used here) determines, then, the emotional and social "equipment" that the adult brings to marriage. If that equipment is such that he can *accept* the ideals, ideas, attitudes, values, and behavior patterns of others for what they are, he can adjust to marriage. If that equipment is such that he can *adjust* his own needs and demands to those of others, he can adjust to marriage. If that equipment is such that he *can be objective* about what he is and what others are, he can adjust to marriage. These are, in our opinion, the *sine qua non* for adequate interpersonal relations in marriage.

SOME CHARACTERISTICS OF MATURITY

What do we mean, in very practical terms, by the word "*maturity*" as it relates to marriage. Many lists of characteristics have

[23] Willard Waller (revised by Reuben Hill), *The Family: A Dynamic Interpretation*, p. 90 f.

been compiled, some with as many as thirty items.[24] Here we shall provide a much less formidable, although equally inclusive list. Each of these will be found to return again and again in our discussions of interaction, both prior to and in marriage.

The Individual Is Adaptable

An important quality in the mature personality is ability to adapt to a variety of situations. Modern life is replete with frustrations; few indeed are the persons who can achieve all their goals or always do as they choose. The mature person accepts his frustrations with good grace, and adapts his thinking and behavior accordingly; he makes the best possible adjustment to any given situation and attempts to profit therefrom. In contrast, the immature person clings to his objectives, even though they are clearly unattainable, and sulks when he cannot have his own way. An example of this type of reaction is seen in the following quotations from an interview.

> The real trouble, as I see it, is that neither my wife or her mother can ever change their minds if they've once started something. We plan to do something this month, like buying a new chair for the house or taking a weekend trip. Then something happens—I have to meet a repair bill we didn't figure on or I can't get away because I have a good prospect—so I have to ask her to cancel our plans. There's trouble every time that has to happen. . . . Marge will get an "upity" spell and make snide remarks that I don't care enough about what she wants to do to stick to our plans, and then we're in hot water for a week or so 'til she quiets down. . . . I can't help it that things happen to our plans, but she's so *rigid* about everything. I don't know how to make her see my side.

This inability to accept a change of plan in small things is symptomatic of Marge's whole attitude toward other people— toward life in general. She has apparently never undergone the type of socialization that would have helped her to develop a concept of her relation to others, to understand that others (in this case, her husband) rightfully have expectations of their own

[24] *Cf.*, for example, Henry Bowman, *Marriage for Moderns*, pp. 100-126.

and of her, or to be able to move as the exigencies of life dictate.

An important aspect of the lack of adaptability rests in its long-time possibilities. If the individual is so unadaptable that adjustment to frustrations is the rule in his life, he may develop ways of compensating that are in themselves further contributions to maladjustment. He may indulge in fantasy (daydreaming) to a dangerous extent; he may withdraw from any social situations that are unsatisfactory; he may even, in extreme cases, utilize illness (of the type that is real but of psychic origin) as a means of escaping from the need to adapt. Whatever form his actions take, the inability to adapt in such cases can only increase his difficulties.[25]

The Individual Can Accept Responsibility

Closely related to his adaptability is the individual's ability to accept responsibility. This is another way of saying that a mature person is one who recognizes that he has a number of roles in every group (including the group of two who constitute a beginning marriage) to which he belongs. He also recognizes that his adjustment in the group requires that he accept and perform these roles to the best of his ability.[26] The mature person has learned through his socialization to be realistic about his responsibilities; the immature person fails to recognize, to accept, and to perform them. The latter has difficulty in making a go of marriage. In the words of a wife:

> I'd say that our main difficulty is in John's unwillingness to see what he has to do to make our home satisfactory. He's had seven jobs since we've been married. Each time, he quits his job without having anything else in mind. He just can't see that his job is to support us, the way husbands are supposed to do. If he doesn't like his work, he just quits. It doesn't matter that we haven't any savings and that we'll have to have money for the rent and food. . . . I'm supposed to go out and get a job until he finds something that's

[25] Where marriage occurs under such circumstances, a vicious circle often results, i.e., the use of compensatory mechanisms disturbs the marital relationship, which in turn encourages further use of the mechanisms.

[26] Cf., Waller, op. cit., p. 282 ff.

more agreeable to him. . . . It isn't only that, though. He just doesn't seem to be able to understand that a man has a lot of other responsibilities as a husband. When I hear the girls talk about what *their* husbands do, I realize that John thinks only of himself and doesn't see that he's supposed to face responsibilities in life. . . . Everything is all right as long as I bear all of the responsibility— when I try to make him see and do his share, he falls apart.

When the husband or wife has a "failing" such as this, it is quite evident that the marriage faces great difficulties. The only way in which it can succeed is if the partner is willing to accept his weakness and to assume all the responsibilities he shirks. This, in turn, places an undue burden upon that partner, who may literally be unable to carry the responsibilities of both.

I finally got a divorce, because I couldn't take it any longer. I had to earn the living, do everything around the house, make all the decisions, and even take care of the baby. Helen just wasn't able to see that she had any responsibility at all. She wasn't sick— she was sweet about everything—but she just sat around and let me do everything. She wouldn't even try to do better. . . . When he saw how it was, the judge gave me a divorce and the baby, even when he knew I'd have to put it out for care until I could make some other arrangement. . . . Even her mother admitted in court that her daughter was a flop as a wife.

This is an extreme case, of course, but it illustrates the way in which failure to accept responsibility can create difficulties in marriage. (One wonders, of course, why any man would marry a woman who was so irresponsible, for she must have shown this characteristic prior to marriage. This we will discuss in a later chapter.)

The Individual Is Emotionally Independent

The earlier discussion in this chapter pointed out the naturalness of the very young child's emotional dependence upon his mother, since she is the major supplier of all his intimate needs. Also, it was shown that his socialization, if adequate, broadens his emotional horizons to the extent that in adolescence he centers the major portion of his affection in a member of the opposite sex—with marriage the usual result. This, however, does not always occur. The strong (and natural) attachment of the girl for her father and of the boy for his mother may not be resolved and replaced by the ability to love a new individual of the opposite sex. In such cases, mating may well be an effort to find a substitute for that parent.

> John W. is a forty-year-old executive in a large company. He is successful in his work, and well liked by his associates, who regard him, however, as something of a "mother's boy." John's father died when he was five years old, and from then until her death in his twenty-eighth year John was her constant companion. She moved to the town in which he attended college, and they traveled extensively during vacations. He was constantly with his mother's widowed companions, and was never encouraged to have friends of his own age.
>
> After his mother's death, John was an extremely lonely individual. He courted several girls in turn, but each time ceased the relationship before it reached a serious point. In his words: "I've just never been able to find a girl who seemed worthy to take my mother's place. I always judge them in terms of what I think my mother would say about them, and they always seem to have something wrong—something she'd find fault with. I suppose we lived together too long for me to be able to think of any woman I could marry as being different from what my mother was."

This account is included to indicate the extreme of emotional dependence and identification. Many individuals have a similar dependence, although to a less marked degree. It should be noted that this is a case in which the mother was apparently unable to help her child achieve complete socialization. She not only used him as a substitute for her earlier emotional dependence upon her husband; she also kept her child from the peer relationships which we have seen help to build a heterosexual maturity.

The marriageable personality, then, is one free to focus upon the chosen mate without having constantly to fight against or to compensate for an immature dependence upon a parent.[27]

[27] Cf., Baber, op. cit., Ch. 6.

The Individual Has Perspective

One of the prime requisites of maturity is the ability to see needs, goals, and events in their proper relation to one another. The individual who is unable to forego the satisfaction of present desires in order to attain future goals is rarely able to meet the demands of marriage. The person who lives on his past reputation and is unable to face the demands of the present is obviously at an equal disadvantage when faced with the problems of family living. The following quotations illustrate the effects of such inadequacies of personality.

> I can't go on with my marriage much longer. We've been married for three years, and I've stood all I can from him. . . . There's only one trouble—he won't look at things realistically. We need a home of our own, and have a big enough income to afford one by buying it on time, but he wants to have an expensive car, and a camera, and all of those things. . . . He can't see that we might better sacrifice now, and have things later, and I can't stand it any longer. . . . The trouble is, his family once had plenty of money so that they could let him have anything he wanted, and he still lives that way, regardless of whatever our real situation is. . . . You just can't plan in a marriage like ours, because he's like a grasshopper—he lives just for today.

Another aspect of perspective is the ability to see values and beliefs in their proper light. The inflexible person, who believes something simply because he has always believed it, and who refuses to adjust his values in the light of human experience and social change, has difficulty in facing the problems of life. The mature person, in contrast, faces realistically the need for adjusting his beliefs where such adjustment is indicated. Most college students, for example, find that as their intellectual horizons are broadened they must discard many of their earlier values and adopt new ones. The emotionally mature student is able to do this; the immature student clings to his outmoded beliefs and finds himself at odds with his social and intellectual environment.

Finally, the individual without a sense of perspective fails to see himself as part of a larger whole. He tends to consider that social prescriptions are not made for him, and therefore attempts to go his own way—to the detriment of himself and his associates. He most often lacks a sense of humor and is therefore less able to adjust to social situations.

The Individual Is Sensitive to the Needs of Others

While it is essential that the individual free himself from the close emotional ties of babyhood and develop relationships with his peers and superiors, the mature personality continues to love and respect both parents and others with whom he has been emotionally identified. He does this not only for his own emotional well-being but, more especially, because he recognizes the part he has played in their lives and the responsibility he bears in this connection. He is, in short, never guilty of using emotional relations for what he alone may gain from them.

The Individual Can Regard (and Use) Sex Adequately

One of the important indications of emotional maturity or immaturity is the individual's attitude toward sex. The mature person sees it as a biological urge and a means of procreation, but more important, he sees it as a means of expressing the deepest and most intimate of human emotions—love. The immature person, in contrast, sees sex as something to be used in the demonstration of one's superiority over members of the opposite sex, as a means of demonstrating one's maturity to his fellows, as a weapon or instrument for bargaining in human relations, or as a means of physical self-gratification. The mature person recognizes the need for sublimating his sex drive before marriage, but also sees sexual relations as an intrinsic part of the marriage relation. The following quotations indicate something of the problem of the immature personality in this respect:

> At first I felt that I could accept sex in marriage. . . . But the longer we went together, the more objectionable I found the whole idea. As we became more intimate with each other, and he wanted to kiss me more often and to make love to me—I don't mean going

the whole way—I found that I just couldn't accept his advances. . . . I know there must be something wrong with me, since I don't believe that most women feel this way, but I just can't help it. I'm sure that our marriage would never have worked for this reason, so I broke it off.

An attitude toward sex such as the one expressed here can hardly be assumed to be that of a mature person. It should be evident to the most casual reader that such an attitude would in no way be conducive to an adequate adjustment in marriage.

Of equal importance in this connection is the individual's attitude toward past sexual experiences. The mature person attempts to see casual factors in their proper light and does not allow past events to influence his present and future behavior. The immature person allows himself to bear a sense of guilt regarding prior masturbation or deviant sexual behavior; as a result, his recognition of the proper role of sexual activity in the marriage relation becomes warped and unsatisfying.[28]

These are six rather inclusive characteristics of the marriageable personality.[29] We cannot, however, assume that every (or perhaps any) individual has them to the fullest degree. There are no absolutes in the matter of such characteristics—no blacks and whites, but only shades between. Every individual is at some point on a continuum *for each of these* six; for example, one individual may be quite independent emotionally but be less mature in the matter of perspective, and have some distance to go in so far as his ability to use sex is concerned. There tends to be agreement among the characteristics in the degree to which the individual has them, but each personality is unique in this as other regards.[30]

Nor can we assume that what now is will always be. The human

[28] This guilt may be "natural," in that it is dictated by a religious or other group to which the individual belongs. While this may explain the situation, it in no way aids the individual in his adjustment.

[29] It must be recognized that this is a necessarily abbreviated discussion, but these six characteristics are believed to be basic to an understanding of interaction in marriage.

[30] *Cf.* Howard Becker and Reuben Hill (eds.), *Family, Marriage, and Parenthood,* Ch. 6.

personality is not fixed, but is constantly being modified as the individual moves from birth to death. Just as no one would expect the child of two years to be able to accept responsibility, so is it unfair to expect that the high school or college student is entirely able to meet all these criteria to the fullest extent. If we compare the high school freshman's characteristics in these six areas with those he possesses when he graduates from high school, and again make the same comparison when he graduates from college, the development he has undergone is seen to be striking. It is only reasonable to expect that further development will take place as he marries, as he becomes a parent, and so on.

SUMMARY

In Chapter 1 emphasis was placed upon the changing nature of our society and upon the new opportunities and responsibilities that consequently confront the individual who would marry. In the present chapter we have outlined some of the ways in which the individual achieves the unique characteristics he or she brings to marriage—characteristics that will in some measure determine how successful he or she will be in achieving the goals desired in marriage. The development of a personality adequate to meet the demands of modern marriage was seen to be the result of interaction of family, peers, and the institutions of the community in the life of the individual. It is in the understanding of how these contribute to personality characteristics that we have the basis for relating background and development to mate selection. In this sense, the present chapter is basic to an understanding of all that contributes to success in marriage.

The discussion of some characteristics of the "mature" personality which closes this chapter is intended to provide some rules-of-thumb for mate selection. It must be understood that few people, if any, possess in the fullest degree these characteristics, but they are the important attributes for which we seek if marriage is to be all that modern youth ask of it.

READINGS AND TOPICS FOR REPORTS

1. Construct your own list of characteristics of the mature personality. How does it differ from that given in this chapter? Read Bowman, *Marriage for Moderns*, Ch. 10, and compare the two lists. In what important ways do these two authors differ in their thinking?
2. Using the list of characteristics of the mature personality given in this chapter, construct a list of behavior traits that are symptomatic of maturity, and another of traits symptomatic of immaturity.

ADVANCED READINGS

Thorp, Louis P., *Personality and Life.*
Lindgren, H. C., *The Psychology of Personal and Social Adjustment.*
McClelland, D. C., *Personality.*

5

Mate Selection

I<small>N A SOCIETY</small> such as ours, where great freedom is available to the individual in the choosing of a mate, there must be some forces at work which cause a particular couple to choose each other. For it is quite apparent that for one reason or another a given man can marry any one of a number of girls but conversely cannot marry one of another number. This chapter will be devoted to a consideration of how the choice of a mate is determined.

HOMOGAMY AND MATE SELECTION

The factors influencing the choice of a mate of like character-istics—the latter is termed "homogamy"—have been studied in a great variety of ways for many years.[1] These characteristics are numerous; here we can consider only a few of the more important. The characteristics which tend to affect the selection of a mate can best be discussed under three general headings: those definitely

---

[1] Authors use different terms—homogamy, assortative mating, endogamous groupings—to describe this phenomenon. The use of the term homogamy places the emphasis upon *like marrying like*.

associated with social-class membership, those of a social nature but not necessarily related to such membership, and those related to personal characteristics which have little or no obvious relation to social-class membership.

Characteristics Related to Social-class Membership

College students are either members of the middle and upper classes, or are lower-class and upwardly mobile—that is, aspiring to rise to middle-class membership. Social classes are variously defined,[2] and their importance is variously recognized,[3] but there can be no question that most college students consider themselves to be members of the middle class. In a society such as ours, many different characteristics have been used to assign class membership. Education, income, and occupation—and sometimes family lineage—have all been used as indices of class differentiation. Residence, in contrast, is primarily a resultant of class membership—that is, people tend to live with others of similar occupation, income, and education.

The important point for us is not so much the actual class position of the individual but the fact that belonging to a class means being conscious that he is like other individuals in his characteristics, that he identifies with them and they with him, and that his thinking and behavior are influenced by their thinking and behavior.[4]

The student must recognize that most studies related to homogamy in mate selection are focused upon characteristics present in the couple *after marriage and as related to adjustment in marriage.* These are studies of homogamy *in marriage* but not necessarily

[2] In general, social classes are "strata within the social structure, each with its own social, economic, attitudinal, and cultural characteristics."

[3] The tendency in a "democratic" society like ours is to deny the importance of class membership in determining human behavior. *Cf.* Ruth S. Cavan, *The American Family*, for examples of the ways in which class membership is related to social behavior.

[4] This in spite of Ginsberg's observation that "it is extremely difficult to say what one is conscious of when one is [conscious of his class membership]."

homogamy *in mate selection*. This places obvious limitations upon
their use in this chapter.[5] One study of a thousand couples, that by
Burgess and Wallin,[6] was concerned directly with those engaged
but not yet married, and is therefore more significant. For this
reason, that study will be drawn upon extensively in the following paragraphs.

Do like people marry?   According to the laws of chance they
should—but only in 50 percent of the cases; the other 50 percent
should marry opposites, that is, follow the old adage that "opposites attract each other." When the characteristics which are
indicative of a similarity of social-class membership were determined—education, income of parents, and "social status of
parents," Burgess and Wallin found that education "acts as a
selective factor in marriage. There is a markedly greater-than-
chance probability that persons with graduate or professional
training will select marriage partners of the same educational level.
The same is true of persons who have had college experience and
of those with high-school education or less."[7] Similarly, in both
parental income and "social status" of parents, the couples
showed "a marked degree of homogamy, but of somewhat smaller
magnitude."[8]

It is not difficult to see why these striking similarities in characteristics should have been found. Young men and women of like
educational experience tend to marry for a number of reasons.
The level of communication between the pair will be higher where
there is comparable educational achievement. Values change as
education increases and the level of sophistication ordinarily rises
as the individual gains in the social experiences related to educational activities. A college junior (age twenty-three) who was

[5] An extensive bibliography of such studies will be found in C. A. Anderson,
"The Sociological Approach to the Study of Assortative Mating," *International
Congress for Studies Regarding Population Problems*, VIII (1949).

[6] *Cf.*, Ernest W. Burgess and Paul Wallin, *Engagement and Marriage*.

[7] Ernest W. Burgess and Paul Wallin, "Homogamy in Social Characteristics,"
American Journal of Sociology, 49 (1943), p. 112.

[8] *Ibid.*, p. 112 ff.

enamoured of a high school senior (age sixteen) high-lighted these in a counseling interview:

> June is about the cutest kid I've ever known. I've been going steady with her since the opening of school, but I'm beginning to see that it won't work. . . . She's just as pleasant as ever, but I've begun to see that we don't have very much in common—something my father has been telling me all year. . . . I've learned a lot in college, and have learned to think about things that are going on in the world. When I want to talk about them, I find she just doesn't *know* anything! She knows Eisenhower is president, but that's all. We just haven't anything to talk about that she understands and that I'm interested in. . . . The world is falling apart, and she thinks about clothes and dancing and things like that. I want to talk about serious things, but she doesn't know anything about serious things. . . . I tried taking her to the concert series, but it's beyond her. Her gang listen to jazz, and read movie magazines. . . . I've learned since I've been in —— that there's serious music that's good to listen to, and that there are important things to think and talk about. But they're way beyond her.

This young man was beginning to see that one result of having dissimilar educational experiences is the development of a "consciousness of differences," and that these differences are important in the way two people think and act. He broke this relationship, at some emotional cost to both, and later told of his new situation in these words.

> I'm going with Anne now, and there's all the difference in the world. She's in one of my classes, and we are interested in a lot of things together. We talk about world affairs, go to concerts together, and there's a lot more than just physical attraction we have together. . . . If I'd married June, the way I planned at first, we'd just have drifted away from each other.

Family background, as expressed in "social status of parents" and "income of parents," is perhaps less obviously related to mate selection. Both, however, contribute to the individual's having distinct attitudes and behavior patterns which are indigenous to the social stratum to which he belongs.[9] A thousand seemingly naïve examples can be given of such distinctions. The middle-class family, for example, reads magazines and books, rears its children to expect to go to college, and provides them with all the "advantages" it can afford. The lower-class family, in contrast, may not even have a daily newspaper in the house, usually rears its children to go to work as soon as they are past the compulsory school age, and sees no reason for all the "advantages" the middle-class takes for granted—and struggles to provide—as part of life. One young woman gave insight into these differences in the following words.

> My freshman year in college was a lonesome one. I didn't make friends easily, but toward the end of the spring semester I met John and we went around together a lot. . . . I took him home one week end, and he seemed uncomfortable all of the time. When I went to visit him for a week end after school was out, I found out why. I was uncomfortable, too. His parents just didn't live the way mine did. . . . They ate in the kitchen; my family eats in the dining room. His father sat on the front porch in the evening in his undershirt; mine wears a coat—at least when anyone's around. . . . His father talked about what John should do to help them after he's out of school; mine doesn't expect me or my brother to pay back what he's spending on our college education. . . . John's mother never even looked at the daily paper; my mother reads a dozen magazines a month. John was the same he'd always been on campus, but I began to see that we just are worlds apart in so many things. I just don't think we're right for each other.

This quotation indicates some of the ways in which economic and social differences can influence mate selection. No one of the differences is of great importance, or sometimes perhaps even recognized for what it is, but in total they represent differences in values and behavior patterns which are effective in creating the milieu within which mate selection will take place.

---

[9] In a society as large, complex, and "regionalized" as is ours, it is difficult to identify such attitudes and behavior patterns as being uniformly class-related. Much study needs to be made in this aspect of class membership as it relates to mate selection.

Several studies have been conducted in an effort to understand how effective residential propinquity—literally, living near each other—is in affecting mate selection. Bossard, for example, found that about one in four among the applicants for five thousand marriage licenses in Philadelphia in 1931 lived within two blocks of each other, and more than five out of every ten lived within twenty blocks.[10] Other students have found similar conditions to exist. Davie and Reeves,[11] in attempting to explain such a high rate of propinquity, refined the technique by outlining areas with homogeneous characteristics—occupation, education, and so on, and discovered that more than 40 percent of the couples lived within an area and another 30 percent *lived in a different but like area*. Such findings, and they have also been found in two replicating studies,[12] suggest emphatically the importance of social class membership, as demonstrated in residential homogeneity, in determining who shall marry whom. None of this means, of course, that social class determines that man *A* shall marry woman *B*, but rather that he will very probably marry a woman—*B*, *C*, *D*, *E*, and so on—who is in his own social class, and that residential propinquity is important only because it is a resultant of living among one's own social class.

Social Characteristics Not Related to Social Class

Certain social characteristics may be important as affecting mate selection, and yet not be part of the social class constellation. Three of these are important enough to be included here.

Religious affiliation. It would be illogical to assume that the individual's religious faith or denominational affiliation, or the extent to which he practices his religious prescriptions, is directly related to social class membership. One is not a Roman Catholic,

---

[10] *Cf.*, James H. S. Bossard, "Residential Propinquity as a Factor in Marriage Selection," *American Journal of Sociology*, 38 (1932), p. 219 ff.

[11] *Cf.*, M. R. Davie and R. J. Reeves, "Propinquity of Residence Before Marriage [New Haven]," *American Journal of Sociology*, 44 (1939), p. 510 ff.

[12] By the writer's students in New York City and Rochester, New York (unpublished).

a member of Jehovah's Witnesses, or a Methodist because he is upper-, middle-, or lower-class.[13] Nevertheless, Burgess and Wallin found a statistically significant relation regarding mate selection as related to religion.[14] Religious affiliation (Catholic, Protestant, Jewish, none), and such indices of religious participation as Sunday school attendance, church attendance, and church membership were all significantly associated.[15]

Here again we must relate this factor to the question of values, beliefs, traditions, and behavior patterns. The Roman Catholic understands better and is better understood by a potential mate who is also a Roman Catholic. A Protestant moves in a different world, in the sense of his religious beliefs and practices, than does a Jew—hence his usual selection of a Protestant mate. An atheist gives short shrift to the beliefs and practices of a devout Protestant —and so on. Religious affiliation provides, then, something of a "wall" within which mates are chosen, especially when the religious faith or denomination places great emphasis upon marriage within the group. Such prescriptions of intrafaith marriage are especially evident in the teachings of the Roman Catholic and Jewish religions.

Propinquity probably also plays some part in this, since youth of like religious beliefs are thrown together in church activities from early childhood, their families associate together in the church, and it is natural to recognize this consciousness-of-kind from an early age.

Ethnic-group membership. Not only do social classes and religious groups have their own value and behavior systems, but ethnic groups—those sharing a national identity (for example, the Irish, Italians, Greeks, and so on)—have cultural characteristics peculiarly their own. Burgess and Wallin reported a significant relation as to nativity (both native-born, one foreign-born, both

[13] There is some evidence, however, of a positive correlation between religious belief (on a fundamentalist—liberal continuum) and economic status, which is itself highly correlated with social status.

[14] Cf., Burgess and Wallin, op. cit., p. 257 f., 289 f.

[15] Ibid., p. 516.

foreign-born),[16] and nationality identification is probably still important, although less so than in the years of great immigration. Nationality groups are most often ethnocentric—that is, they believe in the superiority of their own kind—and exert pressure upon their youth to marry within the groups, even in the second and third generation of American-born. These groups may include members within more than one social class, as well as in two or more religious groups (see Figure 6), and the individual may therefore have not only ethnic but religious and social class membership within which he is urged (consciously or not) to choose—if he adheres to his culture. A Polish Roman Catholic priest described such a situation in these words.

> Among my young people there is great importance to marry inside the Polish population. But it is not enough for a young man or woman who is Polish to marry just a Polish mate. He has also to marry inside his religion, and this can be Catholic or Orthodox or even some Protestants, and he should not marry from one religion to another. But this is not enough yet, because if he is a good Polish boy [first, second, or third generation] he marries too a girl who is like him, not better than him [in terms of socio-economic status]. For a girl it is all right to marry above her; for a boy it is not good. . . . So my boys, if they stay good Polish people, have only *these* girls to marry. . . . It is too bad they do not always do this. When they marry such [a member of another class, religion, or nationality], it is always trouble.[17]

A state of affairs such as is described here, in the Polish colony of Buffalo, New York, means that these Polish young men are sharply limited in the number of girls available as potential mates. It should be remembered that this priest speaks for the older members of the group, those who continue their ethnocentric loyalty to their Polish heritage, and that the youth of the colony may not be sympathetic to such a state of control. This is seen in the degree to which the American-born youth of such nationality groups are marrying outsiders.[18]

[16] *Ibid.*, p. 530.

[17] This state of affairs is vividly described, although in different terms, in Caroline Ware, *Greenwich Village, 1920-1930.*

[18] *Cf.* Milton Barron, *People Who Intermarry.*

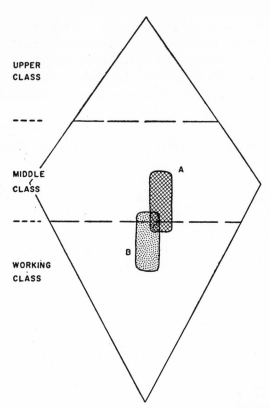

Figure 6. A schematic representation of how individuals from different social classes may be thrown together for mate selection. Group A consists largely of middle class members, but has some from the upper levels of the working class; group B is the reverse. Individuals may also be thrown together where memberships in several groups overlap.

Race. A third social factor influencing mate selection is that of membership in a racial group. The caste system in our country is such that there are legal sanctions in many states against choosing a mate from another race.[19] Even though such legal sanctions do not exist in other states, the social sanctions are usually sufficiently powerful to prevent any such choice. Any minority race has its

[19] See our discussion in Chapter 2.

own class and religious (and sometimes ethnic) distinctions, and these place sharp limitations upon its own members. In effect, members of the minority races are more sharply limited in the available "possible" mates than are those of the majority white race, since there are fewer members from among whom to choose.

Personal Characteristics and Mate Selection

In addition to the social characteristics just discussed, the personal characteristics of the individual can have an important part in the selection of a mate.

Physical characteristics. Burgess and Wallin found a greater-than-chance occurrence of similarity in physical characteristics in their thousand engaged couples. Height, weight, health, and physical appearance were all positively correlated.[20] This finding is in sharp contrast to such folk sayings as "opposites attract"; "tall men marry short girls"; "blonds always marry brunettes"; and so on. Actually, these folk sayings appear to have their foundation in the extreme cases which call attention to themselves. On the writer's campus, as this is written, a six-foot, three-inch basketball player has become engaged to a girl five feet four inches in height. Needless to say, this couple is widely discussed; little attention (in this regard) is paid to some dozens of engaged couples who are of approximately the same heights. Physical characteristics, then, appear to have at least a slight influence in the choosing of a mate.

Psychological characteristics. Much work has been done on the personality characteristics as related to mate selection. Unfortunately, many of these studies have also been conducted with couples already married, which means that personality changes *after* marriage could not be excluded. Burgess and Wallin subjected their thousand engaged couples to a standardized test, the Thurston Neurotic Inventory, and found that among forty-two personality traits, only "14 showed a greater-than-chance expectation for homogamous union of engaged couples. . . . But the tendency

---

[20] *Cf.* Burgess and Wallin, *op. cit.*, p. 207 f. The sole exception was complexion, for which no statistically reliable difference was found.

for persons with neurotic symptoms to be engaged to others like themselves is evident. Correspondingly, nonneurotics unite in engagement with nonneurotics." (See Table 3.)[21]

Winch, however, questions the validity of such a finding,[22] and advances his "theory of complementary needs," which is stated as

TABLE 3. SIMILARITY OF MEMBERS OF ENGAGED COUPLES
IN PERSONALITY CHARACTERISTICS BY REPLIES TO
THURSTONE'S NEUROTIC INVENTORY

	Ratio of Actual to Expected Similarity*
Neurotic Score..	1.13
Do you daydream frequently?**......................	1.17
Are you frequently burdened by a sense of remorse?......	1.10
Are you sometimes the leader at social affairs?...........	1.11
Does some particular useless thought keep coming into your mind to bother you?.................................	1.05
Do you usually feel that you are well-dressed and make a good appearance?..................................	1.04
Are you touchy on various subjects?....................	1.14
Do you feel that you must do a thing over several times before you leave it?................................	1.10
Are your feelings easily hurt?.........................	1.13
Do you often experience periods of loneliness?...........	1.10
Do ideas often run through your head so you cannot sleep?.	1.09
Do your interests change quickly?.....................	1.07
Do you often feel just miserable?......................	1.06
When you were in school, did you hesitate to volunteer in a class recitation?.................................	1.04
Do you get stage fright?..............................	1.10

* The probability that the differences in this table between the actual and expected percentages of similar responses are chance differences is .01 or less.
** All questions could be answered "yes," "no," or "?".

From Burgess and Wallin, *Engagement and Marriage*, p. 208) used by permission of the authors and the J. B. Lippincott Co.

[21] *Ibid.*, p. 208 f.
[22] *Cf.* Robert F. Winch, *The Modern Family*, p. 404 ff.

follows: *In mate selection each individual seeks within his or her field of eligibles for that person who gives the greatest promise of providing him or her with maximum need gratification.*[23] One can accept the general idea that each individual has certain personality-centered needs which he seeks to satisfy by selecting a mate who is capable of meeting those needs, and who in turn is seeking a reciprocal satisfaction. Winch has posited a tentative list of thirteen needs, as follows:

Abasement	To accept or invite blame, criticism, or punishment. To blame or harm the self.
Achievement	To work diligently to create something and/or to emulate others.
Approach	To draw near and enjoy interaction with another person or persons.
Autonomy	To get rid of the constraint of other persons. To avoid or escape from domination. To be unattached and independent.
Deference	To admire and praise a person.
Dominance	To influence and control the behavior of others.
Hostility	To fight, injure, or kill others.
Nurturance	To give sympathy and aid to a weak, helpless, ill, or dejected person or animal.
Recognition	To excite the admiration and approval of others.
Sex	To develop an erotic relationship and engage in sexual relations.
Status Aspiration	To desire a socioeconomic status considerably higher than one has (a special case of achievement).[24]
Status Striving	To work diligently to alter one's socioeconomic status (a special case of achievement).[24]
Succorance	To be helped by a sympathetic person. To be nursed, loved, protected, indulged.

[23] *Ibid.*, p. 406.

[24] The student will want to read Winch's discussion of these two needs for clarification. To the present writer these are especially important because of the ways in which middle-class behavior is patterned in our culture, (see Chapter 1).

Winch is willing to admit at this point that his theory is still in the unproved stage, and that its working can best be seen in unusual or pathological cases. Even without being excessively committed to the Freudian point of view, upon which Winch bases his theory, the student can recognize within himself certain of the needs listed above, and will realize that courting (as discussed in the following chapters), affords him the chance to search for a mate who will satisfy these needs.[25]

Personal Conceptions of Behavior and Mate Selection

Every individual brings to his search for a mate a variety of conceptions of social behavior which are the product of his general cultural background, his relations with his family and peers, and his personal needs. These conceptions are of many forms and degrees, and limit the number of members of his groups who would be eligible as mates. For example, the girl who does not believe in smoking or drinking (for whatever reason) is sometimes automatically ruled out as a possible mate by the male who smokes and drinks. The girl who does not like to dance or play cards automatically tends to exclude from consideration such males as find great enjoyment in dancing or card playing.

Similarly, every individual has a variety of conceptions regarding marriage. Some believe in the wife's working after marriage; others are violently opposed. Some have one attitude toward children; others a quite different attitude. It is impossible to indicate the nature, content, or cause of all of these. Burgess and Wallin questioned their thousand engaged couples on eleven items relative to social participation and seventeen items relative to conceptions of marriage. In all of these, likeness in the characteristic (homogamy) was evidenced to a significant degree.[26] (see Table 4).

It is impossible, on the basis of one study of middle- to upper-class engaged couples, to establish homogamy as *the* compelling

25 *Cf.* Burgess and Wallin, *op. cit.*, p. 205 ff.
26 *Ibid.*, p. 211.

TABLE 4. SIMILARITY OF MEMBERS OF ENGAGED COUPLES ON
Conception of Marriage and Social Participation

	*Ratio of Actual to Expected Similarity**
Conceptions of Marriage	
Should fiancée work after marriage (no; yes, if necessary; yes, desirable).	1.64
Number of children desired (three or more, one or two, none).	1.42
Attitude toward having children (very much desire, mildly desire, object).	1.31
When spouse ceases to be in love (divorce, separate, continue together).	1.28
Object to fiancé(e) having dates during engagement (yes, no, no issue).	1.26
Head of family (husband, wife, neither).	
Prefer apartment to house (apartment, house, undecided).	1.19
Romantic marriages more successful (yes, no, uncertain).	1.19
Negative factors in conceptions of marriage (none, one, two or more).	1.18
Wife keep own name after marriage (yes, no, other or no reply).	1.15
Divorce justifiable if no unfaithfulness (yes, no, uncertain).	1.15
Present sex knowledge adequate for marriage (yes, no, doubtful).	1.15
Ever marry if not in love (yes, no, uncertain).	1.09
Divorce justifiable (yes, uncertain, no).	1.06
Object to fiancé(e)'s going out with opposite sex (yes, other or no reply).	1.06
Positive factors in conceptions of marriage (none or one, two, three or more).	1.07
First sex information (wholesome, partly wholesome, unwholesome).	10.8
Social Participation	
Drinking habits (never, rarely, occasionally or often).	1.81
Smoking habits (does not smoke, will stop if other objects, will not stop).	1.38
Prefer play or dance (play, dance, don't know).	1.31
Leisure time preferences (stay at home, on go most of time, on go all the time).	1.29
Object if fiancé(e) smokes (no, yes, no answer).	1.12
Friends of opposite sex (none, one to seven, eight or more).	1.10
Organizations regularly attended (none, one or two, three or more).	1.09
Offices in organizations belong to now (none, one, two or more).	1.09
Offices in organizations belonged to in past (none, one, two or more).	1.08
Friends of same sex (none, one to seven, eight or more).	1.07
Considered indifferent to the opposite sex (yes, no, don't know).	1.06

* All of these show a statistically significant preponderance in favor of homogamous unions over those that would have occurred in matching *by chance*.

Adapted from Burgess and Wallin, *Engagement and Marriage*, p. 206 f.; used by
permission of the authors and the J. B. Lippincott Co..

force in the selection of a mate. Burgess and Wallin willingly admit that their evidence shows that "like *do* marry like," rather than indicating *why* "like marry like."[27] The point for us is that social class membership, other social characteristics, *and* personal conceptions of what is wanted in a mate (whether consciously or unconsciously understood) all operate to create a "field" from which one mate is chosen—by the process of courtship, which is the topic of the following chapter.

Heterogamous Mate Selection

What about those who do not mate homogamously? The studies referred to above have all shown a better-than-chance occurrence of homogamous mate selections, but this obviously leaves others who do not so mate and must be accounted for.

One group of these includes the "social misfits," who, for one reason or another, have not been helped to reach the maturity usually associated with those of their age, and are unable to participate comfortably in the courtship processes outlined in the following chapter. An example of this type is the girl whose mother's overpossessiveness prevented her knowing members of the opposite sex, and who—when she reached the freedom of college life—"threw herself at the first man she could find." He, incidentally, was in the equivalent possession of his first freedom, and "meant to make up time" for earlier restrictive parental controls. Another example is the "two lost souls huddling together in the dark"—found on every campus at one time or another. Here two probably neurotic people may find the "sympathy and understanding" that each needs. Some students of marriage believe that mate selection based upon the satisfaction of such needs will not satisfy either party.[28] The question may well be raised as to why these are not in fact homogamous selections;

---

[27] It is for this reason that the earlier discussion of our personality needs is basic to our understanding of what mate selection really involves.

[28] *Cf.* Edmund Bergler, *Divorce Won't Help*, for an elaboration of this thesis. *Cf.*, also, Willard Waller (revised by Reuben Hill), *The Family: A Dynamic Interpretation*, p. 210 ff.

the answer is that often these individuals possess violently opposite (rather than homogamous) needs, and that the only element of homogamy lies in their being "unadjusted."

Another type of heterogamous mating results from the purely social situation in which the individual finds himself. It has already been emphasized that social factors limit the number of mating possibilities. In extreme instances, there are no apparent mating prospects. The newcomer to a big city, with its characteristic "anonymity," may have real difficulty in meeting members of the opposite sex who are potential mates. The social and emotional need to marry may well drive such "anonymous" individuals to select mates who are similarly without any peer groups having potential mates.[29] Again, the sex ratio—the number of males per hundred females—may be badly distorted, thus making mate selection difficult. For example, in Tarpon Springs, Florida, the sizable Greek community has lost its main source of income through the waning of the sponge fishing industry. The young men have had to go elsewhere to gain a living, leaving numbers of second-generation Greek girls without prospects of marriage within the ethnic group (which has high value in the Greek culture). The result has sometimes been to "drive" the girls to heterogamous mate selection.

SUMMARY

Despite the fact that the individual is today relatively free to choose a mate—as contrasted with having pressures exerted by his family and community in earlier times—there are still subtle forces which affect the choice of a mate. In this chapter we have seen that such factors as social class membership, similarity of family background, religion, residential propinquity, and physical and psychological characteristics have all been seen to have subtle and often unrecognized importance in determining the choice of a mate.

[29] One example of this is seen in the extent to which "marriage clubs" are used by "the lost and unfound" in seeking mates.

In view of what has been said in earlier chapters, these must be recognized as constituting only a small part of the total forces governing mate selection. They determine not so much the exact individual who will be chosen as a mate; rather, they tend to define or delimit the "field" within which eligible mates will be found.

READINGS AND TOPICS FOR REPORTS

1. Analyze a short story, novel, or movie to show how background factors contributed to the problems of the couple. Would more conscious mate selection have prevented or lessened the problem?
2. List all of the members of your senior class in high school. (You will probably have to refresh your memory with a yearbook!) Remove all those names of individuals whom you could not ordinarily marry because of racial, religious, social class, or other characteristics. What percentage remain as "eligible" marriage partners?

ADVANCED READINGS

Baber, Ray E., *Marriage and Family*, Ch. 4.
Clarke, A. C., "Residential Propinquity as a Factor in Mate Selection," *American Sociological Review*, 17: 17 ff. (1952).
Sirjamaki, John, *The American Family in the 20th Century*, Ch. 4.
Winch, Robert F., *The Modern Family*, Ch. 16.

6

Courtship: I

Viewed functionally, courtship is that process which usually begins in adolescence, and in which the individual readies himself to leave his family of orientation and to establish his family of procreation.[1] It is in courtship that the individual seeks for and selects the person with whom he will mate, and builds an affectional relationship with that person. Courtship begins with dating and ends with the marriage ceremony.

Courtship cannot be considered as an isolated part of life. Its course is influenced strongly by what has occurred earlier in the emotional and social development of the individual, and what occurs in the courtship period will in turn have direct bearing upon how that individual adapts to the later demands of family living. If the situations in marriage are to be understood, the situations in courtship must therefore be understood.

The Rationale for Courtship

We may well ask ourselves why courtship should be an important phenomenon. The answer is to be found, in large measure, in the

[1] See Figure 4.

changes that have occurred in our society in recent decades (see Chapter 1). No longer is mate selection primarily the concern of parents and community; increasingly the selection of a marital partner is deemed the responsibility of the individual himself. This is not to suggest that courting did not occur in other times, for in this country it has been an established practice since earliest Colonial times.[2] A great-grandfather once described his own courtship situation in these words:

> Sure we courted, but it was all settled that we was going to marry before we started courting. If her folks didn't cotton to you, you didn't get the chance to court. If your folks didn't like her or her folks, they just didn't let you start courting, either. What I mean is—you selected the girl, and she let you know she liked you, but you didn't court this one and then that one. The families approved, and you courted. They didn't approve, you didn't court. . . . Courting in my time wasn't picking a girl—it was getting to know her after she was picked. And you didn't back out, either, after you started courting.

Contrast this description with that of courtship in our own time, and it becomes apparent that the *reason* for courtship has shifted. The increased desire and need of young people to know each other's traits and values—if they are to select a mate with whom they can build a satisfying marriage—makes courting much more important functionally than was indicated in this quotation. In that instance, choice was not involved; the marriage was in effect a *fait accompli*, and courtship was something of a luxury rather than the necessity it is today. In the following discussion, therefore, an emphasis is necessarily upon the trial-and-error aspects of mate selection.

The Stages of Courtship

The whole process of courtship is shown graphically in Figure 7. It is, in essence, that process by which male *A* selects and is selected by female *B*, and by which they come to be emotionally and socially

[2] It should be kept in mind that the changes in our culture discussed in Chapter 1 have created a different *rationale* for courtship.

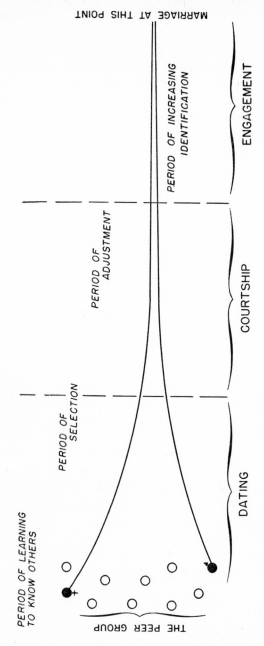

Figure 7. The stages of the pre-marital relationship as discussed in this text. This is a schematic representation, and the three divisions represent basic *types* of relationships rather than fixed and discreet stages.

85

identified with each other and ready for marriage. For present purposes the courtship period is divided into three stages—dating, courtship per se, and the engagement. These are not always clearly distinguishable, as we shall see, but each has rather special functions for the individual and the couple, and each has its special problems as well. For this reason we shall discuss them as separate entities.

DATING

Dating, as understood by today's youth, is a relatively recent phenomenon. Even as late as the turn of the century, most people regarded going together even two or three times as evidence that the couple were "serious." With the freedom afforded youth today, however, this idea has pretty well vanished from the scene. Dating is now a generally accepted activity, but its significance is not always understood.

The Nature of Dating

Dating, especially as it occurs among high school youth, may well be termed pseudo-courtship, but it is impossible to generalize as to the form this pseudo-courtship takes. Dating varies from community to community and even from one adolescent group to another within the community. In some cases, "going steady" is the peer-prescribed way of dating; in others, going steady is frowned upon. For some young people, especially those who have no expectations of a college career, there is little effort to prevent emotional involvement, and the chance of falling in love through dating may be entirely acceptable. Others, who have long-term plans for college or other professional training, may deliberately avoid emotional entanglements and use dating solely as a recreational device.

Whatever the pattern followed, dating may be considered as a trial-and-error period in the whole phase of premarital heterosexual emotional focus (see Chapter 4). It is trial-and-error in that definite commitments are rarely made, the emotional involvement usually is slight (however intense it may seem at the time), and the attachments are more or less temporary in terms of time.

Motives in Dating

Much has been written regarding the utilitarian values of dating. Waller,[3] a sound but sometimes pessimistic student of dating, called it "a period of dalliance which intervenes between puberty and mating," and emphasized its use by youth in obtaining status in the college [and this can also include the high school] community. Other students of the subject have made investigations which appear to verify Waller's emphasis upon dating as a means of exploitation.[4] If these writers are correct, college students use dating primarily as a means for achieving prestige. In contrast, however, both Lowrie[5] and the present writer[6] have found that other motives—the search for recreation, for affection, and as a means of knowing a variety of personalities—are equally, if not more, important to those who date. It may well be, too, that those reporting the status or exploitation goals in dating fail to take into account certain important aspects of the situation. In one university, for example, a socially prominent student made the following comment after reading Waller's article.

> It's very true that we [the fraternity men] only date sorority women—with a few exceptions. But this doesn't mean that we are only looking for sex or prestige. The fraternities and sororities—and their members—get some prestige, and the Sigma ——'s only date the Delta —— ——'s or the Alpha ——'s, but *this is just a fence around whom we'll date*. This doesn't mean at all that we don't date most of all for reasons of companionship or fun.

[3] *Cf.* Willard Waller, "The Rating and Dating Complex," *American Sociological Review*, II (1937), p. 724 ff.

[4] *Cf.*, for example, John R. Crist, "High School Dating as a Behavior System," *Marriage and Family Living*, 15 (1953), p. 23 ff.

[5] *Cf.* Samuel Lowrie, "Dating, a Neglected Field of Study," *Marriage and Family Living*, 10 (1948), p. 90 ff.

[6] *Cf.* E. L. Koos and Harold A. Weinz, *A Study of Attitudes Toward Dating* (processed).

In the light of this observation, which is by no means an unusual one, it appears that we can safely emphasize the importance for most youth of dating *as a means of getting to know members of the opposite sex.* To be sure, there are girls who date the big-men-on-campus for status reasons, and there are men who date the *right* girls (those who have sorority or other prestige value) for similar reasons. But, as Baber has expressed it

> . . . Side by side with this breathless social striving, others are carrying on the normal process of dating anyone who is a good companion, though the thought of ultimate marriage—temporarily dormant—can always be aroused. With the end of formal schooling not far away, most college girls are hopeful that their dating may lead to courtship. . . . Functionally, then, dating [has two motives], *casual* and *serious.* There is no sharp line of demarcation between them, for one may blend easily into the other. . . . The serious type of dating might correctly be called the "questing" type, for it is part of the eternal quest of youth. . . . The central characteristic of serious dating is the process of evaluation.[7]

It is this *process of evaluation* which is to be emphasized in any consideration of dating as functionally related to courtship. The strong need to understand the personality attributes of one's mate, the equal need to know whether values are similar or at least adjustable, and the need to find similarities in behavior patterns—all these require that those who will marry have an opportunity to understand the characteristics of prospective mates.

The Values of Dating

Since dating, even though serious in intent, does not commit the individual to any permanent involvement, the individual is free "to shop around." Since he is so largely the product of his own family, each person's ideas of people are in good measure conditioned by the characteristics of his parents and siblings. Adequate evaluation of a possible mate means, most often, that individuals outside the family need to be known intimately, and the ways in which they think, act, and plan, be understood. Only

[7] Ray E. Baber, *Marriage and the Family,* p. 117.

as acquaintance is broadened to include a variety of personalities does the individual free himself from the limitations of choice and action that are unconsciously imposed upon him by his family associations. It is in this sense that courtship was earlier defined as that process in which the individual readies himself to leave his family of orientation.[8]

Dating is valuable, too, in that it affords the individual an opportunity to develop adequate methods of communication. Few of us are able, even in the first years of college, to deal confidently with all social situations involving members of the opposite sex. For one thing, most youths have too recently entered the hetero-sexual stage of psychosexual development to have a complete feeling of social competence. As dating continues—if it is at all profitable—the individual learns to move more adequately in social situations, and social maturity results.

A third value of dating lies in its mental health function. Whether in high school or college, the young person is constantly con-fronted with tension-creating situations. These may originate in the relationship of the youth to his family, his teachers, or his peers, or other groups such as the church. They may stem from the adjustments he is required to make in his values or his behavior patterns—or from his personal feelings about himself. In any event, there is need for a socially sanctioned opportunity to interact with others with similar tensions, to share with them his frustrations, to be "understood" by those who think as he does. Dating affords such opportunities. A psychiatrist responsible for the mental health of students in a New England college has expressed these needs and opportunities in the following words.

> The students who come to me with the greatest need for tension-releasing discussions are those who do not date. They may be the "grinds," or the physically unattractive, or the emotionally unstable, but in most cases they are men and women who have no oppor-tunity to "talk out" their problems with others of their own age.

[8] This does not mean a complete divorcement of emotional ties, for such is rarely the case (and then only in the emotionally immature). It is, rather, a readying for the new love-centered, hetero-sexual mating relationship.

If these youngsters could only associate more easily with their own kind, the need for seeing me would be greatly lessened.

Dating has, then, a value for the individual quite apart from that of evaluating the characteristics of possible mates. Such a value is of minor importance in the mind of the individual who is dating; he, quite naturally, sees dating as recreation-, status-, or evaluation-centered. Our search for objectivity concerning the processes leading to marriage, however, gives it importance here.

Some Problems in Dating

One of the important problems confronting those who date has already been referred to—that of whether or not to "go steady." Several points need to be emphasized in this connection. First of all, what does going steady mean to the particular couple? If it is simply a peer-dictated behavior pattern in which there is a temporary pairing up for convenience, but with the full recognition that the pair relationship can be broken at will and a new pairing occur, going steady may have its advantages. There is a security in knowing that one is guaranteed a partner for the next football game or dance, and there is a "healthy" status achieved through being able to do what one's peers are doing. A college freshman shows this in the following statement.

> You feel much better when you are going steady, because you are sure that for Friday night's dance you will have a partner. Competition is strong here [because girls outnumber men on this campus] and if you don't go steady it can mean you are left out of something you want very much to go to.

There are, however, problems that may offset the advantages stated here, and the same student makes these clear.

> There is another side, though. If you do go steady, you are typed as being out of circulation, and it isn't easy to get to know other men. . . . Sometimes you are on a double date and think, "Gee, I'd like to know [the other boy] better, but you don't have the chance because you are "assigned" to your own date and the other boy is off limits. . . . If you dated just to be seen with the right people, it

wouldn't matter, but that really isn't the only reason you date. You do want to know a variety of men before you make a real choice.

Another important aspect of going steady should be mentioned here. This pattern of behavior is of advantage to the emotionally or socially insecure individual who is unable to compete for dates with those who are secure. Once having obtained a "steady," of whatever qualifications, he or she is at least able to maintain a modicum of status and to have some of the other satisfactions dating gives. The unadjusted man may find an equally unadjusted girl who will go steady, to the temporary advantage of both, but this may be an ultimate disadvantage, in that it can lead to an undesirable emotional involvement or to premature marriage.

Another problem in dating involves the holding of sex to its proper place and proportion in the total relationship. To many young men, heterosexual activity is a means of achieving status with one's peers; it is also a means of demonstrating one's maleness and of satisfying the need to be aggressive. To many young women, such activity appears to be the price one pays for recognition and status among the males of the community. When coupled with this recognition of dating as a status-achieving device, sex poses problems for youth of both sexes in a culture such as ours. Reuben Hill has indicated the problem in these words:

> Now, these techniques which prove rewarding in the dating game are either not used in marriage or if used make for trouble. Boys must perfect a "line" for accosting, for pick-ups, for date making, which at the same time protects them from involvement; someone has termed it the "circumscribed advance." Girls must learn the arts of coquetry and titillation, of inscrutability, of teasing retreat, the "good-bad girl" allure, appearing to be willing but maintaining standards of high morality. Their armor is also characterized by the circumscribed advance and by their inscrutability—bad costuming for later mutuality in marriage. It is expected in the dating that the girl set the limits of the sex play, that her inhibitions against active petting determine the boundaries of sex conduct. Yet men hope to marry women who give of themselves freely and enjoyably, whose natural receptivity has not been impaired by the experiences of growing up. Perhaps nowhere does dating misprepare its members

more for the spontaneity of marriage-partner relations than in inaugurating this placing of total responsibility on girls for maintaining moral standards during adolescence. Boys are permitted to exercise their spontaneity, but girls are expected, for the sake of both sexes, to inhibit their receptivity.[9]

This problem, as outlined by Hill, appears to the author to be confined largely to those who have a circumscribed attitude toward dating. While not all young people share this attitude, the question of what constitutes acceptable sexual behavior is nevertheless present for all young people in the dating period.[10] The whole religious tradition upon which our culture is based emphasizes premarital chastity; the result, very often, is for the individual to experience a conflict between the sex drive, which has come to the fore at puberty or shortly thereafter, and his emotional conditioning about sex.[11] This poses very real questions regarding sexual behavior in dating. Since comparable questions are necessarily raised in the following chapters on courtship and the engagement, and since the answers are approximately the same for all three stages of premarital relations, the following discussion is elaborated to include the whole of the premarital period.[12]

Sexual behavior must be viewed not only as a highly personal activity but also as one which involves not only the individual but a partner as well, and as an activity about which attitudes are held by the social groups of which the individuals are members. It has already been indicated that the moral standards of our society regard any premarital sexual relations as categorically wrong, and that these are the result of our Judeo-Christian heritage. It must be

[9] Willard Waller (revised by Reuben Hill), *The Family: A Dynamic Interpretation,* p. 218.

[10] This is especially likely to be a problem in a culture such as ours, where *change* is a predominant characteristic.

[11] The emerging sex interest is, of course, reinforced by the widespread emphasis upon sex in our culture.

[12] It is frankly admitted that the following discussion is considered by many people to be "old-fashioned." It is based, however, upon a *total* consideration of the forces at work in our culture, together with considerable experience as a college teacher in attempting to help students solve problems which have stemmed directly from their inability to reach a satisfactory position on the subject of premarital sexual relations.

recognized, however, that there has always been a divergence from these standards, as evidenced in prostitution and in the growing tendency for many individuals to ignore the "moral element" in sex.[13] It must also be recognized that not all cultures have such standards, that they are, in other words, peculiar to certain societies.[14]

Opponents of the official position insist: (1) that sex is an entirely natural and normal drive; (2) that the need to satisfy this drive should take precedence over any man-made moral code; (3) that premarital continence is actually harmful to the individual; (4) that premarital sexual relations serve as training for marital relations; and (5) that such relations serve to test the compatibility of the prospective marriage partners.

Supporters of the traditional attitude are entirely willing to admit the naturalness and inevitability of the sex drive, but they are not willing to see the moral code changed—believing that man must subjugate his personal drives for the good of the social group. They point out, too, that there is as yet no adequate evidence (either physical or psychological) to prove that premarital continence is harmful. They raise grave questions regarding any training value in premarital relations, and point to the vast differences between sexual relationships outside of and within marriage in support of their case. The idea that premarital intercourse serves as a test of possible marital compatibility is also rejected, on the ground that while sexual adjustment is important in marriage, it is only a part of a much larger constellation of adjustments that must be made. The supporters of the traditional standard insist that those who favor premarital sexual relations are rationalizing their own desire to behave sexually as they choose and to be freed from social controls.

In many instances, the traditionalists fail to take into account a number of facts. One of these is that from puberty onward the

[13] This stems in some measure from the lessening control of human behavior by organized religion (see Chapter 1).

[14] For example, the Trobriand Islanders have a completely different moral code; it is, nevertheless, a code with rigid requirements.

young person is deluged with a variety of stimuli leading to sexual interest and activity. Advertising, entertainment, and literature all tend to glorify sex—not as related to the marriage relationship, but as a value in itself. Another is that two powerful brakes upon the desire for premarital intercourse—the fear of pregnancy and the fear of venereal disease—have largely been removed through the dissemination of contraceptive knowledge and the conquering of syphilis and gonorrhea by medical technology. Still a third is the decreasing importance of sin, the devil, and hell in the religious ideology of the younger generation. All these weaken the influence of the traditional standards upon the individual and make it easier for him to ignore the older social controls.

There is little help to be gained from the available research findings on the relation of premarital intercourse to success in marriage. Locke, for example, found that "a larger percent of happily married than divorced women and a larger percent of divorced than happily married men reported premarital intercourse with the future spouse." *However, neither of the differences in percents was statistically significant.*[15] Other studies have indicated a somewhat higher incidence of marital success among those who had not had premarital intercourse, but the evidence is inconclusive and, at bet, impressionistic. It appears that if any realistic position is to be taken regarding this subject, it must be seen *in toto*; the following discussion is an effort to provide such a view.

First, sexual activity cannot be thought of simply as a biological phenomenon but must be recognized as part of a larger whole. It is perhaps unfortunate that society, in its effort to make available a fuller knowledge of sex, has resorted to a treatment of the subject on the same level as other biological phenomena—much as digestion and circulation are discussed. This means that many individuals see it as a purely physical activity and are unaware of its psychological importance. The interpretations of dynamic psychology have, in many instances, been similarly limited, and have led the casual reader to look upon sex as an "instinctive"

[15] *Cf.* Harvey J. Locke, *Predicting Adjustment in Marriage*, p. 133.

drive that should not be denied. In both cases, the emphasis has very often been *upon sex as an individual, rather than a shared, activity.*

Second, whether or not individuals hold to the traditional sexual values of the society, they are unconsciously influenced by those values. Even though they reject moral restrictions as outmoded and unscientific and intellectually accept the idea of sexual freedom, a residue of unconscious guilt can—and very often does—remain.[16] Most young people reared in the family of today have been sufficiently indoctrinated with the traditional moral values of the society that they cannot *completely* accept either the intellectual or the emotional connotations implicit in sexual freedom. To engage in premarital sexual relations under such circumstances is to lay one's self open to anxiety and conflicts, which in turn lay the groundwork for maladjustments in marriage.[17]

Finally, success in marriage implies a degree of trust, a reciprocity of interest, and mutual identification, which are beyond that of any other interpersonal relation. It is these characteristics that give successful marriage the significance it has for individuals in modern society. Sexual behavior plays its part in creating all three—albeit a part often too subtle to be discerned by casual observation. Even where the individuals are engaged to be married, the sexual relation is necessarily incomplete, since it lacks the reinforcement which other aspects of the marriage relationship give. Effective emotional identification and social cooperation in marriage are *built* by individuals, each of whom sees the other as a part of his own self. To expect that premarital sexual relationships provide a sound base for such building—at least in a culture having moral precepts and making the personal demands our culture does—is to be unrealistic. This is neither the time nor the

[16] The term "guilt" as employed here means more than "the state of having committed an offense." It is a variety of deep-seated, unresolved "anxiety," and has serious connotations (often unrecognized) for its possessor. *Cf.* Percival M. Symonds, *The Dynamics of Human Adjustment*, Ch. 16.

[17] The term "anxiety" as employed here means "a state of apprehension and psychic tension," with far-reaching effects when unresolved. *Cf.* Symonds, *ibid.*, Ch. 6.

place to speculate about what should be *if* the moral norms of the society were to change. It is the author's considered opinion that in the present situation, as outlined above, premarital relations present an emotional hazard few people can afford if they desire success and happiness in marriage.[18]

To say, in answer to this statement, that all the evidence indicates that men and women do engage in premarital relations and thereafter do succeed in marriage is to ignore the significance of what has just been said. There is no doubt that marriages have been successful under such circumstances; there is also no doubt that where success has been achieved, our knowledge of the factors contributing to this success is as yet not completely identified. Until such time as these factors be can isolated and understood, the risks in a culture such as this one must be recognized as being too great to be ignored.

The question may then be raised as to "how far one goes" before marriage in any of the three stages of courtship. Sexual drives are cumulative; once having been given some opportunity for expression, they build progressively toward fulfillment through sexual intercourse. If not given complete fulfillment, the residuum is discontent, frustration, and inner conflict. It is this unresolved residuum that makes "heavy petting" the unhappy and unsatisfying experience it is. To suggest that the casual kiss or even the oral activity and fondling commonly known as necking is detrimental to a later love relationship is to approach the ridiculous. Whether heavy petting is physically detrimental is open to question, but its harmful psychological effects can very often be identified, especially where a sense of guilt is involved.

Petting is an unsatisfactory means of satisfying the sex drive in courtship for still other reasons. The sexual stimulation that results from such activity, at least when extreme, may well lead the individuals to forget or abandon their original intent to abstain

---

[18] This is not to suggest that such relations always and inevitably lead to disaster; case materials show the opposite to be true. It is to say, however, that our total psycho-cultural milieu is such that the chances of suffering outweigh those of success in such behavior.

from sexual relations. In such cases, the guilt feelings most often assume significant proportions. Also, if petting becomes *an end in itself*, as frequently is the case, it tends to limit the values expected to accrue from courtship.

None of what has been said above is to be construed as minimizing the problems relating to sexual activity in courtship. They are ever present and cumulative, from the days of the first dates onward—problems that can be solved only by seeing the situation in its totality rather than in its immediate aspects.

The fact that young people enter the dating stage of courtship without previous experience (and usually without benefit of counsel except from their equally confounded peers) means that they face still another problem. How does one act on a date, and what does one expect in the way of behavior by the partner? This text has no intention of providing a series of rules of etiquette, nor does it propose that the student think of dating only in a negative fashion. Nevertheless, there is value in examining research findings from studies in this general area, with the aim of showing some of the characteristics considered objectionable. A study of the attitudes of students in the University of Rochester showed certain of these to be most prevalent among both men and women, although their importance differed with the sex of the respondents. Figure 8 lists the fifteen characteristics most frequently mentioned as objectionable, with their rank order as assigned by men and women students. (It should be noted that the two sexes did not list these characteristics as having the same importance.)

The most important "pet peeve" of men students is with girls who are not satisfied unless the date is expensive; that of women students is with men who want too much "necking." It is significant that these two characteristics held first place, since both are involved in what has been termed "exploitative dating," that is, dating based upon the individual's ability to exploit his own advantages and the weaknesses of the partner. Ordinarily, men have some advantage in that they pay the expenses of the date and have more money to spend; women have an advantage in that

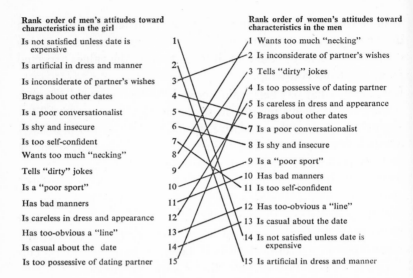

Figure 8. College men and women do not always agree upon the characteristics they find objectionable in dating partners. These differences were found in the answers of 425 women and 345 men in the undergraduate colleges in the University of Rochester to a questionnaire on dating habits and attitudes.

they can give or withhold sexual favors (kissing, petting, or even coitus). Each, then, has something valued by the other—something that can be used to gain an advantage. The fact that they held first place, respectively, as objectionable characteristics indicates something of the aversion both sexes had toward dating as a "way of getting all you can for free."

The characteristic, "is inconsiderate of partner's wishes," ranked consistently among the top three as being objectionable (see Figure 8). In this there is some evidence of a widespread acceptance of dating as a democratic procedure; the old idea that the man conferred a favor upon the girl by dating her is apparently fast disappearing. Only as dating does become democratic and as it is generally accepted as a sharing of the experience will its more positive values assert themselves.

In some rankings of objectionable qualities, important sex differences were found. Men were strongly against artificiality in dress and manner—girls much less so; girls resented "dirty" jokes much more than did men, and were more disturbed by carelessness in dress and manner than were the men. The girls regarded possessiveness as highly objectionable—men were apparently less sensitive in this connection. Men were somewhat more negative about a dating partner who bragged of past dates, who was shy and insecure, or who was too self-confident. Some of these differences undoubtedly reflect the patterns of behavior assumed to characterize the American male and female, others, the still unfavorable position of the female in this society, who must wait to be asked and is therefore not always as critical in her evaluation of the male as she would otherwise be.

None of these findings is to be accepted as definitive. Christensen, in a study of Purdue University students' attitudes, found an extremely high agreement between those of the two sexes,[19] but this may reflect the uniform characteristics of that student body. Each social group, high school or college, has its own characteristics, and hence its own folkways and mores, and these vary greatly from one part of the country to another. For example, the author has studied dating patterns in a small Protestant college and found that one objectionable characteristic of major importance was that of smoking—by either sex. This obviously had only local importance, and reflected the ultraconservative nature of that particular social group. What is important in this connection is the necessity of recognizing the meaning of these attitudes and their psychological importance to the individual and of being willing to take them into account in one's dating behavior.

Even though there is not the degree of psychological involvement in dating that will be seen in the next chapter as a *sine qua non* of true courtship, it is impossible to ignore the emotional qualities of the dating experience. It is impossible for two individuals not to interact to some extent in dating, or in any other interpersonal

[19] *Cf.* Harold T. Christensen, *Marriage Analysis*, Ch. 7.

relationship, and the values of such interaction must be kept in mind. (The exception, of course, is the "gold-digging date, where the only reason for going out is to get what you can in the way of free entertainment and where you don't really have anything to do with your partner except be an escort." This hardly fits our definition of dating as an interpersonal relationship.) If the individual fails to see the contribution dating can make to personality development, he misses an important aspect of preparing for marriage.

There is, however, a note of caution to be entered here. If the same person is dated more than once, both must have in mind the same "definition of the situation." One may regard the dates simply as recreational and social experiences (and see no possibility for the development of a more serious relationship), but the other may view it as an early stage of courtship (and allow himself or herself to become emotionally involved). When such a relationship is broken off, the latter will inevitably suffer. This is seen in the following abstract from an interview in a university counseling clinic:

> I'm here to get help in getting out of a mess. I haven't got a girl in trouble, but I'm in trouble with a girl just the same. I'm an engineering student and I've got three years to go before I can finish my work here and at ——. I don't have a dime, except my scholarship and what my dad sends me. . . . I've been dating [this girl] right along, but I didn't mean anything by it. Just a little fun, and somebody to be with when I don't have to study. . . . I kissed her, but that's all. . . . Now she's all excited about getting married, and says she loves me more than she ever knew she could. She wants to meet my parents and have me go to her home during vacation. . . . I don't know what to do. I didn't have any idea of leading her on, and I like her, but I don't want to marry her—now or maybe ever. . . . It'll break her heart if I quit her cold, but I don't see what else to do.

It is clearly evident that these two young people defined the dating situation in quite different ways. If this girl had recognized that the dating was impersonal, in the sense that it was not expected to lead to further emotional involvement so far as the man was concerned, she would have been spared what later proved to be an embittering experience. She withdrew from all social contacts and avoided what might easily have been a serious breakdown only through the help of an understanding counselor.

Where there is any question in the mind of the individual as to what the date means to the partner, there is every reason to guard against emotional involvement. The chance of such involvement, and of a resulting traumatic experience, is less where each makes clear (if subtly) to the other what his motives are in dating and where his expectations of the future will take him.

SUMMARY

In this chapter we have recognized that the interaction between the sexes is a purposeful one which leads to marriage. Courtship, in the larger sense, was seen to be the process by means of which we find a partner in marriage, and was viewed as having greater importance than in past decades because the selection process is increasingly vested in the individuals themselves.

Dating is here viewed as the initial stage in this whole selection process, and is seen to have both advantages and disadvantages for the individual, depending upon how he views and accepts the process. The appeal in this chapter is for the student who dates to take advantage of the values, that is, the opportunity to learn to know a variety of personalities, to gain self-realization through peer relationships, and to develop skills in social interaction. Conversely, the warning has been given of the disadvantages of following such dating patterns as isolate or limit these values,

READINGS AND TOPICS FOR REPORTS

1. Analyze the folkways of dating on your campus. How do they differ from those of your high school days? Are the functions of dating different? If so, why?
2. Obtain from fellow students a list of what they consider to be the most desirable and least desirable traits in members of the opposite

sex. Analyze these for their importance in determining dating and courtship patterns.

3. What reply can you give to a person who asks for the point at which dating stops and courtship begins?

4. Interview the parents of a number of junior and senior high school students. What do these parents see as the function of dating in the lives of their children?

ADVANCED READINGS

Bromley, D. B., and F. H. Britten, *Youth and Sex: A study of 1300 College Students.*

Hollingshead, August B., *Elmtown's Youth.*

7

Courtship: II

T HE LAST CHAPTER indicated that true courtship differs from both dating and the engagement. It is a relationship more directly focused upon mate selection than is the case in dating; it lacks the definite commitment of the individuals to each other characteristic of the engagement, and the group's recognition of that commitment. In this sense, dating becomes courtship at the point where individuals begin to think of each other as potential mates and continues to the point where they have arrived at a decision to marry. In this chapter the concern is with the special elements of this relationship and with the problems of this in-between stage in the progression toward marriage.

COURTSHIP INVOLVES LOVE

In Chapter 1, it was stated that a major purpose of marriage is to afford the fulfillment of the love relationship of two people. In the last chapter, no mention was made of love—not because it does not appear during the dating period (at least in its most preliminary states), but because falling in love is one of the

significant evidences of progression from the dating to the courtship stage. In other words, one begins to feel that special attraction
for another that is termed love and therefore modifies his activities
and aspirations to meet the special needs of the situation—he
enters courtship. If this strikes the student as too mechanistic an
approach to one of the richest experiences of the maturing individual, he may well keep in mind that it is so expressed simply
because it affords a convenient framework for analysis. Falling in
love is ordinarily not a cataclysmic precipitation into a new state
of being—novelists and scenario writers to the contrary—but a
progression from one relationship to another, sometimes with one
or more false starts.

What, then, is this psychosocial phenomenon that intrudes
itself upon the scene and marks the turning point in heterosexual
interpersonal relations? It is only in recent times that man has
attempted to apply scientific insights to a relationship long considered the province of the poet, and regarded as too personal for
pedantic consideration. Even now, teachers in marriage courses
find many students slightly resentful that such highly personal
feelings as those involved in love should be subjected to classroom
scrutiny. To such students, family budgets, in-law problems,
personality development, and even sex, can be discussed, because
these apply very generally. But love—well, that is something no
one else ever has experienced in quite the same way, nor in so
personal a fashion. Therefore, it should not even be subjected to
academic scrutiny.

Despite this resistance, the question of what love is must be
faced realistically, for three reasons. First, love is the central
requisite of modern marriage; as has been noted earlier, people
marry for love in American society, and, increasingly, stay married
only while love is present in their relationship. Second, love seems
to be a variable element in human relations, since for some people
it is of a fleeting nature but for others a life-long experience and
therefore must be analyzed if its sometimes capricious nature is to

be understood. Finally, love is so variably defined in our society that there is no guarantee of a common understanding unless the various concepts of its nature are reviewed.

WHAT IS LOVE?

We have earlier seen that each individual normally focuses his emotions upon first himself, then his mother, and, after successive stages of change, upon a member of the opposite sex in his years of adulthood. We have also seen that only as the individual gains the satisfaction of his affectional needs at each succeeding stage is he able to progress onward to the mature heterosexual relationship. We do not have to be closely identified with any psychoanalytic system of thought to understand this progression and maturing, for it is easily identified in our own lives and the lives of all about us.[1] Without taking sides in what has been a long and sometimes bitter argument, it can be pointed out that this development is not entirely an innate process. The fact that the individual's emotional growth can be retarded or that it can regress indicates that at least part of this emotional need is affected by the interpersonal relations experienced by the individual—some of which are culturally dictated. The social circumstances in which affection occurs can be so specialized and so powerful that they create vastly different affectional patterns in different societies,[2] and even within social classes in one society.[3] In our discussion love will be considered as having its basis in the "love energy" of which the psychoanalyst speaks, but also as being modified constantly by the prescriptions of the culture and the group membership effects of our social life.

[1] The "extreme" position of the psychoanalysts is set forth in J. C. Flügel, *A Psychoanalytic Study of the Family;* also, in Joseph K. Folsom, *The Family and Democratic Society*, Ch. 11.

[2] For discussions of this cultural dictation of affectional patterns, see for example, Abram Kardiner, *The Individual and His Society.*

[3] There is empirical evidence of class differences in affectional patterns, for example, in the differing ways in which college and working-class youth view the "romance" magazines.

The Elements of Love

We have first of all to recognize that this human sentiment we call love is no uncomplicated thing. One falls in love, loves his children and his parents, has love for his friends, and has still a different love for his mate in the later years of marriage. All these are forms of this "love energy" emphasized by the Freudian, but each has distinctive characteristics of its own. Here we are concerned primarily with that "love energy" which is focused upon the member of the opposite sex who is to assume the role of mate.

Several elements of love can be identified without in any sense overobjectifying it or spoiling its meaning. First, love is *sexual but not sensual*.[4] It would be absurd to suggest that love, in the framework noted above, has no element of sexual desire. It would be equally absurd to suggest that love is only sexual desire, for one may have sexual excitement and find sexual release without any element of affection at all. The man who visits a prostitute has, and presumably satisfies, sexual desire per se, but it is a desire and satisfaction that are physical and lack any quality of emotional interrelatedness; he may, in fact, hate the woman with whom he has sexual contact even as she may loathe and despise him. For in such a relationship the significant element of sharing—of giving and receiving emotional satisfaction—is lacking.

This element of sexual desire varies quantitatively from person to person, but it is always present in some degree (although in exceptional cases it may not be recognized). Without this sexual element, those activities engaged in by youth which are termed "falling in love" would not occur.[5] If the sexual element is not present or is denied, one may well raise the question of whether or not he is in love.

Second, love consists of what may be termed *a mutuality of response*. The couple who love each other are in a continuous emotional *interaction*—not in the sense that "you do something

---

[4] This distinction must also be kept in mind throughout all of this text's discussion of the sexual aspects of marriage.

[5] Even "puppy love" is usually recognized as having its sexual component.

to me," as popular songs would have it, but that "we do something to [and for, and with] each other." What each does is constantly meaningful to the other, but meaningful in terms of the whole life situation in which they are involved, and whether or not they are in constant communication with each other. Each, for example, stimulates the other sexually, but it is a stimulation that also has meaning quite outside the realm of sex. It is a stimulation connoting self-respect and, more important, respect for the other. It is a stimulation which recognizes that each is a person with special needs to be understood and met. It is a stimulation, too, in that it gives a sense of belonging to rather than simply of possessing the other. Mutuality of response means, in other words, that the two individuals cease to be self-centered and independent and become interdependent in all that they are and do. It means, too, that each is constantly sensitive to, and reacts in terms of, the other.

This does not mean, of course, that each never acts as an individual, for this would be impossible unless they were always in each other's company, and did all things together. The job requires the man's attention—making a home absorbs much of the girl's interest and effort. But even as the man is on the job and the girl is in the home, the work put forth is not in terms of "me" but of "us," not of "mine" but of "ours." This sense of "we-ness," then, is essentially a third element of love—*selflessness*. It is primarily this selflessness which makes marriage "a *unity* of interacting personalities."[6]

Motives of Love

Why is one person impelled to love and to seek the love of another? Part of the answer lies in the nature of man and of love itself. The maturing individual has moved through the earlier successive stages of emotional development and is ready—in the

---

[6] This affectional "unit" is the distinguishing element in the modern marriage. See Chapter 1.

emotional sense—for love.[7] At this point our culture dictates that
we shall begin to love, and to love in certain prescribed ways. As
Hill has indicated:

> Love as we know it is a part of our culture, and it is probably
> not found in any other culture in exactly the same form. So much
> is implicit in our conception of love as a sentiment. We love in
> accordance with the customs of our group [including dictates as to
> when we shall love]. . . . We love exclusively—one person only, or
> one above all others and are not supposed to have any real intimacy
> with others; we love not only exclusively but also jealously; how
> different all this [would be] in a polygamous culture! . . . We love,
> then, in accordance with the culture in which we have formed our
> sentiments.[8]

Our culture dictates that we shall marry; while the opprobrious
titles "old maid" and "old bachelor" are no longer heard with
the same frequency as in earlier decades, there nevertheless prevails a sense of the social rightness of marriage. The fact that
children grow up in a family setting that assumes their later
falling in love and marrying is one way in which the individual
accepts the "rightness" of such actions. Individuals, then, are
motivated to marry both by the (perhaps unrecognized) pressures
of their emotional development and by the not-too-subtle pressures
exerted by society, especially through family and peer influences.[9]

It is important to recognize that our culture not only "pushes
us into love," but also helps to do it in a somewhat irrational way.
If one believes the movie scenarist, the short-story writer, and
those who write radio and television scripts, no one ever moves
gradually and rationally into loving a potential mate.[10] Quite the

---

[7] One of the problems in this connection is the fact that in our society individuals
are presumed ready to love some years before they are ready to assume the economic
and social responsibilities of marriage.

[8] Willard Waller revised by (Reuben Hill), *The Family: A Dynamic Interpretation*,
p. 113 f.

[9] Witness the effect of one or two engagements in a sorority or fraternity upon
other members who are only dating.

[10] The writer has recently studied more than two hundred short stories appearing
in women's magazines in which "boy meets girl." The median time between the
first meeting and the declared intent to marry was found to be approximately five
days.

contrary! The young man (or young woman) moves through life quite content with his (her) state of single-blessedness until—suddenly and entirely without warning—he (she) meets that one member of the opposite sex without whom life simply cannot be lived; whereupon, within a period of days (or at most weeks) they are married. (Whether or not they live together happily, or for how long, is rarely revealed.)

This emphasis upon "romantic love" as the real motive to love is a "specialty" of our own culture. Ralph Linton has suggested that "our present American culture is the only one which has attempted to capitalize [violent emotional attachments] and make them the basis for marriage."[11] That such motivations to love do exist goes without saying, for there are people who fall "violently and immediately" in love, and who, thereafter, are entirely successful in their living together. But these are perhaps the exceptions which prove the rule, for most of us, luckily, are motivated to love in a more calm and deliberative manner. Were we all to believe that this "violent emotional attachment," with its concomitant love-is-blind emphasis, is the only way in which two people can possibly meet and mate, many more marriages would surely end in failure, or not occur at all.[12]

Some Mistaken Ideas of Love

That love is *not* a number of things has some bearing at this point. First, it is not emotional dependence, although it is sometimes interpreted as such. The man who seeks a mate because he has need for a woman to take his mother's place in his life; the woman who cannot face an adult world where she must make decisions, and who desires marriage as a sheltered retreat; the individual who must have the constant reassurance of being

[11] Linton might well have indicated that the present American culture has a correlate in its capitalizing upon violent emotional *detachments* as grounds for divorce.

[12] For a more detailed treatment of this point, see Robert F. Winch, *The Modern Family*, Chapter 14.

wanted, and who seeks that reassurance in marriage—all these confuse their desire *for dependence upon someone* with love.

Second, love is not a means of outlet for aggressive tendencies. The man who desires to marry in order to have an outlet for his need to dominate; the woman who seeks a mate so that she can exploit her married-woman status; the individual who seeks to compensate through marriage for all the things he has missed in life—these, too, confuse their psychological needs with love.

Third, love is not just infatuation, for infatuation is the irrational exaltation of the love-object—an exaltation out of all proportion to its characteristics, which are soon found to be veneer-thin and fleeting, and of which one soon tires.[13] Infatuation may or may not be built upon sexual attraction. One has only to contrast the schoolboy in whom sex is not yet an overt driving force, who has a "crush" on his teacher, with the middle-aged man, who yearns after a blond and beautiful (and well-proportioned) chorus girl, to realize this. Each of these focuses his emotions upon another person, whether attainable or not, for the personal satisfactions thereby gained. Neither is in love, for the other important elements are not there.

The Growth of Love

The fact that love is discussed after a consideration of dating and prior to courtship per se indicates that to us love is one of the distinct attributes of this second phase of the courting process. The individual dates one or many members of the opposite sex without being in love; he enters the courtship stage because he is entering a love relationship.[14]

If we are realistic, we must admit that for most of us love is something that grows rather than just happens (see *supra*). Love

[13] The temporary nature of the usual infatuation is one of its most evident earmarks.

[14] As we have indicated in Chapter 6, this entrance into the courtship stage from the dating stage is usually an ill-defined transition. Few people are able to identify the point at which courtship begins; hence our designation of these stages as *ideal types*.

comes to full bloom when the two individuals have found that their personalities blend with each other, that they have mutual interests and common (and shared) aspirations, and have learned that each can see life as completely satisfying only when it includes the other. It is this *learning about the other person in detail*, which courtship provides—as contrasted with *learning about other persons in general* in dating—which gives courtship its special significance.[15]

A Definition of Love

Having noted briefly the origins of love, some of its elements, the motives which move the individual to love, and the phenomena that are not to be mistaken for love, we can now make a brash attempt to define it. *Love is that intense feeling of two people for each other which involves bodily, emotional, and intellectual identification; which is of such a nature as to cause each willingly to forego his own personality demands and aspirations in favor of the other; and which gains its satisfaction through creating a personal and social identity in those involved.* Having offered this definition, let us look at what it really means. It means, first, that *love is a complex whole*, since it is not solely sexual, emotional, or intellectual. It is therefore a very special kind of emotional attachment, and quite different from the love one feels for a spiritual leader, a parent, or a sibling. It means, second, that love is *selflessness*, for the individual who loves puts his mate's needs above his own. It means, finally that there is in love a *"one-ness"* which replaces earlier loyalties to family and peers with a loyalty in this new dyad.

This definition does not imply any absolute uniformity in the degree of feeling or type of experience, but it does indicate that love has these qualities. To expect that every couple, or every individual, would have the same degree or type of involvement when in love is to believe in a uniformity of human nature that is

[15] One of the writer's students has indicated this change in these words ("When I dated, I was interested in girls *plural*. When I began courtship, I didn't care if I ever saw more than *the* one girl again.")

unrealistic in terms of what is known of individual differences. If we accept such a definition, however, we can be realistic about whether or not we really love the potential mate.

COURTSHIP DIFFERS FROM DATING

We have now indicated that courtship involves the element of love, while simple dating does not, and that courtship is a one-to-one relationship, which dating may or may not be. Courtship differs in its intent, too, in that for both parties it promises a deepening relationship. It is almost impossible, as we have suggested, to draw a sharp line between dating and courtship. Love and the intent to develop a more purposive relationship may not be recognized for some time after both have arrived on the scene. Going together may have become something of a habit—the student must remember that habits are good as well as bad—and the recognition of love is often only a gradual awakening rather than a clear-cut acceptance.

The recognition of courtship is essentially personal rather than social. In this it contrasts with the engagement, as we shall see in the next chapter. This personal element is the most important aspect of courtship and must be seen in its several aspects.

COURTSHIP IS ADJUSTMENT

Adjustment is "the deliberate and purposeful procedure of arranging persons . . . into a system of working relations in order to avoid friction or conflict. It must be distinguished from the unconscious process of accommodation, of which it is often the first step. . . ."[16] The couple who are courting are probably both adjusting and accommodating since some of the sharing achieved in successful courtship is undoubtedly unconscious. Our concern here is with the conscious adjustment, with the deliberate clearing away of differences that threaten the success of future relation-

[16] Edward B. Reuter, *Handbook of Sociology*, p. 81.

ships. It is fortunate that a courtship once begun can be discontinued; in this matter, the present generation has not the handicap of those past generations for whom there was somehow a moral obligation once a courtship had begun to consummate it in marriage.

The Need to Know Each Other

The couple who are courting must know each other well before they can make such adjustments as are necessary. Dating has given them some opportunities for knowing each other, but all too often dating has been carried on under circumstances in which the individual could not fully reveal his true self. For example, 78 percent of the high school students who were queried in detail regarding their attitudes toward dating indicated that they did not feel entirely free to be themselves, and that it was necessary to "put the best foot forward."[17] They also indicated that they expected to be able to act more naturally if and when they moved into a courting situation.

From our case studies of working-class and middle-class youth it is possible to say that in true courtship there is a progressive attrition of this "romantic façade," that as the couple learn to know each other better and as each feels more certain about his choice of the other as a probable mate, the need "to be what he thinks the other hopes he is rather than what he is" (to quote one student) diminishes. The simple fact of being together helps in this connection; "intimacy destroys strangeness," but each partner in courtship has the need also to learn purposefully about the other. What, really, does the other think about all of the things that count in marriage and family living? The "romantic façade" may require one set of attitudes to be put forth in the early days of courtship; serious inquiry may later reveal these to be somewhat different from the real attitudes the individual holds. (The fact that this is not always a conscious misrepresentation of one's

[17] Earl Lomon Koos and Harold A. Weinz, *A Study of Attitudes Toward Dating* (processed).

beliefs in no way mitigates the need to gain this understanding.)
An example of this need is seen in the following abstract from an
interview with a college girl who had recently broken off her
courtship.

> In the first months we went together, after we got beyond the
> casual date stage, Bill and I talked a little about families and what
> we expected in family life. He always seemed to agree with the idea
> that a marriage without children wasn't a marriage at all—something
> I believe. . . . Last month it came out that if he ever marries he
> doesn't want any children, that they don't fit in with his scheme of
> things. I don't think he deliberately misled me. It was just that he
> wanted to be the kind of person he thought I wanted, and so he
> didn't reveal how he actually thought about children. . . . If we
> hadn't really learned to know each other, I'd probably not have
> learned this until it was too late—until we'd married. Then I don't
> know what I would have done; probably gotten a divorce. I suppose
> both of us were at fault, but I can't possibly go on now that I know
> how he feels.

The Need to Adjust to Each Other

The interview abstract just reported underlines not only the
need *to know each other* but also the need *to adjust to each other*
if the later stages of the relationship are to succeed. Since human
beings are the product of differing human experiences, it is too
much to expect that there will be no differences. In this case, the
difference was so fundamental that it could probably never have
been resolved. Other differences are no less important, but may be
more susceptible to adjustment.

It is interesting to note in this connection that some textbooks
on marriage apparently consider the engagement to be the time
for certain of these discoveries and adjustments.[18] With this point
of view we cannot agree. Courtship, in the present thinking, is the
time when each person learns to know what the other thinks,
evaluates the chances of being able to find a common ground for
his own and the other's ideas, and then works toward reaching

---

[18] *Cf.* for example, "Problems to be discussed during engagement," in Landis
and Landis, *Building a Successful Marriage,* pp. 186 ff.

that common ground. It is possible, of course, to delay under-
standings about basic points in marital interaction, but to do so
increases the possibility of a late break in the relationship, with
increased damage to both persons (see below).

Certain other textbooks see courtship as

> a period of bargaining, of attempting to involve the other while
> seeking not to involve one's own ego irretrievably. It is a period of
> playing one person off against another, of exploitation and of
> trauma when exploited. . . . Jealousy, depressive doubts about the
> future of the relation, and retreats into misogyny are understandable
> accompaniments of our courtship system. Unless ventilated and
> talked through *in the intervening period of engagement*, these
> ambivalent relations, hurt feelings, and resentments carry over into
> the marriage itself.[19]

Again, we cannot agree with this statement in its entirety. To
place such an emphasis upon courtship is, in our opinion, to
reduce it to the level of an aggressive game and to deny the
element of "sharing," which characterizes at least its latter days.[20]
Hill's further statement is "that dating and courtship experiences
are for the most part poor preparation for marriage, [and] that
they create misunderstandings and distortions of relationships
which require ingenuity to straighten out. The engagement as a
period of transition between courtship and marriage appears to
offer the possibility of just such orientation."[21] If the student
views adjustment as postponed until the engagement, as these
authors appear to do, he fails to avail himself of the great value
courtship can provide.

Adjustment Is Progressive

It should be obvious that adjustment is not present from the
beginning of courtship. The couple begin as relative strangers to
each other; each of their characteristics needs to be explored and,
where divergent, brought into agreement—or at least understood

[19] Waller (Hill), *op. cit.*, p. 219 (italics ours).
[20] It is for this reason that our discussion took the direction it did in Chapter 5.
[21] Waller (Hill), *op. cit.*, p. 219.

and accepted as differences. As the knowledge each has of the other grows, the chances for understanding and sharing, or for seeing that the relationship is not a suitable one, grows. One gains, for example, a knowledge of the personality of the other at an expanding rate; every interchange of personalities sharpens the sensitivity of each to the other's needs and potentialities. We can expect, therefore, that the couple will become increasingly involved with each other, or that they will break the courtship because of what they discover as the involvement has progressed.

It is impossible to say how long adjustment will take, or when a dissolution of the unsuccessful courtship will occur. Too many factors affect adjustment to allow even a guess. Data are available to show variations in the length of time between the first date and the engagement,[22] and to show the relation of the period of acquaintance to marital adjustment,[23] but none of these reports indicates the time devoted to courtship per se or to the length of time between the beginning of courtship and the achieving of adjustment. Social and economic factors may delay the engagement and marriage long after adjustment has been achieved; a variety of factors may delay adjustment in one case or encourage it in another. This is one of the areas in which every couple is a law unto itself. Using a technique suggested by Kirkpatrick and Caplow (see following section) four possible courses of adjustment have been presented to more than five hundred recently-married couples who describe themselves as "well-adjusted at time of marriage." A summary of their descriptions of the progress of adjustment (as selected from graphic presentations of possible variations) is shown in Figure 9.[24] The choices indicated did not vary as much as might have been expected, and almost two thirds reported that their adjustment had been slow to develop in the first one fourth of their total acquaintance prior to marriage, had then risen rapidly during the second one fourth, "and ripened in

[22] Cf. Landis and Landis, op. cit., p. 165.
[23] Cf. Ernest W. Burgess and L. S. Cottrell, Predicting Success or Failure in Marriage, p. 164 ff.
[24] From continuing research now being carried on on Florida State University.

THE PERIOD OF COURTSHIP

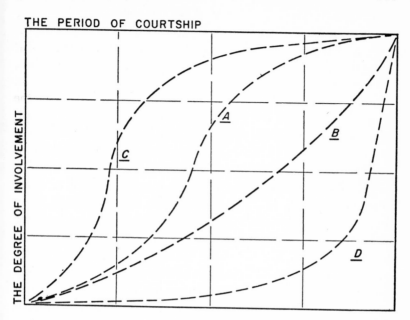

Figure 9. Social and emotional involvement progresses variously in courtship. Among 563 couples, 61.5 percent chose line *A* as representing the pattern of their involvement prior to marriage; 29.5 percent chose line *B*; 5.5 percent chose line *C*; and 3.5 percent line *D*. If these couples are representative, involvement in courtship rarely is either very rapid or very delayed, but is a matter of gradual development. (From continuing research.)

the last one half." The fact that such an experience is reported by so large a proportion of the couples studied indicates that much is yet to be known about how people adjust in the courtship period.

Emotional Trends in Courtship

Not all courtships end in marriage, or even in engagement. This may be interpreted favorably, since it means that many couples have entered courtship only to find that they are not suited to each other and have therefore broken off the relationship.

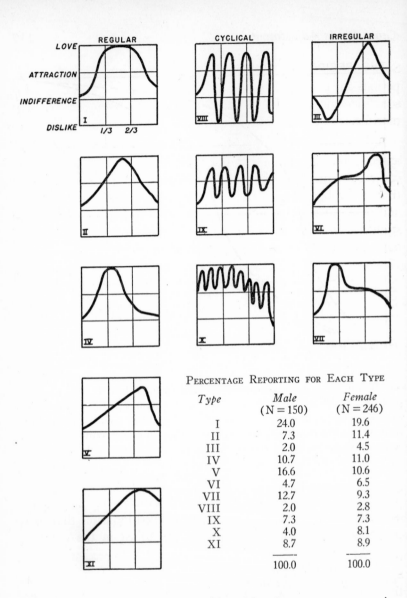

PERCENTAGE REPORTING FOR EACH TYPE

Type	Male (N = 150)	Female (N = 246)
I	24.0	19.6
II	7.3	11.4
III	2.0	4.5
IV	10.7	11.0
V	16.6	10.6
VI	4.7	6.5
VII	12.7	9.3
VIII	2.0	2.8
IX	7.3	7.3
X	4.0	8.1
XI	8.7	8.9
	100.0	100.0

Figure 10. Fluctuations in the emotional involvement accompanying courtship, as identified by 396 college students. (Redrawn from Kirkpatrick and Caplow, "Emotional Trends in the Courtship Experience of College Students as Expressed by Graphs," *American Sociological Review*, X, 1945, p. 621.)

Such action fits well with our thesis that the dating and courtship periods are times of trial-and-error, of exploring different personalities and choosing that one with whom the expectations of marriage can probably best be realized.

But failure to continue the courtship can have its negative aspects, too, since emotional trauma and personal disorganization can result for either or both participants. Some light has been thrown by Kirkpatrick and Caplow, who studied the courtship and postcourtship trends in three hundred ninety-nine university students, on what happens to individuals who have broken their courtship ties.[25] Their findings are shown graphically in Figures 10 and 11. If this study is at all representative, the courtship that

Figure 11. Emotional readjustment *after* courtship. In the Kirkpatrick and Caplow study, 89 percent of the students reported that their post-courtship feeling toward the courtship partner was one of indifference; only 11 percent reported that love had turned to acute dislike. (Redrawn from Kirkpatrick and Caplow, *supra*.)

does not end in marriage is not unusual, since the men reported an average of 2.5 and the women an average of 2.0 love affairs. The aftereffects of these eight hundred ninety-six are seen not to have been too serious, since only 11 percent of the respondents reported dislike of the partner; the other 89 percent reported only a residual indifference. It is evident, at least among this group, that the abortive courtship rarely leaves permanent damage, that people do "pick themselves up" and form new attachments.

[25] Clifford Kirkpatrick and Theodore Caplow, "Emotional Trends in the Courtship Experience of College Students as Expressed by Graphs," *American Sociological Review*, X (1945), pp. 619-26.

SOME PROBLEMS IN COURTSHIP

Many problems are associated with courtship. They vary in importance, but a number are sufficiently prevalent or make such an impact upon the individual as to be worthy of discussion.

Emotional Involvement

A measure of the success of the courtship is the degree to which the two individuals become emotionally interrelated. As courtship proceeds, it is natural for this involvement to grow, but there are dangers associated with this growth. One of the advantages of courtship is that it allows the relationship to be dissolved at no great personal or social cost. It is well, however, that each person guard against an unequal development of the love relationship. If one individual is not to suffer unduly, his progression in this connection should keep pace with that of the courtship partner— neither lag behind nor get far ahead. The girl who falls deeply in love at the very beginning of the courtship and who must be frustrated in her expectations of her partner until his love "catches up" only makes her own situation more difficult. She also places herself in a vulnerable position should his love not mature as she expects.

This may seem unimportant in the light of the Kirkpatrick and Caplow findings discussed in the last section, but from a mental hygiene standpoint it is certainly better to prevent rather than willingly to lay one's self open to emotional trauma. It is not easy to control the rate at which emotional involvement occurs, and the suggestion that one consciously attempt to do so may seem absurd. There is no intent here to minimize the spontaneous aspects of falling in love; we do not subscribe to the thesis that courtship is essentially a battle between the sexes. What is suggested is that the person who is falling in love do so with a clear realization of what he or she may suffer should the love affair fail to develop fully.

One way to avoid too early involvement is to avoid courtship, that is, to remain in the relatively impersonal dating stage for a longer period. We have already discussed some of the negative aspects of "going steady," and wish only to emphasize its danger in this connection. The individual who avoids this particular type of dating and who dates more than one person is better able to prevent a possible hasty or premature entanglement. This is not always easy in view of the special demands made upon the individual by his peer group or by his cultural patterns, but it is something to be kept in mind as one attempts to order his love life.

Personality Problems and Courtship

Is the person's behavior in courtship related to any special characteristics he may have? If an answer can be had to this question, it will not only provide the student with knowledge of how others behave but may also offer him some help in understanding his own courtship problems. Nimkoff and Wood have suggested certain answers in their study of the courtship behavior and personality of four hundred and eighty-nine students in Bucknell University.[26] The norm for dating-courting behavior among these students was to begin dating in the seventh or eighth grade, to begin "going steady" after reaching college, to have two or three dates per week, and to have had two or three love affairs (presumably of varying intensity). The students who did not conform to this norm were of two types. Those who were *socially withdrawn and somewhat maladjusted emotionally* began their dating late, had few or no dates while in college, and had only one or no love affair. Those who were *socially aggressive and somewhat maladjusted emotionally* had been precocious in their dating and often had dated without regard for their parents' wishes, now dated very frequently, and had four or more "steadies" to their credit. While this is insufficient evidence upon which to base any broad generalizations, it appears to indicate that extremes in courtship behavior are probably related to inadequacies of personality.

---

[26] Meyer F. Nimkoff and Arthur L. Wood, "Courtship and Personality," *American Journal of Sociology*, 53 (1948), p. 266 ff.

One of the author's students expressed an extreme view of courtship by calling it "the time when we uncover each other's weaknesses." He might better have put it in a more positive way—when strengths are discovered. In Chapter 4 many of the major characteristics of the mature personality were discussed; courtship, in our scheme of things, is the time each individual is discovering the presence or absence of these in the prospective mate. If they are present, well and good; if absent, the courtship can be broken off without undue damage (see above). Certainly, we repeat, it is better to make the discovery during courtship and to break the relationship if it appears unsuitable than to go on in the hope that things may better themselves.

The attempt to inventory one's own and the prospective mate's personalities is probably the most difficult task faced in courtship.[27] Religious and other background factors are ordinarily uncovered in general conversation, as are most attitudes and values. Parental relationships are often so deep-seated and so value-laden, however, as to defy casual examination. Shall a man not show affection and satisfaction in his relations with his mother? Shall a young woman not be fond of her father and gain satisfaction from being with him? Is there anything wrong in being devoted to one's parents? The answer must be, of course, that filial devotion is in itself a measure of personality development, and that it has been regarded as a moral necessity from Old Testament times. But filial devotion and parental attachment are quite different. If the devoted son (or daughter) cannot see the need to modify the parent-child relationship in the face of the new courtship attachment, and cannot seem to replace it with an equivalent mate relationship, this attachment is not devotion but fixation. If the man (or woman) does not show an understanding of his dependence upon his mother, there is probably very little chance that the courtship can end in successful marriage. If he recognizes his dependence, it can be *hoped* that he will eventually gain sufficient emotional independence for successful marriage;

[27] See the discussion of Winch's theory of complementary needs in Chapter 4.

but even this hope is not enough to allow an optimistic fore-cast.

Only when the individual in courtship is able to assure himself or herself that the prospective mate is free to become an emotional partner and that there is no mortgage of affection to either parent, should the courtship be allowed to proceed. It can be noted that the greatest problem in this connection appears to involve son-mother rather than son-father, daughter-father, or daughter-mother dependency. Winch reports, for example, that "to achieve [emotional maturity in marriage], males must achieve independence which involves loosening their Oedipal attachments to their mothers; females need only to transfer their dependency from father to husband."[28] This suggests that the girl in courtship needs to exercise more care in searching for and understanding her partner's attachment to his mother than does the man regarding the equivalent relationship.

A second aspect of personality involves *emotional immaturity*. How does one evaluate or test for emotional maturity? Obviously the couple do not subject each other to any one of the standard tests designed for this purpose—to do so would be to move courtship into the psychological clinic and probably to destroy it. Here again we must refer to the criteria discussed in Chapter 4. Excluding the one we have just discussed (emotional independence) these are adaptability, responsibility, perspective, sensitivity to the needs of others, and a realistic view of sex. One of the advantages of courtship is that it provides each person with opportunities for seeing the other in a variety of situations. (This obviously excludes the kind of unwholesome courtship in which the couple spend all their time hiding from other people.) It is perhaps easy to hide one's personality behind a "romantic façade" when one is dating; courtship should be carried on so as to expose each individual to a great variety of situations and personal and social demands. Under such circumstances the presence or lack of the character-istics just mentioned can be determined. The habitual behavior of

28 *Cf.* Winch, *op. cit.*, Chapter 15.

each must be given a chance to show itself, and the informality of present-day courtship provides that opportunity—but intentional use must be made of it.[29]

This may again seem to require that courtship be viewed as a period of cold, rational examination of each by the other. Doesn't such an attitude take the joy out of courtship? There appears to be no reason why it should, since such evaluations can be intelligent and searching without being overt and scientific. A man, for example, can learn in courtship whether his girl is primarily interested in him or in her clothes and cosmetic disguise; whether she is demanding of his whole attention when they are with another couple or with his parents. Any and all of these attributes of maturity can be tested in a thousand ways, and not at the expense of normal courtship activities.

Interpersonal Problems in Courtship

Courtships rarely progress without at least a few difficulties. As the two individuals gradually progress from same-sex associations toward marriage, their emotional focus is decreasingly upon themselves and increasingly upon each other—for this is the course of genuine love. It is only natural that this refocusing should have its occasional difficulties.

One of these involves *jealousy*. Someone has called jealousy "an emotional growing pain." In the shift from self-love to other-love, it is not unusual for one to resent a lack of emphasis by the other upon himself. In one student's words, "In the early days of courting, *you* want to be worshipped and are jealous if you aren't." Also, as the early desire to bring the other person into a closer relationship expresses itself, there is likely to be resentment that the other person must be shared with outsiders. Both of these feelings gradually wear away as each becomes more involved with and more sure of the other. Jealousy is replaced by confidence, satisfaction, and the sense of sharing each other.

---

[29] One of the values of the informality in dating and courtship which characterizes our present culture is the increasing avoidance of this "romantic façade."

Where a *sense of perspective*[30] is part of the make-up of both persons, this "growing pain" is unimportant. If, however, one or both lacks this quality, and jealousy cannot be seen in its true light, it is evidence that all is not well and that the suitability of the couple as mates needs to be re-evaluated.

Another difficulty involves *quarreling* in courtship. Quarreling is often thought to be evidence of poor adjustment. One of the problems in this connection is knowing exactly what is meant by the term. If it consists of a persistent bickering over small matters, or of "telling each other off" about personal characteristics, there is good reason to question the presence of quarrels. If, in contrast, quarreling consists of an honest airing of differences—such as are bound to occur as people who are strangers move toward an understanding of each other—it is quite different. Important, too, is the question of whether there are residuals, of whether one or both nurses his hurt feelings, and broods over defeat. Differences of opinion and personality are fruitful sources of tension, and need to be aired and discharged if the growing relationship is to profit. In this sense, a quarrel can be evidence that the tensions are being released and that the couple are moving toward a desired oneness.

If quarrels serve to release tensions only for the moment, and the whole process has to begin again, we may well question the suitability of the relationship. If, however, the release of tension is accompanied by an increased understanding of and adjustment to each other, the quarrel can be said to be a normal part of courtship. It is easy for a couple to rationalize many other aspects of personal behavior. Here again, honesty with one's self and one's prospective mate, and a willingness to look beneath the surface for the meaning of behavior, are essential if courtship is to be productive of adjustment.[31]

A third problem involves relating the past to the present. The possession of a "past"—and who hasn't one?—very often raises

---

[30] See the discussion of this necessary characteristic in Chapter 4.
[31] *Cf.* Waller (Hill), *op. cit.*, p. 186 f.

the question of whether all or part of that past shall be revealed. There is no trite answer, of course, but two questions need to be faced in this connection.

First, why does one feel a need to confess? Is it because of what he may gain from it in the sense that "confession is good for the soul"? If he has a profound sense of guilt about an earlier love affair, is it his hope that by confessing he will somehow release himself from that guilt? Or does he wish to confess his past affairs because he thinks his status will be raised in the eyes of the one being courted? If the purpose of such confession is to achieve any of these aims, its wisdom may well be challenged. (This is not to deny the value of confession, but to indicate that courtship is not necessarily the equivalent of the confession box or the psychiatrist's couch.)

Second, what will confession accomplish for the courtship? Omitting any selfish values, what is to be accomplished by confession of the past? Will the partner be happier in the courtship, or have more understanding in marriage for knowing whatever it is that is to be confessed? There are some things that are necessarily of profound importance: If one has been married before, or is the parent of an illegitimate child, this should be made known during courtship—if for no other reason than that its later discovery may well wreck the marriage. There are other things, however, which may seem of importance to a person who is so thoroughly conscientious that he can hold nothing back, but which may only make the partner uncertain and unhappy. A rule of thumb in this case may well be that confessions that cannot contribute to adjustment and happiness in marriage are unwise. It is not always easy to decide what is or is not significant in one's past as it relates to adjustment in a possible marriage. It is wise, under circumstances where the decision cannot readily be made, to objectify the confession by first discussing its importance with a disinterested person, a marriage counselor or one's minister or priest; very often such an act will prove or disprove the need, to the advantage of both parties to the courtship.

SUMMARY

Having set dating apart from true courtship in the last chapter, we have here directed our thinking to the second stage in the whole mate-selection process—that of seeking out and learning to know and to understand that one person who seems best suited to meet our personality needs, to have values and goals akin to ours, and with whom the intense emotional involvement we call love can be shared.

In present-day society love is considered to be the *sine qua non* of marriage. Here we have recognized that true love is more than infatuation, more than physical attraction—that it has important elements of deep satisfaction in both giving and receiving affection and security, and in appreciating the worth of each as an individual. We have indicated, too, that love is not a way of expressing aggression, of obtaining sexual dominance, or of being submissive. Most important has been the indication that love is not something that is "born mature," but a mutual feeling that has its beginnings in the recognized sameness of interests and values and that grows into an intense affectional relationship only as the personalities of the couple become integrated.

Successful courtship, we have seen, is a time of growing identification, of learning to give and take in the ordinary processes of loving, and of recognizing that marriage is essentially a "oneness" toward which the couple strive—and in the striving find the basic satisfactions of personality fulfillment.

READINGS AND TOPICS FOR REPORTS

1. Secure serious definitions of love from the members of your class; then secure equally serious definitions from couples who have been married for twenty years or more. How do you account for such differences as you find? Are these due to the maturing of the individuals, to their having had years of marital experience, or to other reasons?

2. Using anonymously answered questionnaires, determine the number of love affairs the members of your class have had. What variations

are there in terms of sex, urban-rural background, type of school, etc.?
3. Analyze the contents of a number of "romance" magazines. How do the conceptions of love contained therein differ from those expressed in this chapter?

ADVANCED READINGS

Braydon, Elizabeth, *Women Today*.
Cohn, D. L., *Love in America*.
Levy, John, and Ruth Munroe, *The Happy Family*.

8

Courtship: III

D ATING, USUALLY A recreation-centered introduction to male-
female companionships and courtship, a selective and evaluative
process, lead to the third and final stage of premarital relationships, the *engagement*. It has both social and interpersonal values,
and these should be understood, if for no other reason than that
the engagement is not clearly defined in our society today.

THE SOCIAL ASPECTS OF THE ENGAGEMENT

The engagement, in whatever name and form, is a pattern of
behavior generally used. In every society where the engagement is
found, it is regarded as notice that mate selection has occurred
(by whatever means), and that the couple are no longer available
to others as prospective mates. It serves, then, as a *rite of passage*—
an activity recognizing the movement from one status in society
to another. It also serves, in some societies and in a social sense,
to sanction new types of behavior not previously allowed.[1]

---

[1] The freedom allowed young people in the dating and courtship stages today,
as contrasted with the strict supervision of earlier times, makes this a less important
characteristic today.

It was stated in Chapter 1 that youth in our American middle-class society are increasingly responsible for the choice of a mate. This heightened individualism has been accompanied by a decreasing importance in the group-sanctioned aspects of the engagement. Today, and especially on the college campus, a couple have "an understanding," the girl is "pinned," or an engagement is "announced"; very often, however, what the engagement means is known only to the couple themselves. Gone are the rigid prescriptions of behavior allowable *before* as contrasted with *after* this understanding, or pinning, or announcement occurs. The recognition is now often that of the couple themselves, with less *social* significance attached. The mother of a newly pinned college student (herself a college graduate) has shown some of the differences between the old and the new meanings of the engagement in these words.

> I don't know how to take the actions of this generation. When I became engaged, it meant something. [My husband] and I waited until the end of our senior year, when he knew that his plans were definite and that he would be able to marry after working a year, and then our families announced our engagement at a small party to our best friends. From then on, we were *engaged*, and it meant something to us, to my parents and his, and to their friends and ours. . . . Look at what's just happened. Nancy came home with stars in her eyes, and showed us her pin. It's his fraternity pin. He's a junior and she's a sophomore—they can't possibly marry for years, because he hasn't any money and expects to work his way through law school. . . . She admits she isn't sure that she is going to marry him, but she expects to. . . . We had nothing to do with it, although we know him and like him very much. We haven't even met his parents, although we understand they are fine people. . . . Nancy doesn't see why we should be concerned about all of this. She says everyone in the sorority is pinned, or about to be, and that it's really just being engaged to be engaged to marry. . . . But this *is* an engagement, because they've agreed that they are going to marry and there probably won't be any real engagement—he may give her a ring later, but that will be all there is to it.

This description may have a slightly familiar sound to many college students, for it is not unusual. The weakness of this "event" in determining a new status for this couple is quite evident. Nancy can "back out" of the agreement; the finality of it as the social recognition of a new and sharply defined pair relationship has been lost.[2] This change (especially in the middle class) in attitudes toward the agreement to marry is part of the whole process of secularization discussed in Chapter 1.

Despite this loss of significance, the engagement still has important functions, although they are of a different and (to us) increasingly important nature.

THE PSYCHOLOGICAL ASPECTS OF THE ENGAGEMENT

Even though the engagement no longer has its earlier significance as a "social contract," it is still a contract in the sense that the couple have agreed upon a new status. This new status may be ill defined, easily broken, or understood only by the couple, but it is in effect. It is, in their minds, a new stage in the premarital relationship, and has its special significance.

The Engagement as a Period of Transition

While this writer believes that the evaluating and exploring of each other's personalities, attitudes, behavior, and so on, are logically part of the courtship stage, there is nevertheless much to be done in this connection during the engagement.[3] The need for the "romantic façade" is no longer—and it can be discarded—albeit gradually.[4] The couple enters a new stage of "togetherness" in the engagement that is partly the result of new peer attitudes, and partly due to the increasing strength of love—which can now be brought into the open to a greater extent. The latter is, of

[2] One evidence of this is seen in the fact that the breach-of-promise suit is no longer permitted in most states.

[3] This is not to suggest that the evaluating and exploring of each other's personalities *ever* ends, for it is one of the continuing processes of married life.

[4] This adjustment to reality is a process that requires conscious effort, and is one of the important "planned" tasks in the later states of the total courtship.

course, somewhat the result even today of a changed status of the "pinned" or engaged couple. In one college senior's words:

> Bill and I were never the kind to "neck" in public. We did our kissing when we were alone, and I always made sure I kissed him good night *before* we arrived at the dorm. Now that we're engaged, it isn't quite the same. I don't mind kissing him even in front of the housemother, because everybody knows we're in love, it's official, and it's one of our privileges. . . . I can now admit to anyone that I'm in love, and I can act that way. No one will think it's just cheap necking.

There is evident here a new sense of naturalness and emotional involvement in the relationship that serves as a period of transition in the movement toward marriage.[5] In those cases where parents are brought into the picture, the interpersonal contacts between the couple and both sets of parents are increased in both number and content. One student described this in these words:

> When Joe and I "went together," it was really just us who were involved. Now that we are pinned, we seem to be moving toward what we'll have when married. I'm beginning to be recognized by his parents as Joe's, and my folks think of him as *mine*. We visit each other's homes, and go out sometimes with his or my parents. It's a sort of bridge on the way from just going together to being married.

In saying this, this student sees her engagement in Hill's words: "The engagement as a period of transition between courtship and marriage appears to offer the possibility of [a new] orientation [to being part of the larger psychological whole that includes one's parents]."[6]

The Engagement as a Period of Testing

Certain characteristics of the engagement afford an opportunity for testing the relationship. There is an increase in intimacy, and the possessiveness each feels for the other is more complete. These

---

[5] This is especially important in those cases where "necking" has been viewed as recreation, rather than as love making.

[6] Cf. Willard Waller (revised by Reuben Hill), *The Family: A Dynamic Interpretation*, p. 219.

provide an opportunity for finding out how well each can handle certain personality adjustments, which will be called for in marriage.

One of these has to do with self-management. A successful marriage relationship constantly demands that both husband and wife "give in," gracefully, not grudgingly. During the months of the engagement this ability can be put to the test as never before. Each has definitely declared his intentions regarding the other, and the need for many of the reserves, which have persisted throughout courtship, is abolished. Each can learn more definitely how able and willing the other is to manage himself in the face of the demands of intimate living. Some aspects of married life can never be tested except under the actual conditions of such living, but others can be brought into the bright light of realism and seen for what they are. An example of this is seen in the following abstract from an interview with an engaged student.

> I need very much to talk with someone about what I'm finding since I've become engaged to Johnny. His mother told me once that he is selfish, but I never could see it. When we were having dates—in our Junior year—he was always good fun, and we had no trouble. When we began to go together, and to see ourselves as maybe becoming engaged, things were still fine. . . . We had a few quarrels, but nothing serious. Johnny was always agreeable, and I thought there wasn't any problem. I couldn't see how his mother could have said such a thing. . . . He always seemed to want to do what I wanted to do, although I tried to do what he wanted, too. . . . After we were engaged, though, things were somehow different. Gradually he's let this nice agreeable front slip away. When we talk about what we need to do in order to marry, things are different. He isn't willing to give up things so that we can get ready to have a home. . . . I feel as though I'm up against a stone wall; all of his willingness to go halfway seems to be gone *since he knows he has me.*

This is an extreme example, but it does illustrate the way a person can continue to hide his true self during courtship—only to uncover it in the intimacy of the engagement. Similar examples can be given in most of the areas of interpersonal relations;

suffice it to say here that these very often uncover themselves only after courtship has moved to this final stage.[7]

The engagement can be a period of testing in quite a different way. Engaged people sometimes need to learn how to move more directly toward each other (in both an emotional and a sexual sense). Personal backgrounds being what they are, some men and women still move hesitantly toward each other, despite the greater freedom allowed the sexes in our society today. Shyness and diffidence do characterize many individuals throughout courtship. Even though they have declared their marriage intentions, the test of whether they can move toward the intimacies of marriage must wait until the prescribed freedoms of the engagement confront them. This may be difficult for most students to understand; others will know from their own experience what is meant. In the words of an engaged senior:

> I never could be sure about Joan until after we were engaged. I thought she loved me, but she was cool in many ways. . . . Take sex, for example, I wouldn't want either of us to go the whole way, but she was sort of an iceberg, if you know what I mean. . . . Not until we became engaged and she wore my ring was she really affectionate. There's nothing wrong in what we do now, but since we've been engaged there's all the difference in the world. Now I know she's capable of giving me the same kind of affection I feel for her. I'd never know it, though, if we weren't engaged.

This testing function of the engagement cannot, in our opinion, be overvalued. It is rarely to be expected that a couple will reach *complete* agreement; as Magoun has said, "Two people seldom really love each other until they discover that there are a few places where mutual understanding is impossible, until they accept this, and until it does not seem calamitous."[8] Nevertheless, basic agreement in major areas is necessary, as is the ability to adjust to each other's personalities and to changing demands upon one's own personality. Unless the couple do test for this agreement and

---

[7] It is to be hoped that this type of relationship occurs in only exceptional cases.
[8] Cf. F. Alexander Magoun, *Love and Marriage*, p. 181.

ability, they lay themselves open to possible postmarital stresses, which might otherwise have been avoided.

The Engagement as a Period of Identification

A third function of the engagement is to help the couple to begin to think as *one*, in so far as this is possible and as marriage will demand it. While the successful courtship provides an increasing sense of common purpose, and of understanding and adjustment, it does not give the quality of "we-togetherness" that is needed even in the first days of marriage. Nor does such a feeling ordinarily develop overnight. Any couple who contemplate marriage need time and opportunity to draw together the threads of their two lives—to attempt to do so only after the marriage ceremony requires an unconscious struggle *to think and act in direct relation to each other*, which can be an added burden in their adjustment efforts.[9] We can best illustrate this with a quotation from an interview with a student who had been married for three years.

> Bill and I went together for quite a while, and we somehow knew that things were going to end in our marriage. Probably we would have been engaged in another month or so, and then would have been married in a few months. . . . Then his company decided to send him—quite suddenly—to its Tennessee plant, and so we married after only five days notice to ourselves. . . . I don't want to say that things didn't work out, because they did, but the first months were more difficult than they should have been. . . . The trouble was that in going steady we had just skirted around the idea of really being each other's—it was pleasant to consider but not too real an idea. Then suddenly we *were* each other's, and there just hadn't been any moving over into the same seat, if you understand what I mean by that. . . . As I see it now, an engagement would really have been the time when we got used to the idea of being in a world that consisted just of us, and we missed it. So things were more difficult to adjust to.

One senses rather than sees identification in what this young wife has said. "Moving over into the same seat" is a naïve way of

[9] See the discussion on this point in Chapter 10.

expressing what we mean by identification—the drawing together (with an increasing involvement) of two lives in preparation for the closeness of the marriage relationship. It differs from the transitions discussed above largely in that the latter are essentially social (and involve the whole of the relationship) while identification is essentially a *personal* process. The two are interrelated and interdependent but must be seen to have separate values for the couple.

The Engagement as a Period of Planning and Preparation

In most of the simpler societies, marriage occasions no great physical preparation; after the ceremony the young couple moves in with one or the other's parents, as custom decrees, and life goes on. In American society, the marriage typically indicates the beginning of a new home; this obviously requires some preparation—the renting or purchasing of a place in which to live, the buying of furniture, the accumulation of all the small artifacts that are needed in modern living. The engagement period affords the couple an opportunity to plan for these acquisitions and to ready the place they will call home. It is important that these plans, and at least the major acquisitions, be made jointly. While there is a traditional division of responsibility—at least in the middle class—in that the girl chooses her linens, silver, china patterns, and so on—every effort should be made to have the major decisions arrived at jointly. Where the couple shall live, whether they shall rent an apartment or buy a house [if there is any choice in the matter]—these are decisions of such far-reaching effect as to require full understanding and mutual agreement.[10]

The engagement thus goes beyond the functions discussed above and becomes a matter of *doing* together. In this, there is great psychological value. In the courtship stage, each was more likely to be *doing for the other*; in the engagement period, through this need for planning and readying the home, the emphasis becomes

[10] It is in the making of these decisions that roles and role patterns become more sharply defined.

one of "*doing for us.*" This is one of the more subtle ways in which the engagement serves gradually to introduce the couple to the roles of husband and wife. If both recognize this function and see its true worth, they will be aided in the transition required for success in marriage.

THE LENGTH OF ENGAGEMENT

Since the engagement has the several functions just outlined, we may well ask how long this special relationship should last. Students of adjustment in marriage have shown that longer engagements appear to be related to—if not causal in—the degree to which the couple find happiness (i.e., satisfaction of their needs) in marriage.[11] These findings were based upon limited numbers of cases, but their logic is undeniable. The short engagement, especially if not preceded by a period of intense courtship, leaves the couple without any real knowledge of each other upon which to base their marriage.

In contrast, the extended courtship—which may run into years—can be equally unsatisfactory, but for quite different reasons. The writer knows of one engagement which lasted for ten years. In that period, the couple came to take each other pretty much for granted, and to accept the *status quo* of engagement—without any keen sense of the anticipation of working out and sharing the marriage relationship. Successful marriage includes a continuing anticipation of new facets of the relationship being unfolded—whether at twenty or fifty—and this couple were engaged so long that this anticipation was replaced with a matter-of-factness that certainly held no thrill.

How long should an engagement be? There is no ready answer to such a question. First, it is evident that the ease with which the couple can communicate is an important factor,[12] as is the degree to which they have previously learned to share in their emotional

---

[11] Cf., for example, Ernest W. Burgess and Leonard L. Cottrell, *Predicting Success or Failure in Marriage*, p. 167 ff.

[12] Cf, the discussion on communication in dating, Ch. 6.

relationships. For the couple who have dated a long time but courted only briefly (in the sense used in our earlier discussion), the longer engagement seems indicated. For those who, in courtship, have come to know each other well, a shorter engagement may suffice. In any event, in the situation peculiar to each couple (and no two couples are exactly alike) the psychological functions discussed in this chapter need to have been exercised.

BREAKING THE ENGAGEMENT

We have already indicated that engagements can be broken with impunity.[13] There is—as has also been suggested—every reason why the engagement should be broken, in some cases. The fitting of two personalities together, the adapting of the ideas, ideals, goals, and behavior patterns of each to the other, and (incidentally) the bringing of two persons' peers and families together, can sometimes fail. Where these cannot be done, there seems no justifiable reason today for continuing a relationship that can only come to grief. Happiness in marriage—or even a superficial adjustment—can continue only as long as both persons are equally involved. To say this, however, is not to provide a rationale for the easy breaking of the relationship. The fact that two people have gone this far in the intermingling of their lives means that a break will to some extent be traumatic. Where there are important differences this is unavoidable, but such an action should be taken only after the position of each has been made clear to the other, after they have made definite efforts to resolve their differences, and after they have allowed some time to elapse. This last should not be disregarded; situations that appear to be impossible may well look quite different after a "cooling-off" period. It is well, too, for any couple in this situation to think seriously of invoking the aid of a marriage counselor or other

[13] It should be evident to the student that none of this discussion relates to the quasi engagement, that relationship which is understood by both parties to be only a convenient social assorting. Certainly some of the "being pinned" behavior on college campuses is only quasi-serious in its intent.

skilled (and disinterested) outsider, for many times the discord is of such a nature that such assistance can prevent the loss of a relationship which must have had some merit since it has gone this far.

SUMMARY

The final stage in the progress toward marriage—the engagement—is viewed in this chapter as one of continuing movement toward the "oneness" we have emphasized earlier. It is a period of increasing freedom and intimacy of discussion and behavior, and provides the couple with the final opportunity before marriage of "searching the crevices of the personality" for those qualities that will make (or prevent) the success of the marriage. In some few cases it will be the time when these crevices are found to contain characteristics that will negatively affect marriage. It is, therefore, in these few cases the time when withdrawal from the relationship is still possible. Viewed most positively, however, the engagement is seen as a positive step toward the understanding and sharing which constitute a base for happiness and success in marriage.

READINGS AND TOPICS FOR REPORTS

1. List the circumstances under which you believe an engagement to be unnecessary. Are those you list sufficiently general as to apply to numbers of people, or do engagements appear to be of general value?
2. Select a number of articles on courtship and marriage from current women's magazines. What is your reaction to the general tenor of these articles? Are they unduly optimistic or pessimistic?
3. From your knowledge of "acceptable behavior" today, list the items of conduct which are strongly controlled by social opinion, and those which are left to the discretion of the engaged couple.

9

The Marriage Ceremony
and the Honeymoon

SOME TYPE of social ceremony signifying the marital union is found in almost all societies. In American life the marriage ceremony and the wedding serve that purpose.[1] They satisfy one of the legal requirements of the state, and may or may not be public ceremonies. Whether public or not, their occurrence is generally known, and is often well publicized. Socially, they are rites of passage—a formal moving of the couple to a new social and personal status. Functionally, they have a number of values worth noting.

THE SIGNIFICANCE OF THE MARRIAGE CEREMONY

A major purpose of the marriage ceremony is to have other people recognize the new relationship. Society has a stake in every

[1] The *marriage ceremony* is required by the state, and may be performed by either civil or religious authorities. The *wedding* is a social event, an elaboration of the required marriage ceremony, and is a matter of personal desire. The terms are used interchangeably by many people.

marriage, as has been indicated, and public recognition—by whatever means—gives both husband and wife a sense of social conforming which is psychologically valuable. Very few people can live comfortably while defying or after defying the prevailing mores;[2] participating in the marriage ceremony gives to *all* participants an important sense of social adherence and group membership. There is, in fact, some research which would indicate that secret marriages and elopements have less chance of success than do those that conform to prevailing custom.[3]

The reasons for defying convention are numerous. Some marriages occur on the impulse of the moment (sometimes as a result of intoxication); they may be an attempt to avoid parental control or the censure of friends; they may be an effort to compensate for an unexpected pregnancy. Rarely do they have reasons behind them that would indicate any regularity in, or adequacy of, courtship.

If all concerned, including parents and friends, see the marriage ceremony both as a meaningful part of the whole social drama which is life, and as a high point in the transition of the couple from one degree of personal relationship to another, well and good. But such is not always the case. There are some such ceremonies which are regarded as the opportunity "to pay off social obligations," to collect a dowry for the bride,[4] to gain social prestige in the community (including making headlines on the social pages of the newspapers). The receiving and giving of wedding gifts is a legitimate and happy tradition, despite the strong tinge of commercialism introduced by jewelers and gift

---

[2] See, for example Harvey J. Locke, *Predicting Adjustment in Marriage, passim.* In this study (comparing a group of happily married and divorced couples) there is a recurring emphasis in the happily married group upon behaving in socially accepted ways as contrasted with violations of conventional behavior in the divorced group.

[3] Cf. Paul Popenoe, *Modern Marriage*, p. 222 ff. for a discussion of research in this topic.

[4] An example of this function is still found in ethnic groups (e.g., American-Hungarians) in this country, where the male guests pay for the privilege of dancing with the bride at the marriage celebration. These payments become the dowry the bride brings to her husband.

shops. Having one's relatives and friends share in the joy of the occasion is humanly satisfying. Having an account of the occasion in the papers is very proper recognition of the personal and social meaning of the new status.[5] All these are legitimate and valuable when seen in this light, none is valid when it forces the couple into a "performance" in which ulterior motives are uppermost and which dull for the couple all their shared joys, desires, and needs.

Part of the significance of the marriage ceremony lies in the nature of that ceremony and in the place where it occurs. A majority of the ceremonies in the United States are performed under religious auspices. In some instances this is no more than capitulation to the demands of tradition, but to most people in our society the religious connotation of the ceremony is important. The often-repeated statement, "I wouldn't feel married if a minister didn't perform the ceremony," is evidence of this fact. Whether or not they are active church participants or whether or not they share with the Roman Catholic and certain other churches the idea that marriage is a sacrament, the religious significance of the ceremony is deep-seated, and may well be acknowledged. It is not accidental that contemporary research shows a higher statistical probability of success for marriages which are thus sanctioned.[6] It should be clearly recognized, in this connection, that the significance lies not in who performs the ceremony, or where it takes place, but in the whole constellation of forces which create the attitudes the individuals hold. Religion, whatever the form it may take, is a fundamental part of man's whole value system and hence contributes in an important fashion to the personality he brings to marriage.

It is unfortunate that the state allows its agents to conduct so important a ceremony in so informal (and sometimes uncouth)

[5] It should be remembered that these very often become only elaborate accounts of the clothing and millinery worn by the principal female members of the wedding party.

[6] The researches of Burgess and Cottrell, Terman, Locke, and others bear out this statement. Cf., for example, Harvey J. Locke, *op. cit.*, p. 240 ff.

a way. The significance of this is best illustrated from one of the author's case studies—albeit in a negative way.

> We thought it would be best if we were married without any particular to-do. . . . Neither of us had any parents living near us, and we didn't want a big time with our friends—we just aren't built that way. Neither one of us is especially religious, and we don't belong to any church. So we went quietly to City Hall—we both thought a civil ceremony was enough, and would be satisfactory. . . . I've never been made to feel so terrible in my life. It was just like a business proposition, like borrowing money at the bank. . . . The clerk didn't care a bit that we were ready to get married—all he seemed to think of was getting his forms filled out correctly. He made a mistake, and blotted the application, and swore—more at us, it seemed, than at himself. . . . Then we went across the hall to the man they sent us to, to have the ceremony performed. He called in two clerks as witnesses, and they grinned at us as though we were doing something that wasn't just the decent thing to do. I looked around the office—a calendar with a picture of a nearly-nude woman on it advertising coal, and a spittoon which hadn't been cleaned for a long time—oh, it was awful. . . . The man read the ceremony so fast that neither of us really understood what he said, but we answered as he asked, and then he said, "I pronounce you man and wife." All three of them looked at us just awful, and Harry kissed me, but not the way I had expected at all. He was just as embarrassed as I was, and we got out of there just as fast as we could. . . . We've talked about it often since, and both feel that we missed what we had looked forward to for so long. . . . The whole ceremony didn't take three minutes, and made us feel like three cents.

The casualness of this official and the hurried and negatively suggestive way in which he performed an important rite served to cheat this couple of what should have been a positive and joyous moment in their lives. There was no symbolism, in this case, of a changed and enriched status, of the beginning of a life-long relationship based upon human affection. As a political gesture, it was "adequate"; as psychological meaning it was not only empty but also negative.

Just as the engagement is a time of drawing together, of building an identification with each other, so is the marriage ceremony a psychological device for further uniting the couple. Each has his or her own role to play, of course; each must act according to the folkways current in his life. But neither can do any of these things without taking the other into account. Cutting the cake—together; being congratulated—together; running through a barrage of rice and confetti—together; these and the multitude of other little things which go to make up the total rite (however modest it may be) all serve to bring the couple closer together. Contrast this with the emptiness of the experience quoted above, and the value of the marriage ceremony as a psychological instrument for bringing the couple into a state of "we-ness" is realized.

None of this is to say that a couple cannot be married by a civil servant, or that a formal wedding—with all "pomp and circumstance" attached—is necessary. The simple ceremony at home, or in a parsonage or the church, can suffice. The bride need not be dressed in special finery (never to be worn again); she need not carry orchids imported at great expense. Being congratulated and leaving immediately can be as effective as would a Fifth Avenue *soirée* with its professional caterers, potted palms, and candid photographers. The ceremony can be any of these, and be successful, but only if it fits into the value system of the couple.[7] But also, the ceremony can be most meaningful to the couple only to the extent that it does not exhaust their physical and emotional resources so that the following days are spent in near-collapse. Thus

> I had showers and parties and "fittings" and other demands on me for two months before we were married. It was awful. . . . I had so much looked forward to my wedding that when finally it came I was too tired to know what was going on. It was just a rat race. I wouldn't dare tell mother—she was so happy with it all. But Dave and I saw each other only by fits and starts, and I felt he was a stranger to me when I walked up the aisle in St. ——. . . . When we

---

[7] The wedding is so generally accepted as "the bride's business," and only incidentally as that of the groom, that differences in values in this area are frequently encountered. The secondary place of the male in this connection is sufficiently accepted that there is usually little tension created by these differences.

finally got away, at midnight, I was almost sick—just living on my nerve. Dave wasn't quite as bad, but it took us a week to get over it—and that was all the time we had for our honeymoon.

It is quite evident that this total rite was far less effective than it should have been for the couple. (One might well ask if the ceremony was for the benefit of the couple or of the bride's mother and friends.)

If this chapter were intended as advice-giving (which it is not), that advice might be given in these words: *The marriage ceremony is for the couple's benefit, and should be carried out in such a way that it meets their expectations and needs—but not to the detriment of their relationships in the immediate future.*

THE HONEYMOON

One of the delightful folk patterns of our society is the honeymoon. Like most such patterns it has a sound rationale; in this case, that of aiding the couple to make the transition from individual- to couple-centered behavior. However much the engagement has served to move the couple *toward* the latter, there remain at the time of marriage varying degrees of individual-centeredness. The couple have come to know each other well, and have been joined in matrimony, but they still have major areas of each other's personalities and other characteristics to explore and understand. Not only are they strange in many of each other's ways, but they are now ready for sexual relations—for which they have had only partial preparation and about which their knowledge is still incomplete.[8] The groundwork for all their future understanding has been laid in the courtship and engagement stages, but adjustment—in the fullest sense—can now begin. This is a period in marriage which cannot be given too much importance, yet it is often regarded in the most superficial manner.

---

[8] This is especially true if one or both come from social or religious backgrounds in which sex is considered to be a tabooed subject prior to marriage.

Requirements for the Honeymoon

If the honeymoon is to fulfill its function, it must be a state of mind—not simply a socially prescribed activity. A first requirement, then, is that the couple themselves understand why they are taking the time and spending the money for the honeymoon. The honeymoon planned to coincide with a trip for other purposes defeats *its own purpose*, for as "no man can serve two masters," so the couple cannot have divided interests in this period.[9] A honeymoon in which the girl sat in the hotel room all day while her husband attended a sales-training meeting was admitted by both to be a dismal failure:

> [In his words]: All day long I thought about Grace waiting for me—I didn't learn a thing about my job. I wasn't even there. . . . I got the poorest rating of any man there, and it was because I was so frustrated.
>
> [In her words]: I sat in the lobby or in the room and read all day. I didn't see Jim from seven o'clock when he left for the company cafeteria. . . . When he came back at six, we were both so fed up that it spoiled our evenings. . . . We just didn't have a honeymoon!

Timing the Honeymoon

A couple once told the writer that they were about to go on a honeymoon after fourteen years of married life. This was sheer sentimentality. One can no more delay the honeymoon for fourteen months or fourteen years than one can stop the sun in its course. That they were about to take a trip (which they could now afford), renew something of their youth, and cast off temporarily the cares of the world is not questioned, but their chance of having a honeymoon—in the sense used here—had been gone for fourteen years. Postponing the honeymoon, as many people do for a variety of reasons, is to forego it. Adjustment in marriage waits for nothing—it must begin as soon as the couple begin their married life.

[9] Cf. Rabbi Stanley R. Brav, "Note on Honeymoons," *Marriage and Family Living*, 9:58 ff. (1947)

Choosing a Suitable Place

If they are realistic and at all practical-minded, the couple will spend their honeymoon under conditions that they can afford financially. Beyond this, however, there is the need to choose a place which is suited to their needs, *to the needs of both.* The fly fisherman who takes his bride on a trip to the trout streams in the Colorado Rocky Mountains so that he can fish (while she sits on a hotel porch and reads) is hardly on a honeymoon. The bride who drags her new husband to Niagara Falls because it is an ideal place to exercise her hobby of photography is equally wrong.[10] Such things are sometimes done, of course, and are accepted by the other partner under the momentary urge to do whatever the other seems most happy to do, but this is no honeymoon. The honeymoon, to repeat, is a state of mind, but one that must be shared by both. The proper place for the honeymoon is wherever they can be together constantly and can shut out—at least psychologically—the world about them.

The Personnel of the Honeymoon

It may seem strange that a textbook such as this even raises the question of who goes on the honeymoon, but it is not an unreasonable subject to consider. In a surprising number of cases people report that "daddy and mother," or little sister or Aunt Tillie accompanied them—on what turned out to be a sightseeing trip. Privacy is obviously the prime requisite for at least the first adjustments of two people, and privacy—to talk intimately, to play together, to let down all the barriers that characterize the couple's interaction in courtship and the engagement—obviously cannot be had with a third person present.

ADJUSTMENTS AND THE HONEYMOON

While we can expect that the couple will have reached a high level of understanding prior to the marriage ceremony, we can

[10] The student will by now question the suitability of any marriage in which *one or the other* makes such a decision.

also expect that time will be required for adjustment in many areas.[11] The need is for the adjustment to begin while the couple have the maximum of privacy; while each can concentrate fully upon their pair-relationship.

Realism Regarding Resources

A first is the need to be realistic about money. Traditionally, the honeymoon is as elaborate an experience as the couple can afford. The need to impress, carried over from courtship days, hasn't fully worn off, and the social compulsion to do as one's peers do is great. The honeymoon in which the couple spend more than they can reasonably afford almost surely creates tensions for husband or wife, or both.[12] It is far better to be realistic about what money is available *for this purpose*, and to be frank with each other in the spending of that money, than to lay the ground for tension and frustration when the honeymoon is over. One thing especially to be guarded against, in this connection, is the tendency to regard this as "the only honeymoon we'll ever have and we might as well shoot the works." It is the only honeymoon the couple will ever have, to be sure, but it is an experience which can vitally affect their long-range attitudes and plans, and being careless about the use of money in this first period of the marriage can have untoward effects later.

Realism Regarding Sex

The second area in which there is need for realism is that involving sexual relations. If courtship and the engagement have been adequate, the bride and groom have had an increasing sexual desire for each other. Personal and social values no longer impose barriers against fulfillment of that desire; the consummation of the marriage can now be realized. It is at this point that all the insights each has about the other need to be brought to bear. The

[11] See the discussion of marital adjustment in Chapter 10.

[12] It should be obvious that this is one of the areas in which each other's values and aspirations should have been discovered during the courtship and engagement stages—with plans made accordingly.

intellectual acceptance of sex by the bride has not necessarily been accompanied by an equivalent emotional acceptance. Sex is an experience about which her whole culture may have given her proscriptions which are often deep-seated. Coitus is an experience she desires, because she is human and loves her husband, but one about which she may have reservations.[13] It is an experience she desires, and hopes for, but which she may dread because of its unknown qualities. It is an experience for which her husband may be equally ill prepared, however much book knowledge he may have or how much premarital experience he may have had. All the back-alley talk and the "bull sessions" he may have taken part in have been of little avail in preparing him for this experience, for here are two people engaging not merely in a physical act but in the joining of their whole lives. It is not unusual under these circumstances for things to go wrong. Sexual adjustment comes only with intimate knowledge, and this comes only from extended experience.

It is therefore no wonder that all the understanding and identification that have been built between the couple can be damaged in short order. The male is often more dynamic and aggressive in his approach to sex; if he allows his urgency to carry him faster than his bride is ready to go, the whole marriage can—and has been known to—go on to failure. While such mishandling of the situation does not very often carry through to a complete wrecking of the marriage, it may lead to maladjustments that may take years to overcome. This can well be illustrated from a case record.

I'd really give anything I have, even after twelve years of married life, if I could do over again the things I did on our wedding night, and do them quite different. . . . I was just a green kid; like most kids I thought I knew everything there was to know about sex. I'd been in on all of the things country kids do and talk about, short of having relations. Helen was well brought up—good family, religious, and all of that. . . . Well, that first night I acted like a damn fool. I thought it was natural for her to be afraid, but I also thought if I just carried right on as though it was natural for her to act afraid,

[13] See Chapter 12 for an elaboration of this topic.

everything would work out all right. . . . Well, it didn't. I hurt her a lot, I know, and she didn't have any satisfaction at all. I didn't either for that matter, because afterwards, when she was crying to herself in her pillow I felt like a big heel. And nothing I could say or do seemed to make up for it. . . . Afterwards, she sort of forgave me, and would do what I wanted to, but for the first nine years of our married life she acted just the same—as though it was something she knew she had to do and expected to do because she loved me, but just simply didn't enjoy. . . . It was only after the birth of our second child that I guess she talked to her doctor—although she never said so—because he got ahold of me and laid the law down, and then got me in her room at the hospital and talked to us both like we were small kids. . . . Things have been fine, since, but jeez, I'd give anything to be able to start over again and not make the mistake I did.

To see the importance of what has been said, the student needs only ask himself how different things might have been had this inept handling of the first sexual relations not driven a wedge between this husband and wife. It is probably safe to say, from all available evidence, that had this couple not had superior qualities in the other areas of their married life, their marriage would have been of short duration.

Sexual behavior is treated in more detail in the following chapter; here the emphasis is not upon what the husband and wife do, but upon what they refrain from doing. Each partner comes to marriage with desire, but it is a desire that must be given form and substance and must be keyed to the desire of the other. To act hastily or ineptly, to hurry through to one's own satisfaction without regard for the satisfaction of the mate, to think only of the satisfactions of the moment rather than of the long-time significance of the relationship upon which they are entering— these are the "don'ts" regarding sexual behavior on the honeymoon.

But the "do's" are equally important, and implied above. In the successful honeymoon, each partner recognizes the presence in the other of the basic urge to sexual fulfillment, however harnessed and restricted it may be. Each understands that ineptness is an evidence not of weakness but of humanness. Each knows, too, that what they are undertaking is a summation of their relationship. Both need to work, therefore, to achieve together and for each other all the tenderness, sensitiveness, and passion of which they are capable.

Adjustment to Personal Idiosyncrasies

Each partner to the marriage brings peculiar ways of behaving which are revealed to the other for the first time during the honeymoon. Reuben Hill has said that all couples live in a "habit cage," which they begin to build while on their honeymoon. The idiosyncrasies each brings to marriage have in many instances to be modified, if not abolished, and new habits formed. No man or woman can make over his or her mate in marriage; no sensible man or woman would want to do so. Each needs, however, to recognize the ease with which habits that involve both are formed, especially in the sensitive time of the honeymoon when both are striving to share with the other; further, each must see the need for not allowing these habits to be formed. Not to be "frank" about things on the honeymoon is to pave the way for not being frank in the months to come when little things can become not only unendearing but almost reprehensible. Habits, like oak trees, grow from little things, and the time to stop them is when they are little. In other words, the honeymoon is not a time in which one accepts whatever happens simply because it happens during the honeymoon; neither is it a time when one begins to reform his partner. It is a time, however, when one views the relationship in as clear a fashion as the emotions of the moment will allow, and moves quietly to build the kind of positive "togetherness" that successful marriage requires.

SUMMARY

This chapter has constituted, in effect, a plea for recognizing the values inherent in the marriage ceremony and the honeymoon. Social rites are important, both to the individual and to the larger society in which they occur, and the couple who marry need to recognize the marriage ceremony as a rite of transition to a new status—that of a married couple. This is not to suggest that the ceremony does not have its warm and personal values, but to emphasize that it is a turning point in the whole relationship, and thus has subtle psychological values. Equally important, it is also a point at which the larger families of which the bride and groom are members are brought into a closer relationship.

The values of the honeymoon—as more than simply a "trip" or a bowing to tradition—have been outlined, and these cannot be overemphasized, for it is in this period that the "oneness" of marriage has its most emphatic beginnings. It would be unwise to suggest that a marriage cannot succeed without a honeymoon, but it can be said with certainty that the honeymoon provides an opportunity for a richness of interaction that will be most advantageous.

READINGS AND TOPICS FOR REPORTS

1. Make a study of the cost of a number of weddings. What were the "cultural compulsives" (the expenditures that *had* to be made), and how did they add to the cost of the wedding? What would have been the results if they had been omitted?
2. Interview a number of clergymen and a number of civil officers who regularly marry people. What are the important differences in their attitudes toward the ceremony? From your findings would you suggest that marriage ceremonies be performed only by religious authorities?

10

Adjustment in Marriage

THE PRECEDING CHAPTERS have placed considerable emphasis upon the need for the increasing adjustment of the man and woman to each other as they move through courtship, the engagement, and the honeymoon. There has been no effort, however, to indicate that the couple should expect to be adjusted fully by the time they have returned from the honeymoon—for this would be unrealistic.

WHAT IS ADJUSTMENT?

Adjustment, as related to marriage today, is probably quite different from adjustment in marriage in our society some generations ago. In that time marriage had its very "practical" aspects, as was indicated in Chapter 1. For the man and the woman marriage was usually the "only way out," not only economically but in other ways. The pressures of getting a living, the need to avoid the stigma of being unmarried, the need for children as part of the economic unit—these and other factors made marriage a necessity to a greater extent than today. With the shift to a primary emphasis upon marriage as a means of affording the couple the satisfaction of their emotional needs—both through

husband-wife and parent-child contacts—the concept of adjustment must also be shifted. It is probably not an exaggeration to
suggest that for most families in the eighteenth century, adjustment
meant that each member recognized his obligations and fulfilled
them. For the husband, this meant being an adequate provider, a
person who dealt justly with his wife and children, one who transmitted to his children the skills and values that would stand them
in good stead in adulthood, and one who was a "good" citizen in
his community. For the wife, adjustment meant that she did the
housework (and, in rural families took part in some of the work
in barn and field), bore such children as the natural processes
dictated, reared the children, and submitted herself to her husband.
For the children, adjustment in the family meant accepting such
economic tasks as fitted their age and sex, meeting their parents'
requirements as to disciplined behavior, and in general readying
themselves for a not-too-different parenthood. It is probably not
farfetched to say that when the members did these things, the
family would have been considered a "good" [i.e., adjusted]
family.[1] The family of that time was "institutional," in that, as
Reuben Hill has said, "the welfare and smooth functioning of the
larger society and families *as families* [took] precedence over the
personal needs and aspirations of individuals in marriage."[2]

Marriage at mid-twentieth century is, presumably, something
quite different. We marry for love, we have children for love of
them—not as extra hands for getting a living or as old-age "insurance"—and we divorce (to an increasing extent) *if our needs
and expectations are not met*. In this sense, contemporary family
life is personal rather than social.[3]

We are not primarily concerned here with whether or not
adjustment can be *predicted*. We *are* concerned with what adjust-

[1] As used in this chapter the term *adjustment in marriage* can be equated with
having achieved the goals the couple set for themselves in the marriage.

[2] Willard Waller (revised by Reuben Hill), *The Family: A Dynamic Interpretation*,
p. 344.

[3] This is not to suggest that many of the elements which were important in earlier
marriages are no longer present, but rather to indicate that the *focus* has shifted.

ment means to the married pair. Marital adjustment, i.e., success in marriage, can be judged only within the framework of *the expectations the couple have of their marriage*, and therefore in the degree to which they attain these expectations. One individual may seek in his marriage a well-kept and comfortable home, good meals, a wife who "does him credit" in his business and social activities, and so on. A second may seek in his marriage love, companionship, and children. If each of these achieves his goals, his marriage is (to him) a success—there is *adjustment*. No two couples, in other words, have exactly the same expectations; therefore no two marriages can be judged with exactly the same criteria.

CRITERIA OF ADJUSTMENT

Burgess and Locke have suggested eight criteria by which marital adjustment may be evaluated.[4] These are (1) permanence of the marriage, (2) happiness of the couple, (3) conformity to the community's expectations, (4) personality development of the couple, (5) the degree of companionship achieved, (6) satisfaction with the marriage, (7) integration of the couple, and (8) marital adjustment. As Hill points out in a sharply drawn critique,[5] the uncritical use of these criteria as measuring adjustment may be dangerous. Not only are they not equally applicable for marriages in all social groups, since some are less institutional than others. For example, the use of the single criterion of happiness in marriage automatically includes other criteria of companionship, adjustment, and satisfaction. A second and very important objection raised by Hill is that studies using these criteria have "to date been actuarially focused, reaching prematurely into the realm of prediction, to the net detriment of understanding how actual marriage pairs who succeed in marriage achieve success. They fail to translate traits and factors into mechanisms and

[4] Cf. Ernest W. Burgess and Harvey J. Locke, *The Family*, p. 432.
[5] Cf. Waller, *op. cit.*, pp. 343-370. These pages should be read by every student who would understand the difficulties of measuring "adjustment" in marriage.

processes of marriage adjustment and to show how these operate in a given marriage situation."[6] It is obvious, from Chapter 4, that the Burgess and Wallin study[7] has attempted to overcome this objection, but whether with complete success is debatable.

It is clear that any criteria of adjustment we apply are the reflection of and based in the marriage philosophy and the cultural norms of those who have constructed the criteria. Another way of saying this is that we use yardsticks which measure what we want to measure, and that what we want to measure is in turn the reflection of the culture in which we live. The writer is middle-class; this book is written for college students who are presumed to be middle-class and who hold middle-class values. It follows then that any definition of adjustment and any criteria used will necessarily be those related to a middle-class conception of modern marriage and its aims.[8] The *idea* projected above may well be repeated in these words: Adjustment in marriage is *the achievement of the expectations the couple have of their marriage*. If they expect little but achieve it, the marriage is (for them) a success; if they expect much, and achieve little, the marriage is to them, unsuccessful. This places us in a dilemma in any attempt to generalize about adjustment. In Hill's words,

> When we turn to the topic of marriage adjustment, we encounter a degree of confusion, but the moralistic nature of the norms is quite clear. When we say that an individual is adjusted to marriage, we may mean that he is adjusted to the marriage as a situation, and to his spouse as a participant in the situation. More usually we mean that the marriage itself is adjusted to the moral imperatives of marriage, that the parties are not indulging in behavior that threatens the conventional sort of marriage solidarity. It sometimes happens that the adjustment needs of the individual can be fulfilled only by behavior which runs counter to the accepted mores of marriage. The family adviser not infrequently faces the situation

---

[6] *Ibid.*, p. 349.
[7] Cf. Ernest W. Burgess and Paul Wallin, *Engagement and Marriage, passim.*
[8] For this we make neither apology nor defense, but state it as the position of the text so that the student will have no misunderstanding.

where he must counsel an individual to break up his [failing] marriage for the sake of his own [and his partner's] developmental growth and mental health.[9]

These are stout words, and may be objected to by students who are strongly "institutional" in their concept of marriage. However, since the purpose of this text is primarily *to help the student build a philosophy* adequate for meeting the future demands of his marriage and *to place a high positive value* on adequate mate selection, we need not be defensive about such an attitude.

In the light of the past paragraphs, then, we can propose the following as at least tentative and general criteria we would hope to have the student use in thinking of what constitutes adjustment in marriage.[10] To be successful, a marriage will be one in which

(1) each partner has satisfaction in his and his mate's roles.

(2) each partner has freedom and opportunity to express his own personality so long as it does not threaten or impair that of the other.

(3) each partner is the focus for the affectional relationships of the other.

(4) each partner gains a sense of emotional and physical security.

(5) each partner finds satisfaction in the shared purposes and experiences of their joint endeavor.

(6) the couple are stable but adaptable in their relationships with each other and with those outside the marriage.

(7) the couple are jointly able to provide an emotionally and socially satisfying atmosphere in which each can carry on his roles as parent.

These seven "criteria" fall naturally into three areas, and must be discussed in some detail.

[9] Cf. Waller, *op. cit.*, p. 363.
[10] These are the end products of the writer's and some hundreds of students' thinking together about this topic in college courses concerned with marriage.

Adjustment in Roles

Roles, for our purposes, may be defined as the parts one plays in the groups of which he is a member. Each of us has literally dozens of roles—one or more in each group of which we are a member. In the family, for example, the husband-father is bread-winner, sexual partner, social companion, decision maker, disciplinarian, and so on. The wife-mother is homemaker, sexual partner, social companion, and so on. Each partner in the marriage has his own perception of his roles and of his partner's roles; each evaluates his own and his mate's performance of those roles; both are faced with the necessity of adapting their own perceptions and performances to those of the other.[11] As Kuhn has indicated in another connection:

> In any particular pair, marital adjustment is not so much a matter of discrete traits of personality and separable items of background culture as it is a matter of the adjustment of the multi-fold *common and complementary roles* which each member plays, expects to play, and expects the other to play. It is through function-ing in these distinctive roles that personality traits and background items become meaningful in intrapair interaction. It is in these roles that personality, society, and culture meet.[12]

These roles, then, are shared and—more important—comple-mentary to each other. If adjustment is to be had in the marriage, "teamwork" is indicated; the husband must see and perform his roles as they "fit" with the wife's seeing and performing of her roles. Adjustment of roles is not automatically achieved. Each partner brings to marriage his own unique conceptions of his potential roles. These stem from his cultural background, from the unique experiences he has had in his family, and from his own psychological needs. For example, a man may bring to marriage the idea that he is to be the *head* of the household, with all members subservient to himself. If he is of Prussian background this is to be expected, for this is the Prussian cultural identification of the

11 Cf. the writer's *Families in Trouble*, Ch. 6.
12 Cf. Manford H. Kuhn, "How Mates Are Sorted," in Howard Becker and Reuben Hill (eds.), *Family, Marriage and Parenthood*, pp. 272 ff.

husband-father's roles. He may also bring such a conception, even though he is not a Prussian, but because in his own childhood he learned that "father was always the boss" (for whatever reason). He may bring such a conception, again, because he has a psychological need to dominate others—because his personality can only express itself in this way.[13]

Adjustment, then, requires that each individual make such complementary or reciprocal adjustments as the initial role conceptions may require.[14] It is because of this need that items (1) and (2) are included in the preceding list.

Adjustment in Emotional Characteristics

We have previously studied the importance in mate selection of the emotional characteristics of the individual, and have said that mature love for a mate is of such a nature that it causes "each willingly to forego his own personality demands in favor of the other." We have also indicated that this is an emotional state achieved through *growth* rather than through any one experience. If the marriage is to be successful, this growth does not stop at marriage; it can continue, however, only as each is the focus for the affectional relationships of the other, as each gains from the other a sense of emotional and physical security, and as each gains a sense of status and satisfaction from belonging to the other. These, of course, are items (3), (4), and (5) in the preceding list.

Adjustment and Integration

Integration in marriage has been defined as "the bonds of coherence and unity" running through the couple's lives. These bonds, however, cannot be of such a nature that they exclude the affectional relation of the individual to his own parents, to his friends, or to his children when they come. These bonds, ideally, are of such a nature that they help the person to stabilize his

---

[13] Cf. Winch's list of "needs," Chapter 5.

[14] These are, of course, partly and increasingly conceptualized in the latter stages of courtship.

extramarital relationships—and give regularity to them. For example, the man's affectional ties to his own parents are usually stabilized in direct proportion to the "evenness" and stability he has in the love of his mate. When the latter is constant, he has no need for fluctuation in the former. This quality is included in our items (6) and (7).

VALUES AND ADJUSTMENT

Each partner brings to marriage a set of values which are uniquely his own. Values, in the social sense, are "the things of social life (ideals, customs, institutions, etc.) toward which the people of a group have an affectional (emotional) regard. These may be positive, as cleanliness, freedom, education—or negative, as cruelty, crime, or blasphemy."[15] Values are held, as implied in this definition, in high value, and are the result of the individual's indoctrination by family, peers, and institutions.

Individual values may have little actual significance, as in the case of small folkways; others may, however, be of far-reaching and deep-seated importance. They may be held with small conviction, and easily given up, they may be vital to the individual's whole system of thought, and be held tenaciously. Because they are individually experienced and in some cases so vital, the values of husband and wife must be brought into accord, or at least the differences compensated for if the marriage is to succeed. In the remaining chapters we will deal with areas in which there are possible discordances in values, and will see their importance in inhibiting adjustment.

SOME ADDITIONAL FACTORS CONTRIBUTION TO DIFFICULTY IN ADJUSTMENT

While we can be in total agreement with Manford Kuhn's contention that "marital adjustment is not so much a matter of

[15] Values are very often only partially recognized, even by people who verbalize them most effectively.

discrete traits of personality and separable items of background culture as it is a matter of the adjustment of . . . roles which each member plays,"[16] we must nevertheless recognize that adjustment is made *more difficult in the presence of some differences*.[17]

Age

Where the couple are very young, adjustment may well be difficult.[18] Those who marry while they are still making the major change from same-sex to heterosexual affectional relationships in adolescence, and who are struggling to free themselves from childhood home ties are faced with a dual task if they must also make the adjustments that marriage demands. Similarly, those who marry late in life are often faced with equally serious handicaps. In general, the older the individual is at marriage, the more fixed are his habit patterns and his ideas of his needs, and the less able he is to adjust his ways of living to those of his mate. For the woman there are extra difficulties. Not only does postponement of marriage into the third and fourth decades of life increase the difficulties of child-bearing, but it also tends to have narrowed her choice of a mate, since men in the older age brackets tend to marry younger women. Such postponement of marriages leads to a later adjustment problem—one not always foreseen—in that the older people are at marriage, the less likely they are to be able to adjust to the demands of child rearing (see Chapter 16).

Adjustment can also be made more difficult if the couple are of markedly different ages.[19] The sixty-year-old man who marries the twenty-five-year-old girl is, in effect, faced with adjustments not unlike those of parent and child—but with the complications of having to assume different roles and (presumably) of the presence of love. Adjustment in such a case means bringing the values of one generation into accord with those of another, fitting the

[16] *Ibid.*, p. 252.

[17] One of the dangers in depending too heavily upon prediction studies is that we often confuse *correlation or coexistence with causation*.

[18] Cf. Ernest W. Burgess and Leonard S. Cottrell, *Predicting Success or Failure in Marriage*, pp. 84 f.

[19] This is a finding not unique to any one of the prediction studies. Cf. bibliography.

sexual needs and desires and abilities of the old to the young, and modifying other behavior to meet the needs of both. Such adjustments can be far more complicated than those where such discrepancies in age are not present.

Race

Probably no single set of characteristics is more important than those associated with racial differences. The attitudes in our society regarding miscegenation are strongly negative and inflexible—whether legally defined or not. To enter into an interracial marriage is to flaunt convention and to invite social ostracism.[20] In such cases each partner tends to find himself rejected by his own people, and not accepted by members of his partner's race. Each is deemed, somehow, to have been disloyal to his own kind, and is forced to withdraw into a "shell of loneliness" which includes only the couple. A Negro husband (a chemist holding the Ph.D) and his white wife (of comparable education) showed this in the following abstracts from a series of interviews.

> We knew we'd pay a big price if we married. We fought against our love just as long as we could, and finally gave in to it and married. Everyone was very nice about it. Our friends came to the wedding [in a white church], and entertained us afterward at a reception [in a white home], and we were *so* happy about the way our marriage started. But this didn't last long. We soon found that this was just a nice gesture. . . . Well, we've lost all of our friends—both his and mine. It wasn't anything deliberate on anyone's part; it's just the way things happen. We were just gradually left out of activities with both his and my friends. I'm sure they don't do it intentionally. . . . Now we have to depend almost entirely on ourselves for all of our activities.

The fact that this marriage occurred in a state that did not prohibit interracial marriage and in a community that was not hostile to nonwhites was of little importance. This couple were

---

20 In our own society such marriages are few in number but important in the problems they face. In other societies with different histories of interracial contacts (e.g., among the French), such marriages appear to present fewer problems.

faced with adjustments in the face of a situation which was quite beyond their control—and fared badly as a result.

Parenthetically, we may point out that their adjustment was further complicated by another factor. Even though they might make something of an adjustment between themselves, the attaining of their goals was seriously affected in another way.

> We both want children, desperately, and we're confronted with the fact that "coming events cast their shadows before them." We know, now that we can't have any children, because if we do they will be looked down upon by all other children, kept from any kind of intermingling, and be neither accepted in the white nor the Negro groups. . . . We can't condemn a child to that kind of life, and children are what we want most from each other in this life.

That the difficulties this couple faced stemmed from *social* prejudices in no way eased their problem. In the later stages of their six years of marriage, both realized that adjustment could never be had, and the marriage was broken by mutual agreement—even though each still loved the other.

Other differences which affect adjustment are related to dissimilarities in ethnic background, education, religion, and so on. Each of these will be seen in subsequent chapters to have its effects upon adjustment.

TIME IS REQUIRED FOR ADJUSTMENT

No two people who are realistic about their marriage can expect that complete adjustment will be present in all areas from the very beginning. Adjustment can be had only when the couple have reasonable expectations of marriage, are willing to work to achieve adjustment, when they have personalities capable of adjusting, and where there are no external hazards to prevent it. Adjustment begins in courtship and ends at death. It is not static, but always subject to modification.[21] The coming of each child, each serious illness, each child's being launched, each change of

---

[21] It is in this connection that Reuben Hill employs the very descriptive term "developmental adjustment."

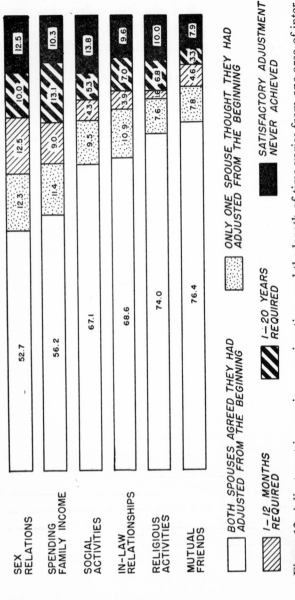

Figure 12. Adjustment in marriage requires time, and the length of time varies from one area of interaction to another. Landis found that 818 spouses varied as shown in this graph in the time required after marriage to achieve adjustment in six areas of marital interaction. (Redrawn from his "Length of Time Required to Achieve Adjustment in Marriage," *American Sociological Review,* XI, December, 1946, p. 668.)

status through shifting jobs or moving from one community to another—each, in other words, requires further adjustment, even in married life. In this sense adjustment *is never final and definitive*.

Nevertheless, couples do recognize that out of the confusion of their interpersonal relations at the time of marriage there does grow (usually) a sense of stability—they become, in their own minds, adjusted. But apparently adjustment comes in different areas of married life at differing rates of speed. Landis, for example, questioned eight hundred and eighteen spouses regarding their "adjustment" in six major areas of married life (see Figure 12). He found that adjustment, as he defined it,[22] was achieved most readily in the area of mutual friendship in these four hundred and nine couples, and that it was less readily achieved (in descending order) in religious activities, in-law relations, social activities, the handling of money, and sexual relations. From one fourth to nearly one half of all of his couples found it necessary to live together for longer than the honeymoon period in order to adjust their values, goals, and behavior patterns to each other. All these will be discussed in later chapters.

SUMMARY

Once having become "a married couple," the need for continuing the adjustment begun in courtship and continued in the engagement and the honeymoon is evident. In this chapter we have indicated that adjustment in marriage lies primarily in two areas— that of the roles to be performed, and in the area of the values held by the husband and wife. Assuming maturity of personality, as discussed earlier, these two constitute the focal points upon which the need for adjustment centers. We have recognized that there are important areas (for example, that of racial differences) which can afford special problems, and have indicated that the fullest degree of adjustment is not necessarily to be expected at

---

[22] Cf. Judson T. Landis, "Length of Time Required to Achieve Adjustment in Marriage," *American Sociological Review*, 11: pp. 666 ff. (1946).

the beginning of a marriage. The emphasis, however, is upon the couple's realization that success in marriage is *something toward which they strive*, rather than something to be demanded from the first days of the marriage.

READINGS AND TOPICS FOR REPORTS

1. Interview a young married couple to learn what roles they identify in their "family drama." Who accepts each of these roles, and what reasons do they give for such a "division of labor" within the family?
2. Interview both an elderly married couple and a couple married for only a year to learn of the values each holds regarding marriage. How do they differ? How are they similar? Are the differences due to changes in the social milieu or to the differences in the period of marriage?

ADVANCED READINGS

Bossard, J. H. S., and Eleanor Boll, *Ritual in Family Living.*
Burgess, E. W., and Paul Wallin, *Engagement and Marriage.*
Lu, Yi-Chuang, "Marital Roles and Marriage Adjustment," *Sociology and Social Research*, 36:364 ff. (1952).

11

Interaction in Marriage

In the preceding chapter we have outlined the concept of adjustment in marriage. There was no indication, however, of the ways in which the couple's relationship will fluctuate as they interact with each other (and with their children).

MORALE IN MARRIAGE

In every marriage there appears to be a characteristic level at which the interaction of husband and wife takes place. In one marriage, the adjustment is great and the expectations each has of marriage are achieved fully. As a result, *esprit de corps* is ample, and the husband and wife enjoy each other's participation in family life and work together successfully. Such a couple can be said to have high *morale*. In another marriage, in contrast, the expectations have not been realized; the couple is not well adjusted—their morale is said to be low. There is a lack of *esprit de corps*, and the interaction is less enjoyed—if not distasteful. Precise instruments for measuring morale in marriage are not yet available; the observer senses rather than measures this level.

Every marriage has a position on the continuum from lowest to highest morale.[1] In that position there may be slight fluctuations from hour to hour or day to day, but these *are normal for that couple in terms of their own expectations of the marriage.* But life is made up not only of "normal events" but of cataclysmic events as well—not all of them bad. The husband's loss of his job—with no savings to carry them until a new position is obtained—would be catastrophic. Uncle Harry's dying and leaving them a previously unrevealed million dollars would be equally cataclysmic, but hardly catastrophic. The first event would result, for most people, at least, in plunging them into depression, in lowering their morale. The second would certainly set them to building "castles in the sky," and give them a strong sense of euphoria. The first of these reactions is especially important, since it is these with which life is replete, although not to the tragic extent given in the example.

Our understanding of what happens when untoward happenings occur is important, for, as Hill puts it,

> The modern family lives in a greater state of tension precisely because it is the great burden carrier of the social order. In a society of rapid social change, problems outnumber solutions, and the resulting uncertainties are absorbed by the members of society, who are for the most part also members of families. Because the family is the bottleneck through which all troubles pass, no other association so reflects the strains and stresses of life. With few exceptions persons in work-a-day America return to rehearse their frustrations within the family, and hope to get the necessary understanding and resilience to return the morrow to the fray.[2]

For the present purposes any lowering of this characteristic level of morale—what Lawrence K. Frank has called "de-morale-ization"—will be called discord.[3]

---

[1] A family with a complete absence of morale would hardly be more than a group of individuals sharing boarding house facilities.

[2] Cf. Reuben Hill, *Families Under Stress*, p. vii.

[3] In the present interpretation, "discord" is a generic term. Its several levels or parts will be discussed later in this chapter.

The Causes of Discord

The student may well ask why discord occurs if people are deeply in love and if the marriage meets their needs and expectations. Hill has given one answer in the preceding quotation. Others are to be found in the conditions in the social *milieu* which affect the couple, and over which they have no control. Industrialization, urbanization, mobility, and the other trends discussed in Chapter 1 have all contributed to a social situation in which the marriage is more vulnerable than formerly.

Still other reasons for discord should be noted, even though they have been discussed previously under other headings. The personalities of the couple may make demands upon their pair-behavior which may be met adequately in "normal" times, but which cannot be met fully when conditions external to the home are unfavorable. All the aspects of personality discussed in the earlier chapters are important when considering marital discord. Where there are temperamental differences—where the wife is vivacious and the husband stolid, where one is quick-tempered and the other slow to anger—discord can easily occur. This can best be illustrated from a case record.

> I like to blow off—it doesn't mean anything—it's just the way I'm built. It does something for me to be able to relieve the pressure. If I could just react with Henry, and get it out of my system, everything would be fine. . . . But there he sits, never letting himself even say a loud word, just sitting and maybe grinning. When he does that, I get madder and madder by the minute. . . . This can go on for days, until sometimes I just have to throw things. Then he finally boils over. If he'd only react, just a little, we'd never reach the boiling point.

> I don't think, if I'd knowed what I do now, that I'd ever have married her. She can't seem to settle down to what marriage means. . . . I like to lead a steady life, and all she wants is to go, go, go, all the time. . . . She gets mad with me because I ain't made that way— it'd kill me to be on the go all the time the way she wants to be. She says it drives her nuts just to sit still all evening. She wants to go to the movies, or anywhere, just so she's on the go. I just can't take it any more. At first, I could, but then it gradually got worse

and worse, and we began to fight about it. . . . Yes, in other things she's a good wife, and I try to be a good man to her, but we're too different, that's all.

These two illustrations do not suggest all of the ways in which personality differences afford an opportunity for discord in marriage; any aspect of personality in which the couple is disparate serves as a possible focal point for tension or conflict.

Whether an inadequate income is a cause of marital discord, or simply provides fertile ground in which other factors can more readily operate, is a moot question. Research indicates that there is a relationship,[4] although this needs further inquiry. Certainly there are marriages relatively free from discord and in which the income is very inadequate;[5] with more than adequate incomes, some others are riddled by dissension. Discord can arise if there are disparate ideas on saving, budgeting, on who shall have certain money-related roles, and so on. It can safely be predicted, for example, that a marriage faces almost certain discord if one partner is a spendthrift and the other a penny pincher.

The causes of discord are relative. It is important in this connection to note that what is to one marriage a cause of discord is to another only a part of everyday life. For example, to some couples the loss of the breadwinner's job can be catastrophic, and have far-reaching effects.[6] To another couple, such an occurrence may be considered as simply part of the pattern of life, and causes no concern—only a reshifting of the living pattern.[7] Discord, then, is as unique to a given marriage as are its expectations and the values held by the couple.

The causes of discord are interrelated. In an earlier document[8] we have suggested that "There is (sometimes) an initial cause which tends to create [discord] in other areas of family life, which

[4] Cf., for example, Harvey J. Locke, *Predicting Adjustment in Marriage*, p. 208 f.
[5] Cf. the writer's *Families in Trouble*, Ch. 5.
[6] Cf. Mirra Komarovsky, *The Unemployed Man and His Family*.
[7] For examples of families which appear to suffer little effects, see the writer's *They Follow the Sun*.
[8] Cf. Reuben Hill, "Plans for Strengthening Family Life," in Howard Becker and Reuben Hill, *Family*, *Marriage and Parenthood*.

in turn become [centers of discord] themselves," and represented this relation as in Figure 13.

> For example, cultural disparity may cause a lack of sexual satisfaction because of the differing ideas and standards of sex behavior, which in turn may lead to suspicion of the mate and lack of cooperation as breadwinner or homemaker, which in turn may create conflicting roles in the family and draw individual members into new positions of responsibility in the family at the expense of other members, all of which so weaken the affectional relationship and integration of the family as to render it unable to meet even a simple departure from its ordinary life pattern.[9]

We cannot, then, view discord as being caused by any one event, or by any one characteristic of the couple.

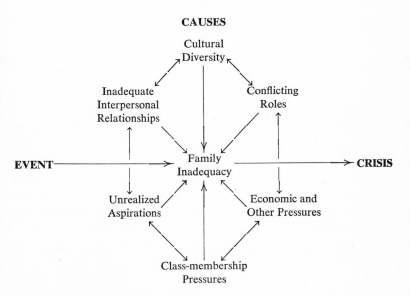

Figure 13. Marital discord rarely has a *simple* or *single* cause. Many factors interrelate in creating what may on the surface appear to be a single cause of tension.

[9] Cf. the writer's "Familes in Crisis," in Evelyn M. Duvall and Reuben Hill (eds.), *The Dynamics of Family Interaction.*

The Levels of Discord

As conceptualized by this writer, discord is not an either-or matter; just as its causes are relative, so do its characteristics vary. Three examples of discord will be presented and then analyzed to show this variability.

In couple *A*, the husband is a die-worker in the —— Company. His work requires that he deal with infinitely small measurements—in 10,000ths of the inch. One day he misreads a blueprint and spoils a piece of work upon which he has spent many hours. His foreman "blasts him out," and he feels deeply the effect of his failure to do his job well. When he goes home, he fails to kiss his wife, snarls at the children, and eats his evening meal in a dead silence. The interpersonal relations are definitely not those of their usual evening meal. The next day his foreman apologizes, admits that he was hasty, and the father's feelings of competency and satisfaction in his job return. That evening life is "back to normal."

In couple *B*, the husband is a graduate student in a university, preparing for a professional career as a dentist. The couple have lived on his savings and his G.I. allotment, but have gone increasingly into debt. The wife is seriously disturbed by this and wants to take at least part-time employment. This her husband refuses to have her do, on the basis that the men in his family have always provided the income and to allow her to work would reflect upon him. The situation goes "from bad to worse"; she is increasingly irritable, becomes slovenly in her housework, and withdraws from their usual social contacts. His slightest wish is no longer her command; he is, in the vernacular, "in the dog house" for his refusal to let her help meet their financial problems. The situation is helped only when he later receives a scholarship which amounts to about one third of their budget.

In couple *C*, both husband and wife work, with the hope of soon making a down payment on a home. Both had little in the way of advantages in childhood, and both are aggressively headed toward the middle class. The husband is an insurance salesman, and, after making an exceptionally good sale, uses most of his commission check for an expensive camera and enlarger—one of his long-time goals. His wife is infuriated by this, and insists that he return the $500 worth of photographic equipment. This he refuses to do; the quarrel becomes more and more bitter; in the end, she packs her things and returns to her parents' home and the job she held before her marriage. Only after several months of separation are they reconciled.

We need not concern ourselves here with why the three husbands acted as they did, other than to say that a variety of needs were involved. There are, however, significant differences in the three examples. There was no change in the interaction in the first example, other than a temporary withdrawal from the usual interpersonal relations. In the second example, the change in interaction involved not only the usual interpersonal relations but also a change in the relative positions in the dominance pattern (or power structure) as well.[10] They no longer looked to each other so completely for satisfaction of their needs; she lost her respect for him, and so on. In the third example the distortion of the relationship was even greater, and involved not only a dis-

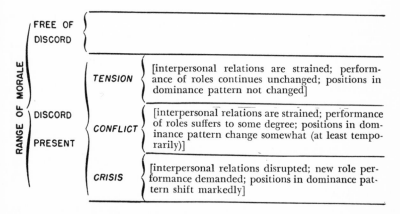

Figure 14. A schematic representation of the several levels of interaction within the whole of morale in marriage, as discussed in this text. These are *types* of interaction and do not have sharply differentiated limits; also, each marriage defines them in terms of its own values, aspirations, and experiences.

[10] This dominance pattern or power hierarchy is the equivalent of the "pecking order" discussed in introductory textbooks in sociology.

turbance of their interpersonal relations and a shifting of their dominance positions, but also an actual change in roles—in that she had broken the relationship and assumed new roles.

The first of these we term "tension," and define as the state of marital discord in which interpersonal relations are strained but the level of interaction is not seriously affected. The individual's performance of his marital roles continues, and he does not lose his recognized position in the dominance pattern. In general, tensions are covert. The second of these we term "conflict," which affects the level of interaction to a greater degree; and in which marital roles and the dominance pattern are distorted, at least temporarily. In sharp contrast, the third of these, which we term "crisis," is a situation quite outside the normal pattern of life, which creates a real insecurity and/or blocks the usual patterns of action and calls for new ones.

It is recognized that the differences among the three are largely matters of degree and that sharp lines cannot always be drawn between them. They are important to us, if for no other reason than that life is full of tension-creating situations (such as what happens on the job in couple *A*). We need to recognize the *relative* innocuousness and frequency of tension, at the same time that we recognize the extremely serious nature and the infrequency of crises. The principles that apply to tension situations in courtship apply equally to tension situations in marriage,[11] and the couple who would succeed in marriage need to recognize the destructive nature of these levels of discordant interaction in marriage.

Some writers consider that tensions follow conflicts and state that they "are the result of conflict situations in which certain basic frustrations are not resolved."[12] This is in line with their concept of a conflict as "a fight of any sort, ranging from a slight difference of opinion to uncompromising warfare."[13] The author's research experience indicates that (1) tensions do follow conflicts

[11] See Chapter 7.
[12] Cf. Ernest W. Burgess and Harvey J. Locke: *The Family*, p. 560.
[13] *Ibid.,* p. 560.

that have not been resolved completely, but also that (2) they are often present in a marriage situation where conflict has never existed, and, more important, that (3) they most often *precede* conflict. The following abstracts from three interviews show the differences among these three.

(1) So far as I can see, some quarrels don't clear the decks—there's some feeling left behind [tension after conflict]. That's the worst kind of fight to have, because it doesn't get either of you anywhere, and you don't get rid of what's bothering you.

(2) We've been married now, two years, and I can honestly say we haven't broken out in a quarrel this far. . . . There have been times when our nerves have been taunt [*sic*], but we've never gone so far as to break out in an actual quarrel [tensions without conflict]. I know we will some day—it's just human nature to do that some times—but I'll put that day off as long as I can, and then be ready to go on again. . . . I think that a quarrel will come when our nerves just build up to a place where things snap.

(3) Things just grow on us! We go along without any real trouble, just the little aggravating things—you know, the letter home he forgot to mail, or my meeting him a half hour late on Saturday noon downtown, or something like that—until finally they build up, and you just seem to need to fight about something. Then one of you does something that seems to the other one really big, and, BANG, then you really fight about it [tensions followed by conflict].... For us that seems to clear the air, and we start all over again fresh. That's why we don't seem to have many real disagreements.

The first and third of these quotations illustrate a fact that is important to this discussion: that there are not necessarily sharp lines between the levels of discord and that a couple may move from one level to the other without recognition of that fact. Also, it is apparent from the second abstract that *tensions can ebb and flow without ever getting to the conflict stage.* The following abbreviated account of one couple's difficulties in the first three years of their marriage will illustrate more completely the ways in which movement occurs from one level to another. (This couple's activities were followed closely during that period; their discord pattern is illustrated in Figure 15.)

In the first six months of our marriage, there was never a bit of trouble. We were too much in love to let anything bother us, or to disagree about anything. . . . We thought our home was wonderful [in a two-room veterans' housing project], and loved every bit of being together. . . . When we had been married seven months, we had our first "tiff." John forgot our seventh monthly wedding anniversary (*A*). He had an important examination coming up, but I didn't think he should have let that get in the way of remembering such an occasion. . . . We didn't fight, or anything like that, but I was hurt and I guess I was a little cool to him (*B*). It only lasted a short while, and then I was all right again, but I *was* disappointed. . . . When we had been married almost a year, I became pregnant (by choice), and then I began to worry about whether everything would be all right. The apartment began to get on my nerves, and I wanted to move, preferably to a bigger apartment, or even better, to a house of our own. I was sick of hearing everything that went on in the next place. . . . When I talked with John about it, I guess I was a little too emphatic, because he was hurt, and that didn't help me (*C*). . . . For two weeks we were just "distant" with each other (*D*). Then I began to feel a little badly in the morning—the doctor said it was nothing important—and I let the whole matter get bigger than it was worth. The first thing I knew, I had told John that I intended to go home to my parents until the baby came and until he got a bigger place for us to live. . . . That was when we had our first fight (*E*). It didn't last long, just a day, and then it was all over.

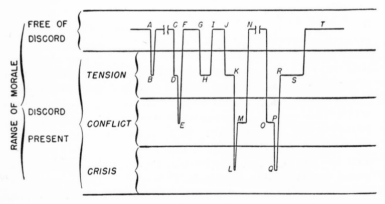

Figure 15. The fluctuations in the morale of one married couple as discussed in the accompanying case illustration.

We both cried, and then felt fine, and we were back on our old footing again (*F*). . . . After that fight everything went all right. I felt better after the first months, and everything was fine. . . . The baby was born on Saturday, and Sunday some friends came from out of town. They couldn't see me, but they took John out to dinner, and had too much to drink. I don't blame him, now, but I was really hurt then (*G*). . . . I cried when he came to see me, and that made him feel badly, so for a whole month things were rather cool (*H*). It was too bad, because that was when the baby was brought home, and it should have been a very happy time. . . . We couldn't have [intercourse], and I think that made things worse, because that would have brought us back together again. . . . Suddenly we just couldn't seem to go on as we were—we cried, and then went back to our old ways. There wasn't any fight; we just seemed to realize what fools we'd been all of a sudden, and everything cleared up (*I*). . . . Two months later, we had another time of being tense and irritable (*J*), because John's G.I. check was lost in the mail, and we were hard up. We really had enough to get along on, but we were short, and it seemed to get us down. This went on for a whole month (*K*), until the check was reissued, and then things really blew up (*L*). With two whole checks in his pocket within two days, John just couldn't stand the prosperity. He went out and bought a camera, so he could take pictures of the baby. Oh, was I mad! I wanted pictures, too, but not that bad. We just had a good fight, and stayed that way for a whole week. We were hardly civil to each other, for that whole time (*M*). . . . Well, we couldn't stay angry, so we had a making-up, and everything was all right again (*N*). . . . Some time after that, John made another silly purchase, or so I thought, and this time I blew right up, and, as he said, "dressed him down like a sergeant (*O*)." We didn't make up right away (*P*), and things were pretty bad. John was under a lot of strain at school just then—he was having trouble with a math course—but I was too dumb to see that that had anything to do with it. Then he did pass his exam, and it was easier than he thought, so the boys all celebrated. They went out on a beer drinking party, and he spent six dollars of our household money. Then I *really* got after him (*Q*), and said we'd have to do something about the way money was handled in our family. I laid the law down, and finally John agreed (*R*), but he wasn't too happy about it. I guess he realized I was really mad, though. Things were quite cool for a while (*S*), but after a couple of weeks, John admitted he'd been a fool in the way he'd spent money; we had a good time making up, and things have been all right for the last several months (*T*).

This abbreviated account illustrates the way in which a couple may move from harmony into tension, back into harmony, direct from harmony into conflict, and so on. It does not, unfortunately, illustrate the fact that the couple may also move directly from harmony into crisis, but case studies indicate that such can be the case. Figure 13 makes no effort to indicate the variations within tension or conflict, nor is the case description sufficiently detailed to portray the differences within each. There are, nevertheless, variations within the levels of both tension and conflict. As one housewife described the differences: "In marriage you can be spiffed, peeved, irked, angry, or plain mad; you can have a spat, a scrap, or a knock-down-and-drag-out fight." Each has—to that particular couple—a special meaning of degree; each couple tends not only to develop their own vocabulary in this connection, but also to recognize the variations in the seriousness and the "form" of the interaction of the particular discord.

THE ADJUSTMENT OF DISCORD

Are the married couple "at the mercy of the elements" when in discord, or can they purposefully move to regain their earlier and more desirable relationship? No rule of thumb can be laid down as to what will relieve marital tension. Only as individuals know themselves and each other well, and are willing to resort to whatever measures seem effective, can they find ways of alleviating discord. Since each disruption of morale has its own unique qualities, each must therefore be solved in a unique fashion. Even so, a number of suggestions applicable in all cases can be offered.

Some Requirements in Overcoming Discord

Even though a couple may work out a variety of techniques for "clearing the air," the results will be unsatisfactory if some basic attitudes and ideas are not accepted and shared. One of these is the idea emphasized earlier—*that discord is not necessarily a sign of failure*. Only as the husband and wife can recognize that each has compulsions and frustrations (many of them outside the marriage relationship) which may provoke and stimulate discord, can they expect to meet situations adequately.

Second, there must be a recognition that *discord is not always resolved as quickly as it appears to have arisen*. If discord is understood to have its roots in personality differences, as is so often the case, it is evident that overcoming these differences requires time. Just as personality is in large part the product of years of the individual's relating to other people, so is the adjusting of personalities to each other in marriage a matter of time. To expect that personality differences, which may not be uncovered until discord appears, can be adjusted overnight is to be thoroughly unrealistic about human relations.

Third, both husband and wife *must be willing to see both sides of the problem at hand*. This is not as easy as it may at first appear, since discord often has its basis in factors of which the individual is not conscious. For this reason, one may never be able entirely to understand the other's position, but a *willingness* makes possible some adjustment—even though it may not solve the basic difficulty.

Closely related to this requirement is a fourth—*the need to be objective*. It is recognized that such a need is difficult to satisfy; it is not easy to be objective about one's self, or to regard the loved one in a completely objective light. Nevertheless, if discord is to be alleviated, it is necessary that each individual be willing to "go outside himself" and look at the facts as they are, rather than as he would have them. It is in this connection that the maturity of personality emphasized in earlier chapters becomes of great importance. The immature person, who lacks any ability to see himself and his relation to his mate in an objective way, has little chance of dealing adequately with discords that are bound to arise.

Finally, there is the need for a willingness to seek help. It may be impossible for the couple independently to arrive at a solution of their discord, either because it is of too involved a nature or because the causes are so deep-seated as to require professional insights and assistance. When such is the case, the help of an outsider must be sought—preferably that of one trained in the field of marriage counseling. Two questions confront the couple under such circumstances. First, can they bring themselves to accept assistance? The idea that a marriage stands on its own feet is so thoroughly engrained in American thinking (and especially American middle-class thinking) that it is difficult for many people to seek outside assistance; the fact that most of the counseling services in this country are or have been associated with charitable agencies, and hence carry the stigma of "charity," is a further handicap. Only as a couple are willing to seek assistance with problems of relationships, in the same way that they seek assistance with a problem of physical illness, can the first difficulty be overcome. In a society as involved and changing as ours, the day is past when seeking help can be considered an evidence of weakness; the couple in trouble must recognize that seeking assistance is an evidence of strength and of a will to succeed in the marriage. The other difficulty is less easily overcome; it is unfortunate that the stigma of "charity" still attaches to many counseling agencies. (It should be recognized, in this connection, that such a stigma exists only in the minds of those who are unfamiliar with recent developments in the whole field of counseling and social work, and that many of the private social casework agencies are ready and willing to work with people who could under no circumstances be considered in need of "charity.")

The second question, of where the couple can turn for help, has in part been answered. Almost all the private casework agencies associated with the Family Welfare Association provide counseling on marital problems—some of them as a separate and well-defined service. Marriage counseling services, which are not attached to any social agency, have been established in a number of cities. In some instances, these are independent, as in the case of Marriage Council, in Philadelphia; in others, they are attached to a church or college. Residents of the larger cities can almost always find professional workers of the highest quality who are available in one capacity or another. In the smaller communities, obtaining assistance with such a problem is more difficult. Ministers, lawyers, and family physicians are usually available, but the student is cautioned against the indiscriminate selection of a person from these ranks. Many such professional people have a bias and a lack of knowledge, which can be detrimental rather than helpful, and they very often tend to oversimplify problems and to interpret them as being entirely within their own field of competence.[14]

Whatever the source of help, it can be of value only as the couple are willing to use it, as it assists them to see the discord *in toto*, as it assists them in identifying the contribution each makes to the total, and as it helps them to work their *own* way to a solution. In the last analysis, no one but the couple involved can do anything about a discordant situation; all others can only help in the interpretation and in the possible adjustment of any external factors.

SUMMARY

Marriage is a *dynamic* process, and as such, one which may well have its ups and downs. If the couple meet each other's personality needs, achieve their goals, and face realistically the exigencies of life, marriage is successful. In the society in which we live, however, there are frequent happenings—many of them entirely unforeseeable—which affect the best adjusted couples. We have, therefore, outlined the ways in which morale can fluctuate, in the desire that the student will be fully conscious of the need for objectivity about what happens in this dynamic relationship. Only as the members of a marriage recognize possible fluctuations in morale for what they are can they be prepared to

---

[14] The same is especially true of the "quacks" who prey upon people in time of trouble. Cf. Lee Steiner, *Where Do People Take Their Troubles*.

assess their strengths and weaknesses, and to adjust to the demands that everyday living makes upon marriage.

READINGS AND TOPICS FOR REPORTS

1. Using your own family for a case study, list the various causes of tension, conflict, and crises as you have experienced them. Do these appear to be peculiar to your own family, or of the kind that all families experience?
2. Interview a number of middle-class families to learn the resources they know of in their own communities to which they could turn for aid in bettering their marital interaction. In general, do these families believe that they should avail themselves of such assistance?

ADVANCED READINGS

Angell, R. C., *The Family Encounters the Depression.*
Cavan, Ruth, and K. Ranck, *The Family and the Depression.*
Hill, Reuben, *Families Under Stress.*
Kirkpatrick, C., "Factors in Marital Adjustment," *American Journal of Sociology*, 43-270 ff. (1937).
Komarovsky, Mirra, *The Unemployed Man and His Family.*
Koos, Earl Lomon, *Families in Trouble.*

12

The Sexual Aspects
of Marriage

THE SEXUAL RELATIONSHIP in marriage has a meaning and function which extends far beyond the reproduction of the species. This is evidenced in the fact that nature limits sexual activity in the lower animals to that short period when the female is able to conceive, while in man such activity can take place at any time in the reproductive cycle. To regard sexual activity as primarily a means of satisfying man's reproductive needs or as a means of securing physical release is to disregard very important elements in the sexual relationship. To give sex an undue emphasis, however, is to err in the opposite direction. Terman, in his pioneer study of factors influencing marital adjustment, found that "the influence of the sexual factor is at most no greater than that of the combined personality and background factors, and . . . is probably less."[1] Harriet Mowrer—a marriage counselor of long experience—in discussing the factors important in creating marital conflict has stated that "sex cannot . . . be considered the basic

[1] Lewis M. Terman, *Psychological Factors in Marital Happiness*, p. 376.

factor [in marital discord] any more than any other factors which make up the conflict pattern."[2]

SEXUAL RELATIONS ARE MUTUAL

All that is to be said in this chapter is based upon the idea that mutually satisfying sexual relations are the one aspect of the whole husband-wife relationship that is based upon the participation of both. The couple can have sharply divergent attitudes concerning religion, the saving of money, or the raising of children, and still live together quite satisfactorily by agreeing to recognize their differences and to honor them for what they are. The very nature of human sexual activity, however, requires a *mutual* concern and participation if it is to be satisfying to both partners. Without this mutuality, sexual relations have no more emotional significance than does the mating of the lower animals—which is a physical meeting resulting from the dictates of an instinct.

It is this mutuality which the persons seeking success in marriage need to appreciate. In Baber's words,

> The first requisite for sexual compatibility in marriage is the abandonment of the self-gratification pattern for the mutual-gratification ideal. This means that each partner instead of seeking a purely personal satisfaction will seek to make the sexual experience *equally satisfying to the other*. This is a high ideal and not always easy to achieve, but the best sex adjustment to be found comes in those cases where this goal is most nearly approached. The very knowledge of mutuality enhances the pleasure of each, as does the appreciation of each for the thoughtfulness of the other. When one partner satisfies his passion without regard for the satisfaction of the other, there is at first bewilderment, then disillusionment, and finally recoil against being called upon to serve without sharing.[3]

The reader will note a close connection between Baber's emphasis upon the mutual-gratification ideal and the emphasis we

---

[2] Harriet Mower, *Personality Adjustment and Domestic Discord*, p. 156.
[3] Ray E. Baber, *Marriage and the Family*, p. 244.

have already placed upon the qualities inherent in love.[4] This, in the writer's estimation, is the *sine qua non* of success in marriage, regardless of the aspect being considered, and must be kept uppermost in mind.

FACTORS INFLUENCING SEXUAL BEHAVIOR

There is a variety of factors which can keep the best-intentioned person from achieving the mutual-gratification ideal discussed in the last section. They are present in some degree in sufficient numbers of cases to be worthy of attention.

Inadequate Socialization

In Chapter 4 it was shown that the individual moves through successive stages of "emotional interest" until in adolescence he or she reaches the mature level of heterosexuality. It was also indicated that some individuals fail, through inadequate socialization to free themselves entirely from the earlier emotional attachment to the parent of the opposite sex, and are therefore incapable of loving completely a mate. Under such circumstances, participation in the sex act is a less total experience than it would be if the individual were possessed of the mutual gratification ideal.

The person may, however, have no such deep-seated inability to love, and still be psychologically conditioned against sex. The child who is caught in innocent exploration of his or another's sex organs, or in masturbation, and who is punished severely and never allowed to forget his "sin," may well grow to adulthood with such fear of sex or guilt feelings that he is unable to resolve them in marriage—unless he has help.

Inadequate socialization in this area of life may result from conditions which are widespread in the subculture to which the individual belongs. Religious teachings, for example, have contributed much to a negative attitude about sex for many young people. The so-called "Puritan" attitudes, carried over into many

[4] See the discussion of this point in Chapter 7.

of the conservative religious attitudes still extant, have acted as barriers to *mutual* sexual expression, or even to a frank consideration of the subject. Within the past year a college student has written as follows.

> My father and mother are really very human persons. I know they love each other and love me. But I know that they are always careful to say nothing about sex, and never show any real evidence of physical affection in the presence of others. . . . I think I can see the reason in the way our church feels about sex. We belong to the —— denomination, and as far as I can remember, the sermons and Sunday school teachings either avoided the subject or mentioned sex as one of the necessary but sinful things in life. . . . There is no effort to help young people to understand this mystery in their lives, and our ministers have always fought the idea of sex education in the high school. The present one went so far as to have the deacons call on the school board to prohibit the use of a sex film in the biology class. . . . I think those of us who grew up in such a religious atmosphere learned to think that it is an indecent part of life, and then we have trouble in adjusting when we get into courses in college which treat it as a natural part of married life. . . . What my friends who don't go to college will do when they marry is something to think about. They won't have been freed from all our church has done to us.

Such religious attitudes are by no means universal; many church groups have been in the forefront in the effort to have young people know the positive values of the sexual relationship. Where the young adult of either sex has been raised in such an atmosphere, however, he or she is scarcely ready to accept the potentialities that sex has to offer in marriage.

Again, the culture itself may inhibit adequate socialization in the realm of sex through the concepts prevalent in the group. One of these is the supposed difference between men and women in their sexual needs—an idea still shared by many older people and transmitted to youth. Biologically, there is no evidence of truth in the statements so often heard: "Women don't want sex as much as men do," and "Women don't have passion as men do." Research, too, shows the falseness of these statements.[5] Where the woman has been adequately socialized and has an understanding relationship with her husband, such statements simply do not hold water. These ideas of the past—that woman was sexually an "inferior" being—were essential to the maintenance of the old double standard of morals so common prior to World War I, in which a man's pre- and extra-marital sexual excursions were excused on the ground of his "need" while the woman was expected to "submit" in marriage.

Early Sexual Experiences in Marriage

Some individuals enter marriage with neither guilt nor fear concerning sex, but with an ignorance of the exact nature of the sexual act. In those cases (fortunately not too frequent) where the first sexual experiences are inept, the reaction—especially on the part of the wife—may be such as to condition her against later adjustment, unless definite efforts are made to overcome that reaction. Such a reaction may result from her husband's lack of knowledge and understanding, or it may result from her own ignorance and tension. This type of reaction can in most cases be prevented through adequate premarital instruction on the nature of the sexual relationship.

Contraceptive Methods and Sexual Behavior

Contraception may be entirely acceptable to both partners and yet create a problem in sexual adjustment. Not all contraceptive methods are equally effective, and the distrust of a particular method—for example, one allowed by one's religion but known not to be of optimum effectiveness—may well operate as a barrier to achieving satisfaction. Similarly, a particular method may be acceptable to one partner but be rejected on esthetic grounds by

[5] See, for example, the work of Alfred C. Kinsey *et al* on this point. Controversial as his work has been, the "Kinsey reports" have given insights into the falseness of many of the folk ideas regarding sex. For an extended discussion of this point, see Jerome Himelhoch (ed.), *Sexual Behavior in American Society*. New York: W. W. Norton Co., 1955.

the other, to the detriment of the latter's sexual adjustment. For example:

> The biggest problem we have is in the matter of contraception. We are allowed to use the rhythm method, but we both know it isn't a sure way, so every time we depended on it, we worried a lot. . . . It made a good deal of difference in the way we felt about each other in those matters. . . . Finally, we decided that we just had to be sure every time, and started to use a method we were told about. . . . I guess it's effective, all right, but Don is very unhappy about it; he says he just can't be satisfied with such a method. . . . We don't get the most out of our sex life. We know that, but what else can we do?

It should be noted that an inadequate sexual relationship, in cases like this, can often be better adjusted if the couple will seek the assistance of a competent physician or clinic.

This dissatisfaction with the means of contraception is likely to be correlated with the fear of pregnancy. Such fear operates, as might be expected, in lessening sexual satisfaction, and therefore hindering adjustment, especially in the important first months of marriage, even though the wife and husband both hope for children. It often becomes very important again when the couple have had their planned-for children and hope to enjoy sexual relations without resulting pregnancy.

THE PHYSICAL ASPECTS OF SEX

With all the emphasis placed upon sex education for youth today, there is still need to review the anatomy and physiology of the male and female reproductive systems.[6] A couple might possibly blunder into an adequate sexual relationship even if both were totally ignorant of the subject, but the purposeful use of sex in working toward the mutual gratification ideal requires an understanding beyond that of simple topography.

---

[6] The discussion which follows is necessarily limited. For a more detailed discussion, see Edith L. Potter, *Fundamentals of Human Reproduction.*

Male Anatomy and Physiology

As compared with the female, the male has a relatively simple genital system, the major portions of which are outside the abdominal cavity. The male sex cells, or sperm, are produced by the testes, which are two ovoid glands suspended in a skin sac called the scrotum. Each testis contains microscopic canals which are lined with undeveloped sperm cells, which develop to maturity at a rate of several billion per month throughout the sexual maturity of man. These canals empty into a larger convoluted tube (the epididymis), which serves as a storage place for the fully developed sperm cells. In turn, the epididymis empties into a duct (the *vas deferens*), which conveys the sperm into the abdominal cavity. In the abdominal cavity the *vas deferens* connects with the seminal vesicle, an irregular-shaped tube, which secretes the seminal fluid. This secretion forms part of the semen—the male discharge—and contributes to the vigor and motility of the sperm. To this point, the sperm have had no power of independent locomotion but have been passed along mechanically. The two seminal ducts combine and open into the urethra, the tube leading

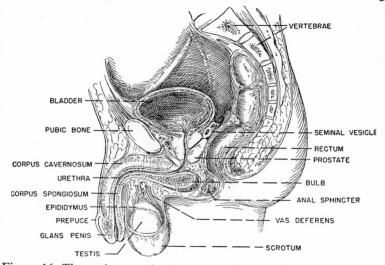

Figure 16. The male reproductive organs (sagittal view).

from the urinary bladder to the external opening of the penis. (This portion of the genital system also serves in the male as part of the urinary system.) Near this junction, the prostate gland empties into the urethra and contributes prostatic fluid to the semen. The semen is composed, therefore, of fluid from the seminal vesicles and the prostatic gland, and it carries the sperm brought through the *vas deferens* from the testes. The function of the prostatic fluid, like that of the seminal vesicles, is to give body to the semen and vigor and motility to the sperm. During sexual excitement the opening from the bladder is closed and minute glandular cells in the lining of the urethra secrete a sticky substance, neutralizing the acidity (caused by the urine), which is damaging to the sperm. Also, during sexual excitement the spongy tissues of the penis are engorged with blood and it becomes erect and rigid enough to penetrate the folds of the vagina. The external end of the penis is hypersensitive during sexual excitement and is one of the chief centers of sexual stimulus in the male. It is ordinarily covered by a foreskin (the tissue removed in circumcision), which is usually retractable during intercourse. After the discharge of the semen during the ejaculation, the excess of blood leaves the penis and it resumes its usual flaccid condition. At each normal ejaculation, some two hundred and fifty to five hundred million sperm are released in the seminal fluid, which is several cubic centimeters in amount.

In addition to their production of reproductive cells, the testes have a function of internal secretion. Testosterone, a chemical substance (hormone), is secreted directly into the blood stream by specialized cells after the onset of puberty and accounts for the physical and psychological changes occurring in the male at that time and characterizing him from that time on. The change of voice, the characteristic growth of hair on the face and body, and (to some extent) the general changes in attitude and behavior toward the female are all attributable to the action of this hormone.

As in the female, the whole of this process of sexual development is controlled by the anterior lobe of the pituitary gland, located at the base of the brain in the center of the skull, which secretes a complex hormone during the whole period of active sexual life. Unlike the female, however, this is a steady influence and has none of the cyclical characteristics that will be seen in the female.

Female Anatomy and Physiology

The female counterpart of the male testis is the ovary. Ovoid in shape and about one inch in length, one is located on each side of the midline of the abdomen and is held in place by a broad ligament running from the uterus to the pelvic wall. Like the testes, the ovaries have two functions: one to produce the female sex cell, or ovum; the other to provide the sex hormones which give the female her special characteristics. Because of their complex nature, these will be considered in some detail.

As in the male, the activity of the female sex organs is dictated by the anterior lobe of the pituitary gland. Two hormones are secreted into the blood stream; one (the follicle-stimulating hormone) is secreted during the first half of the menstrual cycle, and the other (the luteinizing hormone), during the latter half.[7] These hormones act upon the ovary, which in turn produces the female sex hormone (estrone) in certain specialized cells. This process of hormone stimulation is by no means as simple as it may sound in this description; in fact, much knowledge of the interworkings of the anterior pituitary and ovarian hormones is yet to be uncovered. Suffice it to say here that they are interrelated in a very complicated way and that their combined activity results in the processes that will now be discussed.

Each month, under the influence of these hormones, one ovum begins to ripen. At birth each ovary contains many thousands of undeveloped ova, most of which are capable of maturing. As the ovum ripens, the surrounding cells multiply and form a follicle or cavity, which fills with a follicular fluid manufactured by specialized cells in the lining of the follicle and contains the female sex

---

[7] This is an over-simplification. There are probably numbers of hormones (as yet unisolated) which affect the reproductive activity of males and females. But this is obviously not the place for a discussion of endocrine theory.

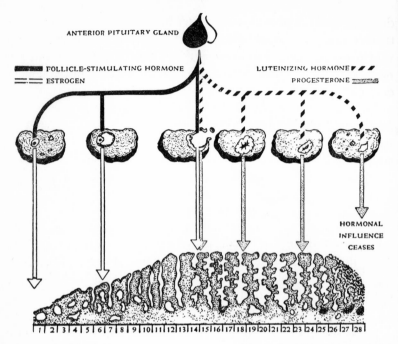

Figure 17. The relation of the pituitary and ovarian hormones to the reproductive cycle. This simplified diagram shows the follicle-stimulating and luteinizing hormones (secreted by the anterior lobe of the pituitary gland) affecting the ovary and the estrogen and progesterone hormones (secreted by the ovary) affecting the uterus. Menstruation is represented as occurring in the last days of the cycle. (Courtesy of the Schering Corporation.)

hormone (estrone). This hormone is absorbed into the blood stream and carried to other parts of the body, where it functions to give the female her special sex characteristics, as noted earlier. As the ovum ripens and the follicular fluid develops, the pressure increases and, about the fourteenth day in the average cycle, ruptures into the abdominal cavity. The fluid is absorbed into the blood stream, and the ovum begins its journey through the remainder of the reproductive system. Where the follicular cells have ruptured on the surface of the ovum, new cells—with a different and vital function—develop rapidly. This new glandular tissue (*corpus luteum*) provides a second hormone (progesterone), which has the special function of conditioning the uterus for its reception of the ovum, should fertilization occur. If fertilization does not occur, the *corpus luteum* grows smaller and its production of progesterone ceases. If fertilization does occur, the *corpus luteum* grows larger and produces even larger amounts of progesterone, thereby further conditioning the uterus for its task of sustaining the developing embryo.

Upon extrusion from the follicle, the ovum passes into the adjacent Fallopian tube. The tube has no function other than that of providing a canal through which the ovum can pass to the uterus. These tubes, one on each side of the midline, are about four inches in length, with the midline end opening into the uterus and the other ending in a number of finger-like projections adjacent to but not connected with the ovary. How the ovum reaches the opening of the Fallopian tube is not definitely known; one theory is that there is a chemical attraction. The rhythmic contractions of the Fallopian tube move the ovum toward the uterus.

The uterus is a hollow, pear-shaped, muscular organ with the larger end at the top, about three inches long, two inches wide, and one inch thick. It lies behind the urinary bladder and in front of the rectum; it functions as a suitable environment for the fertilized ovum as it develops during pregnancy. The two Fallopian tubes open into it at its upper end, and the lower portion (the cervix) opens into the vaginal canal. The muscle of the body of the uterus is governed by the autonomic nervous system; it is therefore not subject to voluntary control but expands and thickens during pregnancy and then contracts strongly to expel its contents at the time of birth.

The lining of the uterus (the endometrium) is directly affected by the hormones produced by the ovary. During the first two weeks of the menstrual cycle the cells of the endometrium multiply rapidly, under the influence of the estrogenic hormone. As the

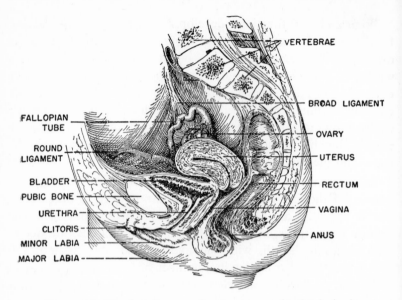

Figure 18. The female reproductive organs (sagittal view).

corpus luteum begins to produce progesterone, following rupture of the follicle and ovulation, the conditioning of the endometrium mentioned earlier takes place; if fertilization does not take place, the production of progesterone by the *corpus luteum* diminishes and the destruction of the endometrial tissue begins. This spontaneous destruction (menstruation) continues for a few days; at the same time the new ovum is beginning to ripen, and the cycle begins again.

The lower portion of the uterus (cervix) opens into the vagina. It is this opening through which the menstrual blood is discharged, through which the sperms enter the uterus, which is sealed with a mucous plug during the pregnancy, and which dilates fully to allow the passage of the infant in childbirth. This portion of the uterus is especially important because of its vulnerability to cancer; it is also sometimes the site of minor bacterial infections and erosions causing a discharge known as leucorrhea or "whites."

The vagina has three functions, all of them of major importance. It serves as a channel through which the menstrual blood is discharged from the body; it is part of the birth canal through which the infant is discharged from the uterus; it is the female organ of coitus or sexual intercourse. It is an elastic canal with convoluted walls, is capable of considerable dilation, and at its exterior end is as sensitive to sexual stimulation as is the male penis. The inner end projects past the cervix, which normally opens into it at an angle.

The vagina is normally slightly acid, because of the presence of beneficial bacteria. This reduces the chance of vaginal infection, but it also reduces the chances of survival for sperm, which require an alkaline environment such as that found in the cervix and uterus.

A fold of mucous membrane at the vaginal entrance (the hymen) is usually found in the virginal individual. (There are numerous folk ideas about the hymen, most or all of which are erroneous.) This may or may not completely surround the opening of the vagina; in rare instances it is completely blocked and requires surgical intervention when the first menstrual flow occurs. Where the hymen is sufficiently developed to prevent easy entrance of the penis into the vagina at first intercourse, it tears or splits— with some discomfort and possible minor bleeding. This, however, is of far less concern than most of the old wives' ideas commonly circulated would indicate.

The external opening of the vagina, with its hymen, lies between major folds of mucous membrane (vulva). These consist of the major and minor labia, or lips, and act as a protective covering for the vagina. The labia are moistened during sexual excitement by a fluid discharged by Bartholin's gland, which has an opening adjacent to the vaginal orifice.

Also enclosed within the labia, and located in front of the urethra (the opening from the urinary bladder) is the clitoris, already mentioned as the counterpart of the male penis. Like the latter, it is extremely sensitive, is composed of spongy tissue, and becomes engorged with blood during sexual excitement. The pressure exerted upon it during sexual intercourse can be an important contribution to the orgasm; it is however, not the only seat of sexual sensation, as will be seen later.

Fertilization of the ovum. The sexual excitement of the male during intercourse ends in a climax accompanied by the discharge of the semen, which contains many millions of sperm. These are normally discharged at the internal end of the vagina, from which point they propel themselves through the cervix into the body of the uterus and on into the Fallopian tube, where they meet the descending ovum. Only one living sperm is needed for fertilization. Upon contact, the head and body of the sperm penetrate the ovum, a change normally occurs which repels other sperm, and cell union takes place—to be followed rapidly by cell division. The ovum continues its descent through the tube, enters the uterus, and soon attaches itself to the endometrium. The specialized development of the round, flat spongy body (the placenta) begins very early. This structure, which develops at the point where the ovum is attached to the endometrium, gathers from the maternal blood (by osmosis) the oxygen and nutrients necessary for the life of the embryo and returns to the mother the embryo's waste products, which are then excreted from the maternal system in the usual way. There is no direct connection between the blood supply of the mother and that of the developing embryo.

Fertilization ordinarily occurs only near the time when the ovum has escaped from the follicle. While healthy, mature male sperm are always capable of impregnating the ovum, provided they are recently discharged and are in a favorable climate, the ovum retains its vitality for only a short period (probably not more than twenty-four hours) after ovulation. There is, however, no guarantee that the ovum will be discharged on the fourteenth or fifteenth day, and fertilization can therefore take place, in exceptional cases, at any time during the cycle. Until the length of time the sperm can live in the genital tract is definitely established, and until more exact knowledge is available of the exact time of ovulation *in a given cycle* and of the length of life of the ovum, definite statements regarding the period during which fertilization is possible are unwise. It is these variations which make the "rhythm method" of conception control relatively unsatisfactory, since too many unknown factors are involved.

Pregnancy. If a sperm succeeds in fertilizing the ovum, and the ovum attaches itself to the endometrium of the uterus, the ovarian cycle is disrupted and menstruation ceases. The failure to menstruate is therefore usually the first sign of pregnancy. Changes in the uterus occur slowly at first, and a diagnosis of pregnancy through examination of the uterus is ordinarily not possible for from eight to ten weeks after fertilization has occurred. An earlier (and more accurate) test for pregnancy, known as the Aschheim-Zondek, can be employed within four or five weeks. This test depends upon the fact that the urine from a pregnant woman contains hormonal substances, which, upon injection into a rabbit, frog, or mouse, produce typical ovarian changes in that animal. The most positive diagnosis, of course, is the beating of the embryo's heart, but this is not evident until some months after conception has occurred.

Pregnancy is certainly a normal part of the woman's life process, despite the disposition of some individuals to regard it as pathological. The toxemias (blood poisoning) so prevalent in earlier decades are now almost a thing of the past. Given adequate prenatal care, and with careful attention paid by the attending physician to her general physical condition, no prospective mother need fear either pregnancy or childbirth.

Pregnancy Failure

No accurate data are available on the number of couples who desire children but are unable to have them, but it is believed that they constitute at least 10 percent of all marriages.[8] The reasons

---

[8] This percentage is an estimate accepted by obstetricians and gynecologists participating in the Second Arden House Colloquium on Human Fertility, but is admittedly a "guesstimate."

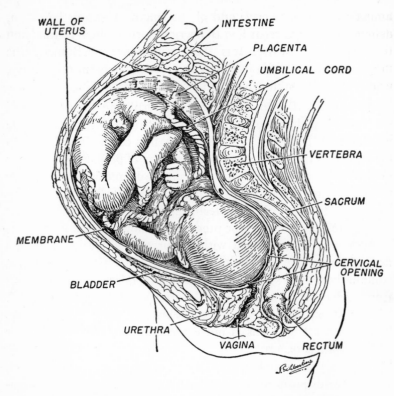

Figure 19. The relation of the unborn child to its mother just prior to birth. This diagram shows the expanded uterus with the fetus attached by the umbilical cord to the placenta, in which the blood of the mother and the blood of the fetus come into close proximity. In the placenta, food is absorbed from the mother's blood stream and transmitted to the child, and waste products are transmitted to the mother for elimination. (Reproduced through the courtesy of the author, artist, and publisher. From A. F. Guttmacher, *Into This Universe: The Story of Human Birth*, The Viking Press.)

for such failures are important to the understanding of the whole marriage relation.

(1) **Sterility.** This condition, in which either the husband or wife is unable to contribute viable cells (sperm or ova) occurs in

an estimated 5 to 10 percent of all marriages. Folklore ordinarily assigns the responsibility for such a condition to the wife; actually the husband is probably the responsible party in one third or more of these cases. In such, the husband's semen contains insufficient sperm, the sperm are lacking in the vitality necessary for fertilization of the ovum, or the tubes leading from the testes are blocked. Sterility in the wife may be due to a variety of causes; the ovum may not develop to the extent necessary for fertilization, because of a hormone deficiency; the Fallopian tubes may be closed, in which case the sperm cannot reach the ovum nor the ovum the uterus; the cervical opening may in some cases be closed by the tipping of the uterus and thus prevent the sperm from entering; or the nature of the vaginal secretions may be such as to kill the sperm before they can enter the uterus. Many of the conditions, in both husband and wife, can now be treated in special clinics, and the couple who find themselves unable to have children can, in many cases, have the condition remedied by a competent physician. Emotional factors are increasingly recognized as a cause of sterility; in those cases where possible physical causes have been ruled out, consultation with a psychiatrist is indicated.

(2) **Abortion**. Medical authorities estimate that about one tenth of all pregnancies end in spontaneous abortion—that is, under circumstances in which the uterus cannot carry the fetus to full term and expels it. In only a small percent of these cases is the condition such that fertilization will always end in abortion. Such abortions are due to one or more of a number of causes: The uterus may be in an unhealthy condition; the development of the placenta may be imperfect due to nutritional or hormonal deficiencies; the sperm or ovum may have been imperfect or may carry abnormal chromosomes; in some instances serious illness may be the cause. Where these are responsible, the fetus is most likely imperfect; in other types of abortion the fetus may be normal and the cause must be assigned to abnormalities in the reproduction system; in still others the cause is unknown.

The folklore of our culture still places great emphasis upon the guilt of the couple in cases of spontaneous abortion; such an attitude is entirely unwarranted. The biochemical processes involved in developing the ovum and sperm, in fertilization, and in the nurturing of the embryo are so complex that the cause of abortion can most often not be assigned. Competent medical assistance can today help most couples to overcome the difficulties that have caused the interruption of the pregnancy.

In most states induced abortions can be performed legally under certain circumstances and with proper medical opinion. These are termed therapeutic abortions, and are resorted to where there is serious mental disease, where organic conditions threaten the life of the mother, or where there is reason to believe that the fetus will be abnormal. The Roman Catholic position prohibits such abortions, as has been indicated in a number of papal documents. The official position of Pope Pius XII, for example, has been that there are *no* medical and therapeutic indications for abortion, however much pity one may have for the mother, or even though her life may be endangered. There is, in this belief, no reason great enough to excuse in any way the murder of the unborn child.[9]

Illegal abortions are of quite a different order. While adequate data are not available, there are authoritative estimates indicating that such abortions number in the millions each year, with a great majority occurring among married women. Many of these are self-induced, but many are performed by physicians with questionable ethics, or—even worse—by charlatans who conduct "abortion mills." Infection—possibly followed by sterility, chronic illness, or (in extreme cases) death—is likely to result because of the circumstances under which such operations are performed. Also, serious psychological conditions resulting from anxiety and guilt are likely to be end products of such abortion. It should be noted, in this connection, that the nostrums widely advertised "for

[9] *Cf.* Sertum Laetitiae, "To the Church in the United States," Encyclical Letter of Pope Pius XII, p. 12.

delayed periods" are of value only in enriching the pocketbooks of their purveyors; there is no known drug that causes abortion.

One cannot be too emphatic in condemning illegal abortions. Couples undoubtedly pay a great price, both physically and emotionally, for such interruptions of pregnancy. If they have reservations about additional pregnancies, their logical responsibility is to avail themselves of the excellent contraceptive advice now generally available rather than to submit the wife to the serious effects and dangers of illegal abortion.

SEXUAL BEHAVIOR

While sexual activity is the result of innate drives in the human being, it is also learned behavior in that it is modified by each couple—who search for mutual gratification—in terms of their special requirements.

Physical Requirements

The physical characteristics of both husband and wife are such that certain requirements need to be fulfilled if sexual activity *is to be mutually satisfactory*. In brief, these are as follows: the penis must be sufficiently erect and distended to allow entrance into the vagina; the vulva and vaginal opening must be sufficiently lubricated to allow entrance without discomfort; the stimulation of the penis must take place in sufficient amount and intensity that the orgasm can occur; the wife must undergo sufficient sexual excitement—by whatever means—to cause her to have an orgasm. Given these four, coitus with mutual orgasm becomes a matter of psychological insight, mutual regard for each other's needs and characteristics, and a will to succeed in the mutual enjoyment of the relationship.

Sexual Excitement

The culmination of the sex act is the orgasm, which is defined as the "height of excitement in coition." In the male this is the discharge of semen; in the female, there is no comparable physical discharge. In both, however, there is during sexual activity a building up of nervous tension. In the male this tension appears to be localized in the genitals, with only secondary effects upon the remainder of the body. In the female, in contrast, the tension appears to be less centered in the genitalia but to be diffused throughout the body. At the time of orgasm, these tensions break, and the body returns rapidly to its nonerotic state. Even here, however, there are reported differences, with the male's tension releasing more rapidly. No dogmatic statement can be made regarding the orgastic experience of the human being.[10] Different individuals of the same sex are erotically sensitive in different parts of the body, and the sexes differ markedly.

In the husband, a quick response to erotic stimuli is usually reported, accompanied by a learned ability to hold a high level of sexual excitement without reaching orgasm too quickly. In the wife erotic excitement is usually reported to be slower in developing but rises to the intensity of orgasm more quickly after arousement does take place. Similarly, there are great variations in the role the secondary sexual characteristics (the lips, breasts, and so on) play in the attaining of an orgasm. To some wives, kissing and fondling of the breasts or genitals are almost necessary if the orgasm is to be achieved; to others, these acts are apparently of little value. There is, then, no law or rule of sexual behavior leading to orgasm; it is essentially a matter of the couple's learning to know each other's *highly individualized* needs and responses. It must be emphasized that this is *learned* behavior—not necessarily or even probably to be expected from the time of the first coital experience, but to be understood as something which *grows* as the couple adjust to each other's needs and characteristics.[11] Each must learn that his own and his mate's erotic behavior is a frank

---

[10] It is this willingness of the "marriage manuals" and "how-to-be-sexually-adjusted-in marriage" articles in current magazines to view sexual behavior in a dogmatic way which makes them of no value in understanding human sexual needs.

[11] *Cf.* Landis' findings as shown in Figure 12, page 164.

expression of the desire for mutual gratification. Each must learn, too, that the human values in sex can be achieved only as both undertake gentle and prolonged experimentation in the search for those acts which provoke the desired reaction *in the other*.

This emphasis upon the mutuality of the experience does not mean that the sexual act will be carried on in the same manner, or that orgasm will always occur for either or both partners. Variations will occur for a number of reasons. Fatigue may make it impossible for the individual to reach the point of orgasm, even though intercourse is desired. Emotional stress may affect the individual in the same way, at the same time that quiet coital behavior is appreciated and needed.[12] There is, in the lay literature, too much emphasis upon both husband and wife reaching orgasm at the same time and upon the presumed need for orgasm to occur.[13] Such emphasis may lead the couple to have expectations of coitus which, when not achieved, leads to feelings of inadequacy and failure. This is not to ignore the circumstances in which failure to achieve orgasm has real significance. Abraham Stone, director of the Margaret Sanger Research Bureau, and an outstanding authority in the field of marital relations, discusses both aspects of the failure to achieve orgasm in these words.

> . . . If a woman responds actively to the sexual embrace and takes pleasure in the sexual union, her inability to reach an orgasm may not be of any serious import. Please understand that even if a woman does not attain an intense culmination, it does not mean that she does not derive a great deal of gratification from the sex act. Some women, indeed, are not at all aware of any orgasm problem until they learn about it from a conversation or book, and then they become greatly worried because they believe that they are not obtaining complete satisfaction from their sex experiences. As a matter of fact, some of the descriptions in the literature about the manifestations of the orgasm are often more poetic than real, and they sometimes lead men and women to expect sensations which are but rarely experienced.

[12] This is evidenced in the fact that many couples report satisfaction with occasional sexual experiences in which no attempt is made to reach an orgasm.
[13] See footnote 10.

If an actual orgasm deficiency exists, however, the effect of this condition upon the woman would depend largely upon the intensity of her sexual desires and the degree of her excitation at the time of the relation. If her sexual impulse is weak, or if she has been aroused but little, the absence of the orgasm will hardly have any harmful effects. On the other hand, if she has been very much stimulated, the failure to reach a climax may leave her in a state of frustration which may prove physiologically and emotionally disturbing. During erotic excitation there is a marked local congestion of the sexual organs as well as a general physical and emotional tension. With the completion of the act, if an acme is reached, there is a gradual release or detumescence, and this is followed by a sense of fulfillment and relaxation. In the absence of an orgasm however, the relief is not complete, and the woman may remain for some time in an unsatisfied and restless condition. Repeated experiences of this kind may eventually lead to various nervous or sexual disturbances.[14]

Variations in the Intensity of Desire

"Highly sexed" and "undersexed" are descriptive terms much used in the American vernacular. In the quotation from Stone above, he speaks of a "weak sexual impulse."[15] There is little doubt that people vary in the level of sexual "energy," just as they vary in temperament and other characteristics. Such differences have to be taken into account as the couple strive toward the mutual satisfaction ideal discussed earlier, but it is more important to remember that many times what is interpreted as a weak sexual impulse is really the presence of inhibitions caused by the factors mentioned earlier, or perhaps the fear of pregnancy.[16] Once these inhibitions have been released and a high degree of understanding achieved, many people who have considered themselves "undersexed" have come to participate fully in the sexual relationship.

There is some clinical evidence to support the idea that in the woman the sexual urge varies within the menstrual cycle. Many

14 Abraham Stone and Hannah Stone, *A Marriage Manual*, pp. 212, 213.
15 *Ibid.*, p. 213.
16 *Cf.* Stone, *ibid.*, p. 209.

wives and husbands report that there is a greater disposition to sexual activity in the period following menstruation and preceding ovulation—at which time the estrogenic hormones are in fullest production. This is not too important, however, since the important goal is that whenever the urge occurs the individual, whether wife or husband, be free to express candidly his or her feelings on the subject.

Impotency and Frigidity

These two conditions are variations in sexual behavior, which need special mention since they are so often misunderstood. Impotency, which is the husband's inability to have or to maintain an erection to the point of orgasm, may be either temporary or permanent. Where it is temporary, it is usually the result of unusual fatigue or worry, as related to emotional conflicts or feelings of guilt, or it accompanies ill health.

Frigidity, which is the lack of sexual response on the part of the wife, is caused by similar factors, or by an ignorance of the need for precoital stimulation. Cultural and psychological conditioning against sex as a normal part of the emotional and physical life, and immature emotional development, can all contribute to frigidity.

Only in rare cases will frigidity and impotency fail to respond to treatment. Often all that is needed is a frank approach to the difficulty by the couple themselves; in more involved cases, however, the help of a physician or psychiatrist may be needed.

SUMMARY

This discussion of sexual behavior in marriage has been based upon the recognition that sex is not all-important in marriage—but also that it is not unimportant. How we behave regarding sex in the marital relationship has been seen to be the resultant of our personality needs, our cultural heritage, the values we seek to fulfill in marriage, and, finally, the extent to which we understand the anatomical and physiological aspects of the relationship. Sexual behavior is emphasized as being more psychological than physiological, more a matter of attitudes than physical dexterity, and it must be understood to have values far beyond the mere fact of procreation. If contemporary marriage has the important function of fulfilling personality needs—and this is recognized by even the most traditionally-minded, then the affection-giving and affection-receiving functions of the sexual act have an important place in our knowledge of what marriage demands.

READINGS AND TOPICS FOR REPORTS

1. Read one of the current how-to-behave-sexually books or magazines, and analyze its prescriptive advice in the light of the discussion in this chapter.
2. After research in the library, contrast the attitudes of the Roman Catholic and Protestant churches regarding sexual activity, both in and outside of marriage. What are the differences between venial and mortal sins as understood by the churches in this connection?
3. Interview a number of obstetricians to discover their attitudes regarding the need for psychological preparation for the sexual aspects of marriage, for pregnancy and childbirth, and for later care of the child.

ADVANCED READINGS

Goodrich, F. W., *Natural Childbirth.*
Latz, L. J., *The Rhythm of Sterility and Fertility in Women.*
Rock, John, and David Loth, *Voluntary Parenthood.*
Stone, Abraham, and Hannah Stone, *A Marriage Manual.*

13

The Economic Aspects
of Marriage

THE COUPLE WHO marry today face vastly different situations
as regards money than did their ancestors of a century ago. As
Chapter 1 has already indicated, ours is a money-centered econ-
omy. The family, whether urban or rural, is likely to earn its
living rather than to make it, and the pressures upon the family
to equip itself with a variety of "necessities" are heavy.[1] This is
especially true for middle-class families where the desire to better
the plane of living is frequently great.[2] The situations which
families face as regards income and expenditures are therefore
worthy of some consideration.

FACTORS INFLUENCING THE USE OF MONEY

The spending of the family's income is not always directly
related to the amount of money available nor to the physical needs

[1] In any discussion of the economics of married living it should be kept in mind
that "necessities" is a relative term, and that the student will, therefore, view the
discussion within a framework uniquely his own.
[2] See the discussion of this important characteristic of the American scene in
Chapter 1.

of the members. Other factors may play an important part in determining how the income will be budgeted.

Values and Expectations

No two families, regardless of income or other characteristics, have exactly the same values, the same goals, and the same expectations in life. We can best illustrate this by describing two families whose incomes, occupations, size, and social class membership are practically identical.

The *A* family, as Mrs. *A* describes it, "exists in poverty for ten months of the year so we can *live* the other two months." Each year the family plans a two-month vacation, using a station wagon and camping out, during which they visit the national and state parks in several states. They have followed this pattern since World War II, and have by now visited all but eight states. They take numbers of color photographs, and in the following months relive their vacation by reviewing the trip for themselves and their friends.

In order to do this, all other expenditures are held to a minimum. They occupy an inexpensive apartment, spend as little as possible on food and clothing, and carry only enough insurance to meet the immediate costs if a member of the family should die. "We know we could always make out some way if my husband should die. . . . What is important to us is that we *live* while we are all together, and we get our fun out of traveling and seeing new places—so that's what we do."

The *B* family, in Mrs. *B*'s words, is "insurance poor." This family, in its seventeen years of existence, has never been away from home on a vacation. Mr. *B* has two months vacation, as does Mr. *A*, but he stays at home "because we never have any money we can afford to spend on a vacation." The *B*'s, like the *A*'s, spend as little as possible on food, clothing, and shelter, and make no expenditures for other items that are not absolutely necessary. They do, however, carry an impressive amount of insurance on Mr. *B*'s life (in endowment policies), and are insured against almost every type of catastrophe for which the family can purchase protection. In Mr. *B*'s words, "I get a check for about $450 a month, and my insurance premiums take almost half of that amount. We're protected, though, and that's what is important."

Both of these families represent very unusual extremes, but they serve to illustrate the point that—for whatever reason—the values and goals of families are uniquely their own. Most students would not agree with the penny pinching of the *A*'s, with one "grand splurge" each year. Also, most would not agree with the *B*'s, whose penny pinching is centered upon being sure of a financially-adequate old age and being protected against crises which may never come. The fact is, however, that in terms of their own needs (as they view them) both families are quite happy (as they view happiness) to live as they do. It is obvious, then, that what constitutes an adequate use of income varies with the values and goals held by the particular family.

Occupational Demands

Few families live completely independent lives from the standpoint of demands upon their incomes. The occupation of the breadwinner may well subject the family budget to special demands. Travel for which he is not reimbursed may be required in the case of a salesman; the doctor or the college professor may need to buy books and to attend professional meetings at his own expense; the insurance salesman may find it necessary to play golf and to belong to a country club in order to have the proper business contacts. Each of these is a sample of the way in which the family income may have to meet special needs. Even such an expenditure as that for clothing may be influenced by the occupation; the farmer can wear dungarees, the businessman must be dressed more formally (and hence more expensively). Family expenditures, in other words, may necessarily vary in terms of demands over which the family members actually have little control.

Social Pressures

Social pressures can well influence the spending of the family's income. If the family lives among and associates with other families of like income and interests, it is sometimes difficult to resist the influence of the social group. If attending the local artist's series is "something that is done," there are subtle pressures upon the family to do the same. If the family's friends send their children to a dancing class, for whatever reason, it is sometimes difficult to deny the children the same experience, at whatever cost to the budget. The total effect of such pressures is rarely recognized; suffice it to say that they do exist and that they help to determine how the family's income shall be spent.

Psychological Needs

It is difficult to generalize concerning the ways in which psychological needs can influence the use of money in the family. It has probably occurred to the student that Mr. and Mrs. *B*, in the illustration used earlier in this chapter, had marked feelings of insecurity, and this was true. Both were worrisome individuals who were, for example, always fearful that someone would fall on their sidewalk and sue for damages. Hence their carrying an unusual amount of insurance to cover such happenings.

Similarly, a husband and wife may fail to achieve the recognition they need, and entertain frequently in order to compensate, to be accepted in the "right circles." They may find it necessary to belong to a certain club for the same reason, even though it means distorting the family budget. Some couples satisfy their need for status (resulting from a feeling of inferiority or insecurity) by being sure that their children are given all the "advantages" they were denied or were ineligible to achieve.

Whether the need is to compensate for insecurity, lack of status, or for some other lack in their lives, these attempts to satisfy do affect spending in some families. It is impossible to indicate all the forms such action may take, and it is important that we understand rather than pass judgment upon a family's concept of its needs.

The Necessity for Agreement

No one of the factors discussed above is all-important in determining how the family income shall be spent. Every couple entering marriage may be confronted with these in some degree and in varying combinations. The important point is not that the needs can and do make demands upon the family income, but that there be recognition and agreement between husband and wife in the way they are to be met. There can be disruption of the family's functioning if this agreement is not present; there can also be disruption if the family ignores its special needs and attempts to conform to some economist's "norms" of family expenditures. For example:

> A husband and wife consulted a family counseling service because they were unable to make their expenditures conform to the standard budget a household-finance specialist had given them. Each recognized that there were tensions and feelings of guilt based upon the fact that they spent (what they were led to believe were) disproportionate amounts for certain luxuries. When they were helped to see that these were necessities in terms of the husband's occupation, and that their needs could fit no standardized budget, the tensions were resolved.

FACTORS INFLUENCING THE CONTROL OF MONEY

Even though there are agreements upon the major goals in the use of the income, difficult situations can arise because of the ways in which the money is controlled within the family.

Role Definitions

Many individuals bring to marriage fixed ideas of how they shall behave in the matter of family finances. These ideas may stem from the loyalties and conceptions gained in childhood, in which case the individual attempts to carry out the same role conceptions and performances that were in existence in his parental family. Such behavior can seem entirely natural and adequate to that individual, but may be a source of tension to the mate. For example, where the husband and wife have been raised with different patterns for expending money, a problem situation can develop as follows.

In the *G* family, the husband brought to marriage the idea that he earned the money and that it was his function to expend it. In his parental family, the father had held the purse strings tightly, and on the weekly shopping trips to town had given each member of the family such funds as were needed. Mr. *G*'s mother had accepted this pattern—had, in fact, known no other in her own childhood—and no difficulties ensued.

Mr. *G*'s wife, however, had come from a family in which no such pattern had existed. Her father and mother had made joint decisions and the family had budgeted in a democratic fashion. To follow any other course would have seemed strange.

In the early years of the *G*'s marriage, both husband and wife had attempted to live according to the roles they had known in childhood—with considerable tension resulting. It was only when Mr. *G* came to recognize (with some help) that his own family's role patterns had been adequate in an earlier time and for a quite different situation, and had met his rural parents' needs but did not meet his and his wife's urban needs a generation later, that the tension was released.

Psychological Needs

Of a quite different dimension in controlling money are the factors arising out of the psychological needs of the *individual*. Just as the family may have a need for security or status (as discussed above), so can the individual have psychological needs which are sometimes met through the use of money in certain ways. The husband who must constantly prove to himself, his mate, and his children that he is the dominant figure in the family can do so by holding a tight rein on the family's expenditures. The wife who demands that she control the finances and who arbitrarily doles out a small allowance to her husband because she resents his nominal headship in the family is another example. Situations such as these are most often the result of deep-seated emotional problems and can be adjusted only with the help of a psychiatrist or a skilled marriage counselor. They are, also, most often accompanied by a failure to adjust in other areas of married life.

Changes in Patterns of Control

One of the realistic goals of any marriage is to have it meet the needs of the members as they move through the life cycle. This means, as we have pointed out earlier,[3] that what is satisfying and satisfactory at one point in the family's existence may not be at all suitable at a later date. The pattern for control of finances may change radically as the members' needs change. In the words of a middle-aged, middle-class mother:

> We worked hard at sharing the responsibilities in our early [married] years. Now I find that with the children and all of my responsibilities in the P-TA, the church, and my other community work, I'd rather that [my husband] simply took care of everything. I don't *need* to spend the money, and I would rather just leave it all in his hands. . . . I use charge accounts and am careful to keep them from being too high, but I've ceased to have any share in how our money is spent—something that would have been very important to me once.

The point to be emphasized here is that every couple must recognize that such changes can and do occur as the family relationships undergo change. If such changes are taken into account, there is little reason for concern. When there is little insight or an unwillingness to adapt to new situations, however, this aspect of money management may well plague the marriage.

USING THE INCOME

The use of the family's income may vary from one family to another and for one reason to another, but certain general principles have been found to be effective regarding its use. These—need we repeat—are always subject to personal interpretation and to variation from one stage of family life to another.

Budgeting

One principle applying to the family's use of its income is that it have some idea of where the money is to go—and when. Budget-

[3] This need for adaptability to changing needs and aspirations is closely tied to the personality characteristics discussed in Chapter 4.

ing is by no means the rigid division of the income into amounts to be placed in little cubicles in a locked box, as some couples think. It is, in Bigelow's words,

> ... not a hard and fast list of predetermined expenditures, not an ironclad arrangement allowing no . . . flexibility in the use of income. The family budget is *a spending plan*. It is a tentative estimate of the family's income and expenditures for a realistic list of items. It is a guide to *intelligent planning*.[4]

The intelligent use of a budget—not to freeze expenditures within definite limits but to incorporate foresight into the matter of spending—enables the couple to set realistic goals for the spending (and saving) of what they have. It has, however, a further benefit, as Landis and Landis point out.

> Keeping a budget has value in the early years of marriage for it brings family spending into the open and encourages talking money [and hence other things] over. It has been suggested that a young couple work out a financial plan before they marry. This is an excellent plan, for it means that they will discuss their attitudes on the spending of money and discover some of their points of agreement and disagreement at a time when they can discuss their differences more objectively than might be possible later, after they are married and are faced with baffling financial problems. It should also help them to be more realistic about how they will be able to afford to live after marriage so that there should be less tendency to blame each other if they later feel a financial pinch.[5]

A further value in employing a budget lies in the fact that it affords the opportunity to clarify conflicting views on values and wants and to arrive at new ones, which are mutually satisfying. If one partner wants a television set and the other a healthy bank account, the need to provide for one or the other (or both) within the budget provides a framework within which the contrasting views can be adjusted. A budget is not a sure solution for "money problems," however. It can become, for some people, a source of major irritation and constant tension, as seen in the following account.

4 Howard F. Bigelow, *Family Finance*, p. 341.
5 Judson T. Landis and Mary G. Landis, *Building a Successful Marriage*, pp. 317 f.

The *F*'s have an income adequate for their needs, but Mr. *F* is an accountant and believes that a full set of books should be kept on all income and expenditures in the home. Mrs. *F* is far from systematic in her account keeping, and is likely to omit minor entries regarding small purchases. These omissions are a constant trial to Mr. *F*, and he spends considerable time attempting to improve his wife's bookkeeping methods. This serves only to frustrate his wife to a greater extent, and there are periods of tension in the family as a result.[6] "I get so darned mad at him I sometimes just have to go away and cry. That budget doesn't do us one bit of good, and just makes us unhappy. And there isn't a thing I can do about it. Joe is so set about it and so stubborn that I just have to put up with it. . . . It's the one thing about our marriage that makes me *very* unhappy."

It is obvious that this couple did not benefit greatly from using a budget under circumstances such as these; it is also obvious that at least one member of the family missed the true purpose of the budget—that of planning for expenditures—and apparently considered it as an exercise in detailed bookkeeping. Under circumstances such as these, some other plan for controlling family expenditures should be worked out; whatever the means employed, it should always be acceptable to both parties, or it will become simply another source of tension and conflict. There are, of course, some cases in which no practical means of managing the family finances can ever be worked out; in these a permanent lack of adjustment seems inevitable.

Buying

Some of the more important problems faced by the married couple center around the purchase of food, clothing, and equipment. In a society that in a variety of ways exerts constant pressure to buy—through high pressure sales campaigns, advertising, and installment selling—the beginning family is especially vulnerable. While the buyer enjoys a certain amount of protection through the activities of governmental agencies in his buying of

---

[6] See the discussion of family de-morale-ization in Chapter 4.

foods, drugs, and the like and is similarly protected against fraudulent sales by Better Business Bureaus and merchants' associations, there are still many instances in which the young couple need to exercise considerable care. In addition, there are some business practices, which are entirely ethical and legal (and under certain circumstances justified), that need to be understood if the family is to make the best use of its income.

Intelligence in buying. The family shopper is constantly urged by advertisers to buy certain brands of foods and other household needs and may be greatly influenced in her purchases by such practices. "Nationally advertised brands are best" might have the word "known" added to that slogan. The quality of a product depends upon more than its widespread recognition and distribution, and a number of other factors are pertinent in family buying. Why is the cost of brand A somewhat more than that of brand B? Is the quality of the first brand actually better than that of the second? The family shopper who buys by name only often loses out because she fails to take into account the reasons for the difference in price. Very often there are local food products which are not widely known but which are the equals of those with national reputations, and which are less expensive. To choose an item simply because its name or label is featured in advertisements in national magazines is sometimes a way of spending money foolishly. The shopper needs to acquaint herself with brand names, but above all she needs to acquaint herself with the quality of the goods she buys.

The cheaper item is not always the best, however. Just as a brand name does not connote quality, so does a bargain price not always connote a bargain. The family buyer finds it necessary, therefore, to learn to judge quality for herself, and then to relate that determination to the price of the article. Where durability is essential, as in the case of items that must be expected to serve for a number of years, the importance lies in the materials, workmanship, and available future repair services, rather than in the present price alone. Item A may cost 10 percent more than item *B*, but that 10 percent may be well worth spending when one considers the durability and workmanship available in item *A*, plus the fact that the manufacturer stands ready to offer repair and reconditioning services throughout the lifetime of the article.

The family buyer can avail herself—women do more than two thirds of all the buying for American families—of technical assistance in judging major items for family use. Several private testing laboratories now make their services generally available to subscribers (and at least one does so through a monthly publication found on most newsstands). Two of these are the Consumer's Union[7] and Consumer's Research.[8] Neither is related in any way to the products they evaluate, nor are the products specially selected for testing. Several brands of one article are tested, and the impartial (and sometimes highly uncomplimentary) findings are published. This is not a suggestion that their recommendations be taken at face value, but their discussions of quality do provide the family buyer with guides for her own decisions.

Intelligent buying involves a sense of timing, too, and here the planning of expenditures through "budgeting" can be especially helpful. If, for example, the husband needs a new topcoat—an article that varies little in cut and material from one year to another —foresight in planning that expenditure plus knowledge of when topcoats will be "cleared" from the sales racks through "end of season" sales can mean substantial savings to the family. The same is true of items such as canned goods, which are reduced in price in certain seasons to clear the shelves for the new pack. Planning family expenditures so that advantage can be taken of such sales is part of successful budgeting.

Finally, intelligent buying requires that one view the setting in which sales are made. Many items are price fixed and therefore cost as much in the small neighborhood or off-the-main-street store as in the luxurious specialty shop. Others, however, can be purchased at substantial savings—and with no sacrifice in quality—

[7] *At* 17 Union Square, New York, N. Y.
[8] *At* Washington, New Jersey.

in the smaller store. The larger store, with many extra services, high rents, and generally greater overhead—all of which are paid for by the consumer—may well put the family buyer at a disadvantage.

Charge accounts.   The practice of "charging it to our account" has a nice sound but is a mixed blessing. A charge account properly established and regularly paid is, of course, almost a guarantee of credit with other stores in the future. It has the advantage, too, of allowing purchases to be made and payment deferred to the end of the month or even longer; also, it allows shopping by telephone —which is certainly a convenience. It has some disadvantages, in that it weakens sales resistance for many people—"I really can't afford it just now, but then I can pay for it next month, so I'll take it." Selling on credit is expensive, however, and its expense invariably finds its way into the cost of every article. Having a charge account encourages purchasing at one store (which is one of the things it is intended to do), and therefore lessens the likelihood that the family buyer will shop around; this is inevitably a hindrance to good buying practices. For the family of unlimited means, these objections are not serious; for the beginning or growing family, which must stretch every dollar to the utmost, the charge account has real disadvantages.

Installment buying.   Conservative estimates indicate that from 12 to 15 percent of all purchases of major household items are made on the installment plan. "Only 10 percent down; the rest in easy monthly payments" has a nice sound to the family buyer who has limited funds. But is it good business for the family budget? The interest one pays on an installment purchase is almost always hidden and, when identified by the seller, is very often not truly represented. The test in such cases is to ask the price if paid in cash and to determine the rate of interest from the difference. Ordinarily it will be found to range from 10 to 25 percent.

It must be remembered, too, that in installment buying the advantages are all on the side of the seller. In rare instances does the article become the property of the purchaser until the last payment has been made; what happens in the interim is important. Should the family have an emergency, and find it impossible to meet the monthly payment, what happens? Will the company claim its right to repossess the article, in which case the family loses what it has already paid? Will additional—and exorbitant— fines be levied against the buyer for his delinquency? Has the family actually given other items it owns outright as security for payment? What if the family has a financial "windfall" and wants to complete payments ahead of schedule? These and other questions need to be raised, and can be answered only by reading the fine print in every contract. "Read before you sign" is good advice when buying on the installment plan—if you must buy in this fashion.

The Purchase of Security

Security being as valued, and as important, as it is in our society, the question of insuring the family against a variety of crises is of importance. This is not the place to enter into a detailed discussion of insurance problems of the family, but some facts need to be emphasized.

Life insurance. The expenditure of money for life insurance may well be an important part of every family budget; it is, however, one that is very often determined by the special pressures and interpretations of the insurance salesman rather than by the family's needs. Those who marry need to understand something of the several types of insurance available to them.[9]

1. *Ordinary life insurance*. The most common type of policy issued is that termed ordinary or "straight" life insurance. Its purpose is to provide a stated sum at the death of the insured. There are several ways in which this is done.

(a) *Term insurance*, which is written for a stated period of years (usually one, five, or ten), is the least expensive way of

[9] A brief but adequate discussion of the types of insurance best suited to family needs will be found in *Public Affairs Pamphlet No. 134*, "How to Buy Life Insurance."

obtaining protection for the family. The premiums are figured on the probability of the individual's death within the stated period (rather than upon the whole of his life expectancy); also, term insurance affords *protection only*, with no dividends and no sum returned at the end of the period for which he is insured. It can therefore be purchased at comparatively low rates.

5-year Term	$$
Ordinary Life	$$$$$$$$$$$$$
Endowment at age 65	$$$$$$$$$$
20-payment Life	$$$$$$$$
20-year Endowment	$$$$

Figure 20. The "insurance purchasing power" of $10 a month for a 25 year-old husband, by type of insurance. (Dividends are not taken into account, but would increase the total somewhat if left with the company. Data from the averages of reports by five of the largest mutual companies.)

This type of insurance has both advantages and disadvantages. It provides a maximum of protection for the family at a minimum cost per dollar; it makes possible the carrying of a larger amount of insurance for the family with less strain upon the budget; the family can protect itself for limited periods where the need for long-time protection is not present. Many families, for example, carry term insurance to cover the outstanding portion of the home mortgage, and reduce the amount of insurance as the mortgage is reduced. One of the disadvantages has already been mentioned— that it affords protection only and gives the individual no other return for his money. Another is that it becomes more expensive each time it is renewed.

(b) *Straight life insurance* is a second type; in this type of policy the individual pays a fixed sum each year of his life (to the age of ninety-six when all insurance policies automatically become endowment policies), and the company pays the face value of the policy on the individual's death. Since the payments are always the same and are calculated on the life expectancy of the individual at the time he buys the policy, the cost is higher than in the case of term insurance. After the first or second year this type of policy has a cash surrender and loan value; in other words, the individual not only has protection but can—if his plans change or a crisis occurs—have a part of his expenditure returned.

The chief advantage of this plan is that it provides a fixed amount of insurance for which the cost is constant throughout life; it is therefore easily fixed in the budget. Its serious disadvantage lies in its relatively high cost in the early years of marriage when one is raising a family and its relatively low cost in later years when the dependents have gone from the home. Also, the cash surrender or loan value is relatively low.

(c) *Limited payment life insurance* differs from straight life only in the number of payments made. In this type, the insured contracts to pay the total cost in a specified number of years (for example, in 20 years); after that time the policy remains in force and is paid at the death of the insured, but there are no additional costs. Since the premiums are confined to a specified number of years the cost is obviously greater than for straight life insurance. Such policies have cash-surrender and loan value, but the disadvantage to the beginning family lies in the relatively high cost per year.

2. *Endowment insurance.* There is no investment or savings value in the above three types of insurance. They are purchased for protection—not for any return they will bring to the insured. Endowment policies, in contrast, are intended to provide an element of savings and investment as well as protection.

(d) *Endowment policies* are those in which the individual pays a higher premium for a specified number of years (usually to the age of sixty-five) and receives the face value of the policy when he reaches the stipulated age. If he dies before that age, his estate receives the face value of the policy. The individual buys this type of policy with the expectation of outliving the contract and therefore receiving his money. Such a policy works to the disadvantage of the family in that much more term or even straight life insurance could be purchased for less money and the difference invested in other savings plans, which pay a higher rate. If this were done, the amount of protection afforded would be greater through the years when protection is of primary importance to the family. This type of insurance provides the investment feature, but it is one which usually works more to the advantage of the company than of the insured.[10]

(e) *Retirement income insurance* is definitely a matter of investment. In this case the individual buys insurance against his death, but in addition pays, in effect, an additional sum, which is invested by the company to be returned in guaranteed monthly payments after a stipulated age is reached (usually sixty, sixty-five, or seventy). The insurance company is, in effect, an investment banker for the individual, and guarantees the return he will receive from the money he invests. Such insurance is obviously expensive and of questionable value to the *beginning* family.

Life insurance is today so varied and so varying in cost that the insurance buyer will do well to examine the many plans and provisions that are made available by different companies. The control of insurance companies by state governments is such in most states that the individual can be reasonably sure of the company's soundness; the buyer—rather than the insurance agent—must be the one to decide what insurance will best meet his needs and at what level he can afford to set his annual expenditures for insurance.

Life insurance can be written for many special purposes and standard policies can often be adapted to special needs. For example, the family can purchase policies on the life of the wage earner, which will guarantee the children's college expenses should he die before they are of college age. (One of the mistakes sometimes made in this connection is for the insurance to be carried on the child's life, which obviously does nothing for him if the wage

---

[10] This is not to discredit such insurance policies nor the companies which write them, but to indicate that they do not best meet the needs of the average married couple.

earner dies.) The family wishing to guarantee the carrying out of almost any program for itself can find a policy to meet its needs.

Other types of insurance. Our country is so "insurance conscious" that the family can buy protection against almost any type of risk. Only a detailed book-length treatise could cover all types—here we can mention only a few of the more important.

1. *Health insurance.* Insurance against hospital costs is readily available in this country, either through commercial insurers or through cooperative "Blue Cross" plans. Where the wage earner can be covered through payroll deductions, the cost is somewhat less than where the family must enroll independently. Since hospital costs can be a tremendous drain upon a family's resources, especially in the case of prolonged illness, the family does well to provide itself with this type of protection—especially where there are small children involved.[11]

Cooperative insurance against medical and surgical costs is increasing in popularity and is usually associated with Blue Cross plans. Until now, the expense of premiums for this coverage has been too great for many families, and the purchase of such insurance by families with low or even average income is questionable. There is as yet no evidence to show whether the family is better off if it carries such insurance or saves regularly in its budgeting for medical and surgical expenses.

2. *Property and liability insurance.* The point beyond which a family can go in *not* insuring itself against certain possibilities has never been clearly established. Ideally, of course, the best solution of this family problem would be to insure against any eventualities, but few indeed are the family budgets that can allow such a coverage. Certainly, the family home, whether owned outright or mortgaged, needs to be insured against fire; the contents, too, need at least a minimum of coverage. Similarly, the family that owns a car needs liability insurance; if it feels that this is an

[11] For the moderate-income family suffering the usual short-time illnesses, the Blue Cross plans ordinarily provide adequate financial protection. In the case of long illnesses, especially of a chronic nature, however, the family can rarely expect full insurance protection.

unreasonable charge against the family budget, it may well question its right to own a car. One criterion may well be applied for determining whether or not a certain type of insurance must be fitted into the family budget, to wit: What will the consequences be for the family if it has no insurance, and a loss occurs? If being without a house in which to live and losing the investment therein will result from a fire, then fire insurance is a necessity. If having a serious accident with the car, and being held liable (perhaps to the extent of one's earnings for the next ten years), is even a remote possibility, then automobile liability insurance is a necessity. Here, again, a realistic evaluation of the family's situation—and not the importunings of an insurance salesman—must be the criterion applied.

Savings and Investments

Every family has need for some money which can readily be available in case of emergency. The savings account is a major means of holding such funds in readiness, at the same time that it is earning interest. The commercial bank's rate of interest is ordinarily between 2 and 3 percent per year, and such accounts are therefore not important from the standpoint of "having money earn money" for the family. Such funds are readily available in time of need, however; moreover, they can usually be left in the account (drawing interest) while used as security for a loan up to the full amount of the deposits. In such cases the cost of the loan is reduced by the amount of interest earned.

Building and loan associations, which are to be found in every community of any size, most often pay a higher rate of interest. Placing the account in such an organization can serve two purposes, since identification with the organization through a savings account can facilitate later borrowing for home ownership. An official of one of these organizations indicated this in these words:

> In a city as big as ours it is difficult to know many of the people who apply for mortgage loans. We have recourse to the usual credit information, but we also pay a good deal of attention to the saving

habits of a young couple. If they have an account with us and have saved regularly, even if the amounts are small, we are likely to be especially cooperative when they are ready to seek a loan for a home.

Investments in stocks and bonds are ordinarily not a part of the young family's concern. Many factors enter into such use of the family's money, and cannot be discussed here. The investment of funds in a home is, however, a popular way of both having a home and saving money—that is, building an estate. The last twenty years have seen rapid changes in methods of financing such purchases. The Home Owner's Loan Corporation (a federal agency) will now guarantee lending agencies against loss from defaulted mortgages on homes, and home ownership loans are now made with much smaller initial payments than was formerly the case. Also, payments are now so devised that the amount paid is the same each month. In this way, a home can be owned in fifteen or twenty years with monthly payments no greater than the usual rent.[12]

Whether or not the family is better off if it owns or rents a home is a moot question. Home ownership under today's banking practices is relatively easy, and the family's equity grows with each payment. In contrast, there is no value and small satisfaction for most people in the collection of a bundle of rent receipts. In contrast, the family which rents has no responsibility for insurance, taxes, or upkeep. No decision can be made regarding the relative merits of the two for any family without taking into account the values held by that family, the chance of their having to move because of job demands, and so on.

Social Security and Job Benefits

The last two decades have seen the development of Old Age and Survivors Insurance—commonly known as social security. About 64 percent of all workers in the United States are now covered by

[12] The loan officer of any bank, especially of the "Federal Savings and Loan" type, will be glad to show any couple how they may own a home "by paying rent."

this federal plan for benefits for the aged. The worker who is in a "covered" occupation pays 1.5 percent on the first $4200 of his income; the employer contributes a similar amount. The details of Old Age and Survivors Insurance coverage are complicated, subject to rapid change, and constantly being extended to new groups; these cannot be discussed here.[13] The important point in this connection is that the benefits afforded are substantial when the worker has been covered for the required period, and their contribution to the family's security should be taken into account in planning the family's protection and savings program.

An increasing number of employers are also providing "fringe benefits," especially in the case of large corporations. These benefits should be clearly understood by the family as long-time financial planning is undertaken, for the benefits derived therefrom are important parts of the total income.[14]

Borrowing

Few indeed are the families of moderate income who do not at one time or another find it necessary to finance the cost of a crisis outside the regular income or savings. Illness, death, or other unexpected demands upon the family purse create situations in which the money must be had—at whatever cost—if the emergency is to be met.

Borrowing is closely related to credit; those whose credit is sound have less trouble in borrowing, as do those who can borrow against property, savings, or life insurance policies. Many families whose credit is sound still use poor borrowing practices simply because they do not know any better. This is true partly because the widely known means of obtaining money—through borrowing from "personal loan companies"—are cloaked with misconceptions. Such companies are set up primarily to meet the needs of individuals whose credit is not too good or whose job prospects

[13] In every community of any size a district officer of the Social Security Administration is available and will give full details on the present status of OASI.

[14] In many instances, corporations have made available "fringe benefits" of such a nature that the family is able to divert much of its "security dollar" to other needs.

are not the best; therefore their rates (3 or more percent per month) are increased to cover a relatively high percentage of losses. For the family—except those who qualify under this description—to borrow from such an agency is unsound family financing.

The growth in recent years of small loan departments in established banks provides the ordinary family with a more satisfactory source of funds in time of emergency. The rates charged are somewhat higher than those for loans made against adequate security, but are substantially lower than those charged by personal loan companies. In many instances, too, the bank insures the borrowing family—for the amount unpaid—against the death of the breadwinner. This is a small but important part of the whole transaction.

Here again the caution about reading the fine print in the contract is important. While the personal loan companies are subject to state control in approximately two thirds of all states,[15] many small abuses of the family (in case it is unable to meet a payment) are possible. The borrowing family needs, therefore, to investigate thoroughly the terms and practices under which it will borrow—if borrow it must.

SUMMARY

Important as money is for the married couple in providing the necessities of life, its basic importance as emphasized in this chapter lies in the *meaning* it has for the couple. Money in itself is only a means to an end, and that end lies in what the couple value and what they expect from marriage. Psychological and social needs help to determine how the income shall be spent, and it is in the full assessment of the values and expectations, together with the recognition of the pressures of life, that the ability to be

---

[15] Personal loan companies ordinarily lend to people who are unable to meet the credit requirements of the banks, hence the high rate of interest. The established and responsible family will likely find the banks sufficiently receptive to meet their financial needs.

happy in marriage—as regards its economic aspects—comes. If the larger aims of the marriage are to be realized, the economic aspects of life must be viewed in terms of the underlying psychology of the couple.

READINGS AND TOPICS FOR REPORTS

1. Interview a lending officer from a local bank to learn of ways in which the commercial bank can serve the beginning family. What does he see as the differences between the services his organization offers as contrasted with those of the savings and loan association, the credit union, and the small-loan company? Are these important to the young family?
2. Study the budgets of a number of families with whom you are acquainted. How do these differ in their allotments for various items? What are their explanations for the special emphasis they place upon certain items?
3. Shop in a small neighborhood store and in a large downtown store for a standard household item such as an electric or gas stove. How do prices differ? How do the stores differ in the ways they will finance deferred payments? Are there interest charges? What are the stipulations in the contract you would be expected to sign?
4. Interview the credit manager of a large store. What does he view as important family characteristics which will determine whether or not he will extend credit? What means does he have for determining the family's financial responsibility?

ADVANCED READINGS

Bigelow, H. F., *Family Finance* (rev. ed.).
Household Finance Corporation, *Money Management Series.*
Nickell, Paulena, and Jean Dorsey, *Management in Family Living.*
Troelstrup, A. W., *Consumer Problems.*

14

Religion in Marriage

RELIGION PERFORMS a quadruple function in the life of man. (1) It enables him to account for things for which he has no other rationale, by conceiving of a deity who has ultimate power over man and his destiny. (2) Religion gives man a sense of security (or vice versa) in what lies beyond his own life expectancy, through the concepts of a rewarding heaven and a punishing hell. (3) Religion provides man with a set of ethical patterns for his behavior (e.g., the Ten Commandments) and a dynamic for service to his fellows—"thou shalt love thy neighbor as thyself." (4) Finally, religion—through the church as an organization—affords man a social group or groups from which he may gain status, companionship, and so on.[1]

The nature of religion in our society, with its separation of church and state, is such that people vary in their acceptance of the functions listed above, in their interpretations of each function, and in the way and degree to which they participate in religion. One individual may place his primary emphasis upon the first

[1] Many members of the more conservative religious groups ignore or deny this fourth function, yet its effectiveness is well recognized by social scientists. Cf., for example, Leonard Broom and Philip Selznick, *Sociology* pp. 440 ff.

three of these functions, and ignore the fourth, while another places high emphasis upon the third and fourth, and practically ignores the first and second. One individual may place a rigid and fundamentalist interpretation upon God as an anthropomorphic creator and ruler of the universe, while another views God as a motivating "spirit" in the progress of the world. One individual may be a "good" Roman Catholic, or Methodist, or Baptist (and take the pre- and proscriptions of his church literally); another may consider himself a member of a church but in practice ignore its dictates. It is from these differences that problems may occur regarding adjustments in marriage.

RELIGION AND THE INDIVIDUAL

If we are to discuss interpersonal relations in marriage as they are affected by religion, we must understand some of the distinguishing features of religion which affect man's behavior. Ours is a Judeo-Christian culture, in that most of our ideas, ideals, attitudes, and behavior patterns that relate in any way to religion have had their genesis in Jewish and/or Christian religious experiences of the past.

Among the three major faiths in our society (Jewish, Roman Catholic, and Protestant) there are significant differences. For the contemporary Jew, only the Old Testament is important, and then when combined with the teachings and interpretations of the Talmud. Every religion constitutes, in effect, a subculture, in that it has its distinct traditions, mores, values, and behavior, but modern Judaism—more than its Gentile counterparts—is a culture of its own in a very special sense, since it is at once a system of religious beliefs *plus* a system of prescribed behavior patterns related to hygiene, social customs, and so on. For the Roman Catholic, both the Old and New Testaments are important, but the pre- and proscriptions of belief and behavior set down by the succession of Holy Fathers are of equal or more importance. In the case of the Protestants, there are such differences as to defy detailed description. Each denomination within Protestantism (which means in practice each group that cannot be called Jewish or Roman Catholic) has its own special conceptions regarding the authority of the church over the individual, the relations of that individual to God, and so on.[2]

We need not belabor this topic of religious differences among the faiths except to point out that their fundamental concepts are such as to make adjustment in marriage difficult. A Roman Catholic priest has indicated this in these words:

> In politics, government, and other relations which go to make up modern life, and where religion may enter into question, the Catholic position is generally known and usually taken into account sufficiently that the Roman Catholic has to forfeit nothing of what he cherishes in his faith. But in marriage all of this is different. One does not "avoid the issue" over a lifetime. Nor does one merely "experience embarrassing moments" and gloss over the difficulty, for the difficulties which religion represents are there permanently. Paths cross, definitely contradictory stands are taken, on every question Catholics and non-Catholics are trained to different views. The Church says "you must"; the non-Catholic husband or wife says "don't." There is no escape, the Catholic must go one way or the other. One goes to Mass, or one does not. Children are either baptized and sent to Catholic schools, or they are not. Birth prevention is either practiced, or it is not.[3]

The authoritative interposition of the Roman Church between man and his God, as seen in this quotation, is in direct contrast (as Father Sause would admit) to the freedom of the individual Protestant to approach his God without such interposition.[4] In the case of the Jew, the problem is of a different dimension. He has the freedom to approach his God directly, but he—whether Reform, Conservative, or Orthodox—has very practical cultural

---

[2] These conceptions are difficult to specify for many denominations, since they are subject to local interpretations which vary sharply.

[3] Cf. Bernard Sause, O.S.B., *Why Catholic Marriage Is Different*. p. 74.

[4] It is this interpretation (which is rarely understood to the fullest degree by Protestants) which affords much of the intellectual conflict between Roman Catholics and Protestants.

dictates (*re* holidays and other religiosocial matters) which set him apart from both the Roman Catholic and the Protestant.

Each religious faith believes in its own superordination to all others, and hence struggles to preserve the isolation of its group through proscribing marriage with an outsider.[5] For interfaith marriages appear, from available research, to have poor chances of success,[6] at least over a period of years. As Father Sause has said,

> All this trouble does not necessarily happen in the first year of marriage. It is a gradual process. It begins with an occasional compromise "to keep peace in the family." It makes headway by observing silence where silence can be interpreted only as the policy of cowardice. Indifference comes easily when the ground is so well prepared. Positive neglect in religious obligations is next, and finally there is too often the total abandoning of the once cherished faith.[7]

We have, to this point, only set the scene for the discussion of the relation of religion to adjustment in marriage. Our thesis in this chapter is a dual one—that religion has positive contributions to make to success in marriage, and, second, that religious differences have negative aspects that can be important.

POSITIVE CONTRIBUTIONS OF RELIGION

To both the Christian and the Jew, the human being is a person of high worth.[8] This is in sharp contrast to such an idealogy as that found in communism, where the individual is of value only as he serves the state, and where human life is cheap. It is probably safe to say that this emphasis upon individual personal worth is in part reflected in our changing ideas regarding the purposes of marriage and the family, although the direct relation is a

[5] Cf. Chapter 10.

[6] Cf., for example, the findings of Harvey J. Locke, *Predicting Adjustment in Marriage*, pp. 240 ff. Such findings are, of course, not to be interpreted as showing that any *one* interfaith marriage will fail.

[7] Cf. Bernard Sause, *op. cit.*, p. 72.

[8] Cf. Henry Bowman, *Marriage for Moderns*, pp. 355 ff.

beclouded one.[9] The recognition of personal worth is inherent in this text's concept of love, and there is little question that strong adherence to the Christian or Jewish ethos means that the individual is motivated to "other-ness" or "we-ness." Peterson has called attention to the fact that religion has such a function in these words:

> Life is often frustrating and irritating. Storms of temper and depressions born of fear and anxiety disturb most men and women. They react emotionally and hurt each other. . . . One of the most difficult lessons to learn in life is to accept our own imperfections. When this is done we are able to forgive others. Forgiveness promotes growth in togetherness in the family. . . . Self-examination in prayer stimulates growth and induces humility. And the person who is humble, who recognizes the grossness of his own egocentricity and the wilfulness of his own personal aggression, may truly forgive others. Thus, religion helps overcome those egocentric blocks to happiness in marriage that are well-nigh universal.[10]

Religion has a further contribution to make to adjustment in marriage in that it provides a series of opportunities for family rituals.[11] Such rituals are not to be thought of in a formal but rather a psychological sense—when the couple or parents and children worship together, say "grace" together, go to Sunday school together, they share in a togetherness-of-purpose which in turn strengthens the underlying "we-ness" of the marriage and the family.[12]

Religion, again, has still a further function, that of challenging man to rise to new levels of interpersonal behavior through personal and group challenge. In Peterson's words, religion

> . . . contributes to the growth of the spirit of the family by consistently holding up to its members aspirations that demand growth.

[9] It must be admitted in this connection that many of the more conservative religious groups appear to ignore the current emphasis of family life in their attempts to hold to "the old-time religion."

[10] Cf. James A. Peterson, *Education for Marriage*, p. 332.

[11] Cf. James H. S. Bossard, *Parent and Child*, pp. 270 ff.

[12] This is not to say that we can accept wholeheartedly the statement that "Families that worship together always *succeed*," for too many other factors are important to success in achieving family goals.

The ideals stressed by churches are brotherhood, reconciliation, peace, kindness, and redemption. In worship one endeavors to relate oneself to the meaning of existence and to the core reality of life. Hours of worship are hours of the uplifted heart and the questing spirit. The frontiers of conscience and mind are pushed outward and the concern for others is sensitized. This experience may bring to a man and a woman a sense of trust, or faith, and of destiny that changes meaningless drifting into purposeful living, that transforms the confused, ambivalent individual into a person with perspective. In saying this we are not unmindful of the morbidity of some overly puritanical faiths which are barren of beauty and destructive of tenderness. Nevertheless, worship of God, the searching of conscience in prayer, the singing of hymns of brotherhood, and the relating of our experience to ideal goals and aims constitute for many a moving and constructive growth experience.[13]

This is not to suggest that all men find these things in worship, nor that such religious participation as Peterson suggests in these two quotations is a *sine qua non* for success in marriage.

Religion is only one of the important parts of the values system each partner brings to marriage (see Chapter 10). Its content is so varied and so differently interpreted—as was earlier suggested—that we cannot be dogmatic about its presence in marriage.[14] It is quite conceivable that, *within their own values system*, two agnostics can meet their needs in marriage without prayer, family, religious rituals, or worship. If we were to suggest the absolute need for these in marriage, we would impute to human personalities a uniformity which would not stand scrutiny.

SOME NEGATIVE ASPECTS OF RELIGION IN MARRIAGE

Having indicated that religion has a positive contribution to make to success in marriage—*where it is part of the shared values of the couple*—we need to look at ways in which religion can serve as a divisive force.

[13] Cf. Peterson, *op. cit.*, p. 333.

[14] We are faced with the need for research which will more clearly outline the contributions of other factors *which accompany* the presence of religion in the family. The actuarial studies of success in marriage have not provided this understanding.

Interfaith Marriage

The fact that each of the major faiths—Roman Catholic, Protestant, and Jewish—prescribes and proscribes certain behaviors means that the interfaith marriage must face more than simply different ideas about theology. The Roman Catholic Church, for example, places a strict ban on certain child-spacing practices, has rigid rules on the rearing of children born to interfaith marriages in which one member is a Roman Catholic, and (in some parishes, at least) places great emphasis upon parochial education. Modern Judaism places emphasis upon the indoctrination of Jewish youth with the cultural values inherent in Judaism, and holds firmly to certain customs (e.g., circumcision of the male child). Protestantism is equally emphatic if only in that it does not prescribe but resents such prescriptions. (This is seen in the usual Protestant belief that no religious group has the right to forbid child-spacing, and in the attitude toward parochial education.)

In practice, then, the interfaith marriage (at least for those who adhere firmly to the tenets of their separate faiths) is one confronted with the need to adjust something which cannot be adjusted. The "good" Roman Catholic, for example, will accept without question the Church's dictates on contraception; the "good" Protestant will resent this intrusion into what he or she deems to be none of organized religion's affair. We have no intent to belabor religious differences, nor to accuse any faith of being insincere or unwise in its dogma. It is necessary, however, to indicate that these differences are of such importance as to cause concern about the interfaith marriage. For one thing, religious values do not exist in a vacuum, but are usually related to other values. For another, few persons are unable to predict at any one point in marriage how they may feel about certain values at a later time. For example:

> I married a Catholic boy I knew well in college. It never occurred to me that we'd have any trouble over his religion. . . . My parents and our minister all told me it was a mistake for me to marry a

Catholic, but I was in love and couldn't see it. I signed a paper in which I agreed to a lot of things, one that I wouldn't practice birth control, and I wasn't bothered a bit. I was in love, that was the main thing. . . . Now we have five children [in eight years] and I can't have another. I won't have another. But Joe won't use any prevention, and won't let me, so we're just growing apart over it. . . . I do love him, and he loves me, to him what his church says comes first. This I can't take any longer, and I'm going to have to leave him. . . . I know I agreed to everything the priest asked me to,[15] but I couldn't look far enough ahead to see that I'd have to change my mind.

This woman signed the antenuptial agreement (Figure 21) in all sincerity, but after some nine years of marriage found herself both unable to keep to that agreement and at the same time seriously disturbed by her own need to violate it. As she said at another point in the interview, "My word is worth something, and this makes me break it."

Another aspect of interfaith marriage—that relating to in-law relationships—is almost equally important, and will be dealt with in the following chapter.

Intrafaith Marriages

Within the same faith, in the case of both Jews and Protestants, there are also chances for difficulty in adjusting in marriage. Judaism has its Reform, Conservative, and Orthodox subdivisions—Protestantism is split into literally hundreds of groups.[16] Some of the latter bear the same name, but differ, for example, from North to South. Others bear the same name, but the urban congregation is vastly different from its rural counterpart. Still others differ as they meet the needs of differing social classes.

These Protestant groups vary on a continuum from "liberal" to "fundamentalist." At the liberal end there is an acceptance of the Bible, but an acceptance blended with human knowledge. The extreme liberal rejects the Biblical story of the creation, and

[15] See copy of the Agreement she signed, Figure 21.
[16] See Footnote 2, this chapter.

ANTE-NUPTIAL CONTRACT AND PROMISES

To be signed in duplicate in the presence of the priest by the parties entering a mixed marriage, and by two witnesses.

To Be Signed by the Non-Catholic Party

I, the undersigned, not a member of the Catholic Church, wishing to contract marriage with the Catholic party whose signature is also hereinafter affixed to this mutual agreement, being of sound mind and perfectly free, and only after understanding fully the import of my action, do hereby enter into this mutual agreement, understanding that the execution of this agreement and the promises therein contained are made in contemplation of and in consideration for the consent, marriage and consequent change of status of the hereinafter mentioned Catholic party, and I, therefore, hereby agree:

1. That I will not interfere in the least with the free exercise of the Catholic party's religion;
2. That I will adhere to the doctrine of the sacred indissolubility of the marriage bond, so that I cannot contract a second marriage while my consort is still alive, even though a civil divorce may have been obtained;
3. That all the children, both boys and girls, that may be born of this union shall be baptized and educated solely in the faith of the Roman Catholic Church, even in the event of the death of my Catholic consort. In case of dispute, I furthermore, hereby fully agree that the custody of all the children shall be given to such guardians as to assure the faithful execution of this covenant and promise;
4. That I will lead a married life in conformity with the Law of God and the teaching of the Catholic Church regarding birth control, realizing fully the attitude of the Catholic Church in this regard;
5. That no other marriage ceremony shall take place before or after this ceremony by the Catholic priest.

In testimony of which agreement, I do hereby solemnly swear that I will observe the above agreement and faithfully execute the promises therein contained, and do now affix my signature in approval thereof.

_____
Signature of the non-Catholic party

_____   _____
Address   City or Town

To Be Signed by the Catholic Party

I, the undersigned, a member of the Catholic Church, wishing to contract marriage with the non-Catholic party whose signature is affixed above to this mutual agreement, being of sound mind and perfectly free, and only after understanding fully the import of my action, do hereby enter into this mutual agreement, understanding that the execution of this agreement and the promises therein contained are made in contemplation of and in consideration for the consent, marriage and consequent change of my status, and I, therefore, hereby agree:

1. That I shall have all my children, both boys and girls, that may be born of this union, baptized and educated solely in the faith of the Roman Catholic Church. I understand that in case of my death, or in the event of a dispute, the custody of all the children shall be given to such guardians as to assure the faithful execution of this covenant and promise;
2. That I will practice my Catholic religion faithfully and will strive, especially by example, prayer and the frequentation of the Sacraments, to bring about the conversion of my consort;
3. That I will lead a married life in conformity with the Law of God and the teaching of the Catholic Church regarding birth control, realizing fully the attitude of the Catholic Church in this regard;
4. That no other marriage ceremony shall take place before or after this ceremony by the Catholic priest.

_____
Signature of the Catholic party

_____   _____
Address   City or Town

Signed in the presence of:

_____   _____
Witness   Witness

I, the undersigned, do hereby attest that the parties whose signatures are affixed to the above agreement and promises appeared before me personally on the given date, and fully understanding the import and meaning of the aforementioned agreement and promises, freely entered into this agreement and signed the above in my presence.

Date:_____   _____
(Pastor - Assistant)

TWO COPIES of this form should be filled in and sent to the Chancery. One copy, when duly signed, dated and sealed by the Chancellor, will be returned to the priest to be kept in the parish archives; the other copy will be retained in the Chancery. See "Synodus Dioecesana Sancti Ludovici Septima—1929" (Page 54 No. 95 under 2).

Figure 21. Ante-nuptial contract of Roman Catholic Church.

questions such dogma as the virgin birth, the physical resurrection, and the second coming of Christ. In contrast, the fundamentalist accepts the Bible as the inspired word of God, and rejects all man-made interpretations of that word. More important, the liberal is "cool and intellectual" in his beliefs, while the fundamentalist "takes his religion seriously." The first is "intelligence-centered," the second "emotion-centered"; the liberal "can take his religion or leave it," while to the fundamentalist religion tends to be the central focus of all his thought and action.[17] Between these are a variety of religious positions, no two exactly alike. Where the couple share the same conceptions and convictions, these differences need cause no concern. But where marriage involves the "blending" of two (especially when extreme) points of view, adjustment becomes something of a problem. It is, for example, difficult for one who is "liberal" to be entirely sympathetic with the views (and behavior) of his mate who is a fundamentalist. This is seen in the following quotation.

> We are both Protestant, and never thought very much about our differences before we were married. . . . I am a religious liberal, and she is pretty far to the right. I don't believe in the virgin birth, or the return from the tomb, or any of that type of thing, and she does wholeheartedly. . . . It means that there are things on which we don't agree. It isn't that they themselves are so goshdarned important, but they seem to be associated with the whole way we think, all of the attitudes we have about a lot of things. It's as though our religious beliefs were surface indicators of what we think about other things, underneath.

This man indicates a further important point in this connection—that religious attitudes are seldom separate and distinct from other attitudes. It is this interplay of all values which causes us to be concerned about adjustment in some marriages, even though they are within the same faith.

A problem such as the one just illustrated high-lights again the need for adequate communication and understanding in the

---

[17] This discussion should be understood as an effort to describe rather than to ridicule any particular religious point of view.

courtship and engagement days. Had these ideas been uncovered and thoroughly talked out, this couple might well not have gone beyond the courtship-stage—to the benefit of both.

THE RESULT OF RELIGIOUS INTERMARRIAGE

Several research projects throw light upon the relation of religious affiliation to failure to adjust in marriage. These may all be regarded as exploratory studies, since they involve relatively small numbers of cases and probably do not represent genuine cross sections of our society.[18] Landis, reporting on 4,108 families with children, found that only 4.4 percent of the Catholic × Catholic,[19] 5.2 percent of the Jewish × Jewish, and 6.0 percent of the

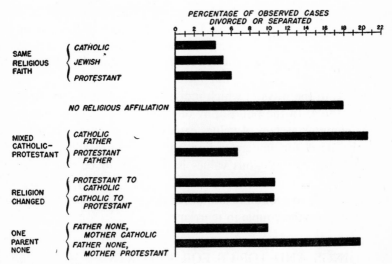

Figure 22. The frequency of divorce and separation as related to religious differences; reported by Landis in his study of "Marriages of Mixed and Non-Mixed Religious Faith." (*American Sociological Review*, XIV, June, 1949, p. 403.)

[18] This is one example of the difficulty faced by students of the family in doing research. Cf. Reuben Hill, *Families Under Stress*, pp. 3 ff.

[19] In such descriptions, the religion of the husband is always stated first; hence, a Catholic × Jewish marriage is that of a Catholic husband and Jewish wife.

Protestant $\times$ Protestant marriages, had ended in separation or divorce. Among the mixed Catholic-Protestant marriages, 14.1 percent had so ended, and the "no religion" couples were reported to have had 17.9 percent end in this fashion (see Figure 22).[20] Weeks[21] and Bell[22] reported slightly different percentages but substantial agreement in somewhat similar studies. It must be remembered, of course, that *these studies only show what happened, not why it happened.* We have already stated that religious values are only part of a larger values system, and there is no way in which these studies could have ascertained the underlying reasons for the differences. However, it is apparent from these studies that our earlier pessimism regarding interfaith marriages is not unfounded.

SUMMARY

In this chapter we have viewed religion as one of the compelling forces in the life of man, but have indicated some of the wide variations in the ways in which individuals recognize, accept, and use this force. In the philosophy of this text, religion is one part of the complex system of values each partner brings to marriage, and the need for understanding and conscious adjustment of differences in the religious values is therefore to be emphasized. In this sense, religious values are different in kind but comparable in importance to economic and other values which are brought to and shared by the couple in marriage.

READINGS AND TOPICS FOR REPORTS

1. Read Milton Barron, *People Who Intermarry*, and have a class discussion on the characteristics of such individuals. Do they

[20] Cf. Judson T. Landis, "Marriage of Mixed and Non-Mixed Religious Faith," *American Sociological Review*, 14:401 ff. (1949).

[21] Cf. H. Ashley Weeks, "Differential Divorce Rates," *Social Forces*, 21: 334 ff. (1943).

[22] Cf. Howard M. Bell, *Youth Tell Their Story*, pp. 220 ff.

constitute a distinct group in our society? Is there a good chance that they have special needs and differences in values which they attempt to fulfill through intermarriage?

2. Interview clergymen who represent different faiths and different denominations in your community to discover what they believe to be the functions of religion for the married couple. How do they differ in their interpretations of these functions? Under what circumstances would they discourage or encourage interfaith or interdenominational marriages?

3. Read George Joyce, *Christian Marriage*, and Regina Wieman, *The Modern Family and the Church*. What are the possible sources of discord for a couple who hold such opposing views of the function of religion?

4. What efforts do the churches of your community make to foster marital adjustment in their families? To foster marital adjustment among young couples in the whole community? Are these efforts, or their lack, consistent with the representations made by clergymen (see Question 2)?

ADVANCED READINGS

Baber, Ray, *Marriage and the Family* (2d ed.), Ch. 5.

Burgess, E. W., and Paul Wallin, *Engagement and Marriage*, Ch. 6.

Kane, John, *Marriage and the Family: A Catholic Approach*, Ch. 8.

Slotkin, J. S., "Adjustment in Jewish-Gentile Intermarriage," *Social Forces*, 21:226 ff. (1942).

15

In-Laws and Marriage

IN CHAPTER 1 we pointed out that the trend in American society has for some decades been away from the inclusion of more than the married couple and their children within the home. The frontier and earlier rural patterns, in which the son brought his bride home, is now the exception rather than the rule. Too, the old patterns, in which the aging father and/or mother lived with their children—sometimes being passed from one to another, have now been outmoded. The desire is "for a home of one's own from the start," even if it means helping to support one's parents in their own domicile or in a home for the aged. This is not necessarily a violation of the Decalogue's command to "Honor thy father and thy mother"—for they may be as anxious to have their "freedom" as are their children.[1]

SOME POSITIVE ASPECTS OF IN-LAW RELATIONSHIPS

It would be unfair to discuss the in-law problem without first indicating the positive values to be had in in-law relationships. It

[1] One of the positive effects of the federal "Social Security" program and of the Old Age Assistance programs sponsored jointly by federal and state governments has been to enable many people to stay in their own domiciles in the later years of life.

is true that we do marry today with the idea of setting up a home of our own, but this is not to say that we must thereafter build a wall around it which excludes either set of parents. The man marries a girl (and vice versa) who, if wisely chosen, is the product of a home in which love and security have been the rule and in which the emotionally mature aspirations of the parents have included his or her marrying. The parental group with such characteristics can be a boon to the new couple, for they can bring to the new marriage much in the way of emotional support.[2] For example, one wife reported the positive aspects of her relationship with her in-laws in these words.

> What we would have done without them, I don't know. They have kept away from us and made us face our own problems, but they've always been there in the background ready to help if needed. . . . My folks are dead, so Bob hasn't had the same help on my side. . . . When the baby was on the way, they bolstered us up with constant encouragement, and I always felt that we could turn to them for understanding. . . . We've never had to borrow money from them, but I know they'd give us the last cent they had if we needed it. But that's not the important thing. It's knowing they love us *as a couple*, and are willing to share their love with both of us, that makes our marriage richer.

This is, of course, the expression of a mature wife's attitude toward mature in-laws. It is unfortunate that not all in-laws are as mature and understanding as these; it is also unfortunate that too often we are culturally influenced to enter marriage "with a chip on the shoulder"—ready to have our in-laws "start something"—and from that point on fail to interpret them in the best possible light. This negative attitude is culturally defined, in a sense, since it is expressed in our cartoons, our jokes, and our media of communication (radio, television, the movies, and so on). We are, in other words, *expected* to align ourselves against our in-laws, and sometimes do this without reason and without realizing the inanity of our attitudes and actions.

[2] Cf. Evelyn M. Duvall, *In-Laws: Pro and Con*, Ch. 9.

SOME NEGATIVE ASPECTS OF IN-LAW RELATIONSHIPS

We shall pay what may seem to be disproportionate attention to the negative aspects of in-law relationships, not because we expect the couple to encounter them, but because an understanding of the problems that *might* be faced can help in both mate selection and the building of a successful marriage. For, "being forewarned is being forearmed," and troubles can often be prevented if we know what lies behind the surface. Each of these "causes" will be considered in turn.

Cultural Causes of In-law Problems

We have just indicated that our culture defines the in-law (more especially the maternal mother-in-law) as a trouble maker. There are, however, other reasons for assigning "cultural loyalty" as a cause of in-law discord. Each family possesses, in effect, a culture of its own, and there is inherent in man a loyalty to his own culture. Where the cultures of two families differ markedly, as in the case of internationality marriages, the couple can quite naturally be pulled in the direction of the culture they will tend to reject, and the in-laws will resent—even though unconsciously—the son-in-law or daughter-in-law who is an "outsider." Slotkin, for example, found that in only 57 percent of one hundred and eighty-three Jewish-Gentile marriages was the outsider either partially or wholeheartedly accepted by both families. The Gentile families (less likely to be strongly oriented to a distinctive cultural pattern) were less rejecting than were the Jewish families.[3]

Religious intermarriage may well have in-law problems for the same reasons, since religion is intrinsically part of the family's total culture. In such cases, there may be little or no understanding of the *meaning* of religion to the individual, but the fact that he or she is a Roman Catholic, a Mormon, or other "different" believer is enough to create misunderstanding and discord. For example,

[3] Cf. J. S. Slotkin, "Adjustment in Jewish-Gentile Intermarriages," *Social Forces*, 21: 226 ff. (1942).

My folks just won't take Barbara into "the family." I know they didn't want me to marry a Catholic, but I did anyway, because the differences aren't important to me. I can't get steamed up over whether my kids are Protestant or Catholic, as long as they are good kids. . . . My parents are old-fashioned, though and were brought up to think Catholics are a different breed of cats. They don't know what Barbara believes different from us, but she's a Catholic—and that's enough. I can't pin them down to why that's so bad—they just say "she's a Catholic, that's why."

One could substitute Republican or Democrat, Italian or Czech or Irish, Methodist or Jehovah's Witness, or practically any other descriptive word in the above quotation and have it fit one or more cases. In no sense is it always directed at the particular characteristic; the thought behind it may be illogical and inane, but it is symptomatic of a generalized distrust of people who are culturally different. Hence the unwillingness or inability to accept the in-law(s) who is/are "different" in this respect.

In-law problems may also arise because there are intergeneration differences in particular aspects of the culture content. Parents are likely to have values and aspirations not entirely in sympathy with those of the younger generation. The older person may be inflexible in his attitudes regarding such things as spending money, entertaining friends, religious practices, and a host of other personal values; the fact that these change rapidly from one generation to another makes intergeneration differences highly probable.[4] The problems that can ensue from such value differences are illustrated in the following abstract.

Bob and I do love my mother very much, but she can be an awful trial. She is dead set against drinking and card playing—most of her people were—and while we don't drink often or much, we do sometimes have cocktail parties as part of Bob's getting business contacts, and because that's one of the things our crowd does. Neither Bob nor I can see anything wrong in what we do. . . . Every time we have such a party or go to one, she arrives the next day with a hurt look on her face and a beaten tone in her voice. You'd

[4] Cf. Robert M. Dinkel, "Parent-Child Conflict in Minnesota Families," *American Sociological Review*, 8: 412 ff. (1943).

think we had personally mistreated her. The whole tone of the conversation will revolve around the theme "How can we possibly do this to her?" . . . We feel so guilty after one of these sessions that we have a terrible time—if she lived with us I don't know what we'd do.

Our concern here is not with the psychological reactions of the parent but with the fact that the cultural patterns of the two generations are sufficiently disparate to provide a fertile field for tension.

Another culturally caused in-law difficulty centers in child-rearing practices—which have changed radically in recent decades. Grandmothers rarely spend much time in keeping up with new theories in this field, if for no other reason than that they have raised one brood (satisfactorily) and this is sometimes conceived as giving them an "expert" status. In all fairness it must be said that their interest is genuine and vital, but this does not make it easier for the couple when she intrudes her ideas on the subject. Such intrusions may even be unconscious, but her well-intentioned efforts can do much to damage the interpersonal relations of the couple. Thus (from the same interview last quoted):

> Another problem we have revolves around how we care for the children. Mother is old-fashioned and believes in the old ways— "spare the rod and spoil the child"—and she is constantly at both of us because we don't keep at the children all of the time. . . . If she lived with us instead of just coming over two or three times a week, I know she'd have us in a constant turmoil.

Role Interpretations and In-law Problems[5]

"Jane is my baby, the last one I've got"; "John is my big boy." These are horribly embarrassing descriptions when applied to twenty-two-year-old Jane or twenty-five-year-old John by a parent, and are symptomatic of a role relationship that once was acceptable—but is hardly valid in a married partner. John, in marrying Jane, has certain expectations of how she will relate to

[5] Roles are structured both by culture and by personality need. Here we are primarily concerned with the latter.

him and he to her. Jane is now his wife, and perhaps a mother, and John now has complementary roles to accept and perform. Their role expectations (and demands) are usually quite different in such cases from those of the parent(s). While one set of expectations is being met, the other is almost surely being either violated or fulfilled incompletely. Herein lies a source of in-law difficulty, for the man or woman who can at one time meet such dual role expectations of parents and mate is rare indeed. The result is very often tension, if not conflict, or even crisis. Thus:

> We have the darnedest time sometimes. Jane's mother and father think of her as their "little girl," and don't seem to understand that what Jane is trying to be is *my wife*. She can't be both at once, and we [married couple and parents] get in each other's hair occasionally. It isn't that they want to keep her a baby at home—it's just that they don't see she has to act different in a home of her own.

Psychological Causes of In-law Problems

We have earlier called attention to the fact that the maturing child has need to be released emotionally by his parents as he enters adolescence. This does not always happen, and the child can go on through the mating stages and into marriage itself with a residuum of the earlier emotional attachment still intact. The reasons for such a continuance are many and varied,[6] and are of two types.

Parental attachment for the son or daughter. In this type, it is the parent who has been unable emotionally to release his "child," and must either live with him—usurping many of the roles in the former relationship which should have been transferred to the marital partner—or at least maintain a maximum of dependence upon him or her. This was illustrated in one case, for example, in these words.

> Joe's mother won't let him alone. She lives only five blocks from us, and she's here every night, calls him at work, and in general takes over. I don't even manage our household affairs. Last Saturday

[6] Cf. Percival Symonds, *The Psychology of Parent-Child Relations*, especially pp. 3-52.

she took him downtown to pick out a suit. She's always planning the meals *he* should have. . . . I'm just a hanger-on. Instead of my making a lot of the decisions a wife usually makes, she's always doing it first. . . . No, Joe doesn't like it, either. He wants us to have our own home, but he doesn't want to hurt her. He's all she has— she says—and so she tries to act as she did before we were married. . . . I think this is the only way she gets any satisfaction in life. . . . She comes over, too, with the littlest questions for him to answer. Does *he* think she should get a new winter coat? Does *he* think she should have her car greased? Does *he* think she should go this place or that with her dear friend, Mrs. Smith? She can't even think for herself. . . . We surely didn't expect—either one of us—that she'd be this way after we were married. She's fooled us both.

The solution in such a situation as this is not readily at hand. Had they been able to foresee such a dependency, Joe's wife would probably not have chosen him as a mate. Unfortunately, however, it is not always possible to predict the direction or the degree to which a parent will either cling to the earlier relationship or depend upon the child after marriage. A change in circumstance can alter the older person's emotional and physical security, and hence lead to such a condition. Chronic illness, for example, can set in motion a whole chain of reactions which create dependency; the loss of one's own husband or wife can cause the individual to transfer his or her dependence to the child—forgetting that the latter has in the meantime set up a whole new affectional and role structure in his own marriage.

Attachment for the parent. The vicious counterpart of the parent's inability to be independent of the husband or wife is the latter's inability to free himself or herself from the parent. Where the husband cannot free himself from "his mother's apron strings," or where the wife must run home to her parents at every sign of tension (even though the parent quite honestly tries to prevent this) in-law problems can arise. The inability to enter marriage ready to assume the interdependency that characterizes successful marriage is tragic, but it does occur. The occurrence of such a situation may well be charged to poor mate selection, since an overdependency would probably have evidenced itself in a variety of ways.

Reuben Hill[7] has suggested a possible reason for in-law interpersonal problems—based upon the affectional relationship—which is of still another dimension.

> It may be that a number of subconscious factors are at work, especially in the relation between the man and his mother-in-law. The man's mother-in-law, perhaps cut short in her own emotional life, lives vicariously in her daughter, and tends, therefore, to fall in love with her daughter's husband. Her inhibitions lead her to resist any such attachment strongly, and accordingly she turns toward him the hostile side of her ambivalent emotions. On the side of the man, there is apt to be a strong transference upon the mother-in-law as a mother substitute, but ingrained inhibitions lead him to react strongly against this attitude. In addition, the mother-in-law arouses some interpersonality conflict because she resembles the wife in many respects but lacks her youthful charm, and this is a further source of hostility.[8]

Whether or not we can accept in its entirety this highly Freudian explanation of the cause of in-law difficulties, it has some merit in pointing up a further area in which these can—and do—occur.

Other contributions to in-law problems. However adequate the relations of husband and wife may be to their in-laws, there are still other causes of interpersonal tension which have sometimes to be faced. The family, for example, which lives in a house no larger than will meet their needs (and which is all they can afford) may suddenly find that they are overcrowded because a parent has to live with them. Forced retirement, a physical ailment which prevents the individual's living alone—these and other exigencies of life can throw together people who are well adjusted but whose physical resources are entirely inadequate to meet the needs of a family *plus* an in-law. Under such circumstances, tension (and even conflict and crisis) can result—if for no other reason than because the normal needs in family living are denied.

---

[7] Cf. Willard Waller (revised by Reuben Hill), *The Family: A Dynamic Interpretation*, Ch. 7.

[8] *Ibid.*, p. 291.

SUMMARY

Despite the "shrinkage" of the family—from being a several-generation group to being a husband-and-wife-plus-children group—in-laws still play an important part in the life of the married couple. It is unfortunate that the contemporary emphasis is so often upon in-laws as "problems," for it provides expectations for many married couples that are unwarranted by the facts. In this chapter we have discussed both positive and negative aspects of the in-law relationships, but hope that the student will view the in-laws in an essentially positive light. The major ways in which in-laws contribute to marital difficulties have been outlined, and the recognition of these as possible in any given marriage is essential to their avoidance as causes of discord. In short, "forewarned is forearmed"—not against in-laws but so that problems can in most instances be avoided.

READINGS AND TOPICS FOR REPORTS

1. Interview a number of middle-aged couples to determine who among in-laws they consider to be the most frequent source of difficulty. How many report no in-law difficulties? To what do they attribute the lack of such difficulties?
2. Interview a number of young married couples to learn of ways in which in-laws have been most helpful in their own adjustments to marriage. In those cases where children have entered the picture, do they see the relationship becoming more or less favorable?
3. What advice, to use the term loosely, would you give to a young bride who wanted to know how best to get along with her husband's family? Would this differ to any extent from equivalent advice given to the young husband about getting along with his wife's family? If so, why?

ADVANCED READINGS

Duvall, Evelyn, In-laws: Pro and Con.
Wallin, Paul, "Sex Differences in Attitudes Toward In-Laws," American Journal of Sociology, 59:466 ff. (1954).

16

Children and Marriage

THE AVERAGE MARRIED couple of a century ago had no reason to be concerned about parenthood. Fertility was not controlled, in most cases, and the child had a positive value through his potential economic contribution to the family. In recent decades, the picture has changed completely; fertility can be controlled, and the child's economic role has become one of consumer rather than producer. Along with the developing concept of marriage as an affection- and need-centered relationship has come the emphasis upon the child as primarily an affectional asset to the married couple. Children are increasingly born not because of biological chance but because of the parent's desire for them.

A BASIC ATTITUDE

The possibility that a child will be born to a couple confronts them with three questions: What will the presence of a child do to our relationship? What will the effect of our relationship be upon the child? Are we a couple who should have a child or children? The first hint that a pregnancy is under way immediately affects the relationship of husband and wife; no longer can their

251

attitudes and behavior be governed solely by their own needs—there is a third individual to be taken into account.

There is much confusion today regarding the whole matter of family limitation and child spacing. While there is evidence that child-spacing measures are widely employed among married couples,[1] the idea is still current that large segments of our population are denied the right to decide whether or not they shall have children, and at what intervals. This is not entirely in accord with the facts of the case. The Roman Catholic Church—often considered to be the most virulent opponent of family limitation—places its stamp of ecclesiastical approval upon one means of contraception (the rhythm method) and allows Latz—a chief proponent of this method—to advance a number of reasons. Contraception by this method, he says, allows such economic burdens as inadequate income and unemployment to be lightened, which in turn makes it possible for parents to provide more adequately for their children and themselves. It also serves to lessen the physical burdens of depleted energy resulting from earlier pregnancies, from serious illness, or from conditions which would threaten the woman should she become pregnant. Finally, says Latz, contraception serves to lessen unfavorable psychological effects that may result from severe demands being made upon the mother.[2]

This is by no means the only point of view expressed by the Roman Catholic Church, but it—together with approval of one method of family limitation—does indicate that even official Catholic opinion sees the need for a reasoned approach to the problem of the place of the child in the family.[3] The quotation

[1] Uniformly, public opinion polls show that a majority of Protestants and substantial numbers of members of other religious groups subscribe to the idea of child spacing or contraception. This does not mean, of course, that all such respondents have effective measures at their command. Cf. Abraham Stone and Norman E. Himes, *Planned Parenthood*, p. 30.

[2] Cf. Leo J. Latz, *The Rhythm of Sterility and Fertility in Women.*

[3] There is much confusion on this point, and Roman Catholic clergy offer varying interpretations of the position of the Church. Cf. Henry Bowman, *Marriage for Moderns*, pp. 263 ff.

well states the basic rationale upon which this chapter may proceed—taking for granted an ethical acceptance of the idea that parenthood should be a dignified and voluntary function rather than the blind acceptance of biological chance.[4]

DECISIONS THAT MUST BE MADE

We can best discuss the decisions that must be made regarding the having of children by posing a series of questions—each to be answered in the framework of our earlier discussion of what marriage and family living involve.

Couples Planning to Have Children

The old idea that *every* couple was obligated "to have children as part payment of their debt to society" appears to have failed of acceptance. As students of human development have explored the factors contributing to personality growth, they have increasingly emphasized the need of the child for a home environment that provides emotional security and affection and is free of conflict.[5] The child absorbs the attitudes, aspirations, joys, anxieties, and tensions he feels in his home, and will tend to breathe out what he breathes in. If he is raised in a happy home, he will tend to be a happy child; if he is raised in a home which lacks happiness and affords little emotional security, he will in turn tend to be unhappy and insecure.[6] Further, as studies of adjustment in marriage show, there is at least an unconscious tendency for the individual to repeat in his own marriage the major characteristics he found in his parental family.[7] This is another way of saying that parents assume at least an indirect

---

[4] This position is essentially that of the major Protestant groups. Cf. The Federal Council of the Churches of Christ in America, *Moral Aspects of Birth Control.*

[5] Cf. James H. S. Bossard, *The Sociology of Child Development*, pp. 73-95.

[6] This is not intended to deny the effect of extrafamilial relations but to emphasize the primary nature of the family's contribution to his personality. See Chapter 4.

[7] Cf. E. W. Burgess and L. S. Cottrell, *Predicting Success or Failure in Marriage*, *passim.*

responsibility for the success or failure of their children's marriages—as well as for other adjustments they must make.

The significant question in this connection is whether or not the couple can provide such an atmosphere of affection and security. If there are serious maladjustments in their relationship, it is not unlikely that these will be reflected in any children they may have.[8] If they are themselves well adjusted, and there are no hereditary or physical obstacles to parenthood, there seems no reason to doubt their suitability as parents. It should be pointed out that the decision to have or not to have children cannot always be arrived at in the first year of marriage. Earlier chapters indicated that adjustment in marriage is the result of a process that will require both time and effort. Some couples adjust well to each other in marriage, but have personalities and values that are not compatible with the demands of child rearing. It is customary to describe many childless couples as "selfish and thinking only of themselves"; these may, in fact, be more concerned with the long-range effects of their having children than are other couples who present to society a full complement of offspring. An example of this insight and concern was given by a high school teacher in these words.

> Before we married we faced very frankly this whole question of whether or not we should have children. Don and I love each other very much, and it is a great deal more than just physical attraction. We think alike, have hobbies that fit together nicely, and enjoy each other in every way. . . . We are both quick-tempered, and are likely to be very irritable at times. Our courtship was very much of a "tempest in a teapot" sometimes, but we always made up, and always will. . . . Don just doesn't like children—I'm sure there are a lot of reasons in his own childhood that make this the case—and is very uncomfortable when he is with them. I like children of high school age, but I don't care very much for small children, and the idea of handling a baby—even my own—doesn't make me very happy. . . . Each of us is a college graduate with a master's degree, and we are both very much interested in our work. We saw no

8 Cf. Bossard, *op. cit.*, pp. 338 ff.

reason to sacrifice that interest, or to sacrifice whatever we can give in the way of service through our jobs. We also saw, from our knowing each other very well, that we might make a home for a child that wouldn't give him what every child brought into the world has a right to have. . . . All in all, when we weighed every side of the question, we decided not to have children, and have kept to that decision. Our parents don't understand this, and think we are cold and selfish. Actually, I think we have done what is best for all concerned.

It is impossible to say, with the evidence at hand, that these two people would have been good or bad parents, but the fact that they considered the factors, rather than arbitrarily having children simply because they were married and biologically capable, is to their credit. Were more people to weigh carefully their potentialities as parents, and to abide by their honest feelings, fewer children would probably be born, but more of those born would be born into adequate homes.

Such a statement will undoubtedly raise a further question in the minds of many students. Is this an argument against the having of children? The answer is yes, but a very qualified one, and that confined to those people who can achieve only a limited satisfaction in life for themselves, and who can provide little or none for the children they may bear. The value of a child lies not in his economic contribution to his parents, but in the enriched living that his presence in the family brings to his parents *and that they in turn contribute to him.*

Couples Ready to Have Children

The decision to have children is not a simple one. We have already indicated that the couple needs a period of time in which to make the necessary postwedding adjustments. Those who must face all the adjustments required by pregnancy at the same time that they face the adjustments required by their first years of living together are unduly handicapped in attempting either. Other factors must be given equal consideration, however, since they tend to be interrelated.

The bearing and rearing of children are expensive, no matter how carefully the couple may plan their expenditures. While the old saying that "it isn't the initial cost but the upkeep that counts" applies here, the initial cost is high and must still be taken into account.[9] The couple who are in the process of adjusting their needs to the husband's income, and who must add the initial and continuing cost of a child to their budget are faced with handicaps they may never be able to overcome. If the wife has worked in an effort to help balance the budget, or to set up an adequate home, the problem is especially great—since pregnancy requires her to stop work some weeks or months before confinement, and to remain away from work for some time after. Even then, if she goes back to work, it is only in the exceptional case that she earns enough to offset the total cost resulting from her absence from the home. (What the emotional costs to the child of having foster care may be is another matter.) Whether or not the family will have a child in circumstances such as these is a question demanding careful study.

It is in situations such as this that the complexities of adjustment (see Chapter 11) are to be found. The financial burden may create situations in other areas of the relationship which are in turn tension-provoking. For example, well-established and highly valued patterns of recreation may have to be foregone because of necessary shifts in the budget. These may not have been taken sufficiently into account in the planning of the first conception, and may show themselves only after the child has arrived. A couple is ready, then, to have a child *only when both really want it and have faced all the ramifications in their relationships* which will result from its coming. For all but the most affluent, child rearing involves sacrifices—of time, freedom, money, and aspirations. It is worth while, certainly, but it demands the giving up of many things. Unless *both* husband and wife are ready to make

---

[9] In a carefully controlled study made in 1948-1950, Helen Bouche found that sixty-nine families with $3,000-$4,000 income spent an average of $371.92 for a first child to his first birthday.

these sacrifices, and *want* to make them, numerous difficulties are sure to present themselves. Where, for example, the wife is very anxious to have a child and the husband agrees only because he thinks it will make his wife happy, there is no way of predicting accurately the reception the child will receive from its father. Its presence may stimulate affection permanently, which is all to the good; it may stimulate affection which is temporary and later changes to resentment—to the detriment of the father-child relationship; it may arouse resentment immediately. Both of the latter situations can only mean insecurity for the child and strained husband-wife relations for the parents.

Despite this seemingly negative approach to the problem of when to have a child, it must also be emphasized that a couple can wait too long before having the first child. Childbearing under proper medical supervision today involves negligible risks, but delaying the arrival of a first child until the mother is in her late thirties is no advantage to her—or to the child. While the problem of a first pregnancy in later life is obviously a physical one for the mother, it also has psychological aspects which involve both parents and child. Parents who are in their early twenties when the first child is born will be less than forty years old when that child enters adolescence; those who are over thirty-five will be nearing the age of fifty as their offspring approaches adolescence.

The problems inherent in the latter situation are self-evident. At the advanced age of fifty, adaptation to new ways is not always easy, and roles are well fixed. Intergeneration differences in values and behavior patterns are likely to be found, and parents may have difficulty in being at all sympathetic with the "antics" that are normal adolescent behavior. This is not to suggest that older parents do not make "good" parents, for many are in their fifties when the last of their children are in the adolescent stages, and succeed very well. Having only one child, and that in the latter years of the reproductive period, is a quite different matter.[10]

---

[10] The student may well raise questions about the personality needs and characteristics of those who wait this long to marry or to have a child.

It should be remarked, too, that there is no wisdom in deciding to have a child in order to hold a marriage together. The wife, or husband, or both, who believe that waning affections can thus be restored, or that a child can be "the moral equivalent" of other needs the marriage has been unable to fulfill, is expecting more from a child's presence in the family than seems wise.[11] It is true that children do cement husband-wife relationships, and do enrich the lives of both, but only when the child is genuinely wanted.

How Many Children?

Unfortunately, no couple can predict absolutely what their income will be throughout their married life. Nor can they say specifically at the beginning what aspirations they will have, or what demands will be made upon them for their children. All these factors determine, in some measure, how many children a couple shall have. Children must be fed, clothed, housed, and educated—at what seems to be an ever-increasing cost—and the decision to have two, three, or more must be made not so much in terms of the small-child costs as of those in later years. The boy of two can be fed and dressed rather inexpensively; the boy of fourteen, with a prodigious appetite and the need for man-sized clothes, presents a different problem. This is not to be construed to discourage a couple from having children—quite the contrary. It offers, however, a reason for looking at the *total* situation, viewing the family's prospects objectively, and being somewhat rational about the whole matter.

Most couples can predict within reasonable limits what their earnings will be over a lifetime.[12] The high school teacher, for example, knows that the "ceiling" for his annual earnings will probably be in the neighborhood of five thousand dollars; the average minister, the same or somewhat less. (Everyone hopes not to be "average," but a realistic approach to life makes such

[11] Couples who resort to childbearing as a source of stability in marriage may well be challenged as to their insight into their own personality needs.

[12] Even though earnings may rise, costs have the unfortunate tendency to keep pace.

estimates practical.) It is not difficult then to project the cost of rearing a child into the future, and to relate it to the goals the couple have for him. If these goals include a college education for each child, they can be met only by having an income or savings commensurate with the needs during the years he will be in college.[13] Realism demands that these factors be taken into account. An example of what can happen is seen in the following quotations from an interview with a mother who "looked too late."

> We love kids, both of us, and always wanted a big family. Both Bill and I come from big families, so I guess that is a natural way for us to feel. . . . The six we have are close together and wonderful, and we thought we'd have others right away, while we're both young enough to be with them. . . . We've just begun to wake up, though, and it's quite a shock. Bill gets $3,400 a year, and I don't think he'll ever get much more. If he had a college education, he might go on up, but now that's out. . . . We figured up the other night, and we'll have twenty-four years of college to give our six youngsters in just eleven years. We're "insurance poor" now, trying to carry an endowment policy on each of the children for a thousand dollars, and that won't be a drop in the bucket toward what a college education will cost for each. Just as soon as they are old enough I am going to have to go to work, and save every cent of what I earn, for their college money. Even then, I don't see how we can make it. . . . I'm not sorry that we've had them, but we should have looked ahead a little, and had less in so short a time, and been able to give them what they need.

The spacing of pregnancies is always a part of the picture in determining how many children the couple shall have. The untoward physical effects of too-frequent conceptions are emphasized by many physicians. For example, in a survey of medical opinion on this subject, Dr. Alan F. Guttmacher found that among 3,782 physicians the average time believed to be minimal between one childbirth *and the beginning of the next pregnancy* was fourteen months.[14] If for no other reason than that the

[13] It should be remembered that the *minimum* cost of a college education for one year is usually estimated by college authorities to be in the neighborhood of $1,200.
[14] Cf. Stone and Himes, *op. cit.*, p. 26.

mother's health is important for the welfare of the family, adequate child spacing is therefore indicated.

The psychological effects of having children at less than the advised interval are of equal importance. The mother who has no time or energy to cuddle and love and care for the small child— because another has already arrived or is on the way—is very often paving the way for that child's unhappiness and emotional maladjustment.[15] If parents want children, they surely must also want their needs to be fulfilled as well as is possible; to fail to space children's births is to neglect to see the child's needs in true perspective.

One rule should be underlined here for the young married couple: *have as many children as you can care for and love adequately*. The values of the sizable family—for both parents and children—tend to be obscured in our society by financial and social pressures. The emotional problems associated with being an only child have often been identified, but the values of growing up among siblings have had less emphasis.[16] It must be emphasized in this connection that the couple who wait until they are entirely ready—in a financial sense—for childbearing, rarely have children. Few are the couples who have or ever will have all the money they need; such a condition might even be boring. Marriage always involves taking some financial risks; what we have suggested is that risk-taking be tempered with reality.

What If the Couple Cannot Have Children?

The best estimates by specialists in this area indicate that approximately one couple in every ten is involuntarily childless.[17] There are also women who have a pregnancy and then find further pregnancies impossible. For both these groups, the adoption of one or more children can be the answer to the unfulfilled desire for children.

---

[15] Cf. for example, David M. Levy, *Maternal Overprotection*.
[16] See Chapter 4.
[17] See Chapter 12.

People may desire to adopt a child for quite invalid reasons, however. The Cadys suggest that the following are among such reasons:

> (1) Do you want a child to vicariously fulfill some unattained ambition of your own—to paint or to write, to win fame as a musician, or just to enjoy the advantages of higher education?
>
> (2) Do you want more than anything else a son to carry on your business or a child to "perpetuate your name" and inherit your worldly possessions?
>
> (3) Are you a childless wife, nearing the menopause, never before much interested in offspring but now suddenly spurred by the panicky feeling that a lonely middle age stretches before you, who wants to adopt— and to do it as quickly as possible?
>
> (4) Perhaps your marriage seems to be foundering and, grasping at straws, you are impelled to act on the erroneous but, unfortunately, not uncommon notion that a child will "hold it together."[18]

Because of just such motivations—and there are probably others—adoption is no longer a simple matter. As children's needs have been more specifically formulated and as the family's effect upon the child has been more generally recognized, the taking of a child into a foster home for adoption has been overlaid with a number of safeguards. These are intended to protect the child against being placed in a family environment that will not meet his physical and emotional needs; they are also intended to protect the couple from incurring the responsibility for a child who is unsuited to adoption. Not only have children been emotionally starved and physically exploited through adoption into unsuitable homes, but well-meaning couples have adopted young children, only later to find them feeble-minded or otherwise incapable of benefiting from the love and care they were prepared to give.

[18] Used by permission from Ernest and Frances Cady, *How to Adopt a Child*, pp. 8 ff.

Concurrent with the development of adequate adoption safe-guards has come an organized effort to keep children in their own homes, whenever possible, or to resort to temporary foster care in the hope that their own homes can be rehabilitated for their eventual return. Governmental and private social agencies now administer a variety of programs designed to strengthen the family and aid parent(s) to keep children at home; as a result, the orphanage is little used today, and children available for adoption are proportionately fewer. Thus, not more than a fraction of the couples who hope to adopt children are able to do so. This does not mean that they should not apply, but that they should not be too optimistic in their expectations.

Where every effort is made to safeguard the interests of the child and the couple (and an adoption should not be sought where such efforts are not made), the latter may well expect a searching examination of their potentialities as parents. Their reasons—both overt and covert—for wishing to bring a child into their home will be explored thoroughly, as will their emotional states, their degree of integration as a couple, their integrity, and their sense of responsibility. They will, as one couple expressed it, "be almost turned inside out," and they must accept such violation of their privacy since it is for their own as well as the child's good. If they cannot stand such a searching examination, that in itself is evidence that they are hardly suited to the role of adoptive parents. They can expect, in return, that the agency will make every effort to guarantee the mental and physical status of the child and that both will be safeguarded by the fact that an adoption does not ordinarily become final until after a period of adjustment and trial.[19]

Having received a child for adoption, what can the parents expect? The answer depends in the largest measure upon them, just as in the case of the so-called "natural" child. While there are cases in which an adopted child does not adjust (and these always

---

[19] This is not to be resented since it is intended as protection for both parents and child.

receive the greatest publicity), it is safe to say that in general the adopted child is little different from a couple's own child—provided that the emotional atmosphere of the home is equivalent. If the adopted child is loved, given security and recognition, and in every way drawn into the couple's life, the result should be entirely satisfactory.

WHAT PARENTHOOD DEMANDS

A couple may genuinely want a child, may plan for and attempt to give him every possible advantage, and still not be the best of parents. In the remainder of this chapter an effort will be made to outline briefly what parenthood in the present-day family requires. First, however, we need to understand what parenthood is.

In recent decades the conceptions of parenthood held by many people have undergone a radical change; no longer are the traditional ideas universally accepted.[20] The traditional conceptions were somewhat as follows:[21]

> (1) The family centers upon a strong father to whom the child is submissive and obedient.
> (2) The father knows what the child should become and prescribes the activities that will lead the child in that direction, and are therefore best for him.
> (3) The parents find satisfaction in the child's indebtedness to them—an indebtedness best repaid by obedience and bringing honor to the family.
> (4) The mother is a self-sacrificing martyr to the needs of her family, who "works her fingers to the bone for her children," and who acts as a surrogate for the father—but never shares his authority.

[20] Cf. for example, Margaret A. Ribble, *The Rights of Infants: Early Psychological Needs and Their Satisfaction.*
[21] The following discussion has drawn liberally upon Reuben Hill's discussion of the changing conceptions of parenthood. Cf. Willard Waller (revised by Hill), *The Family: A Dynamic Interpretation.*

(5) The child is "good"—which means obedient, cleanly, orderly, and quick to master and adhere to the patterns of his elders.

Recent developments have tended to outmode these concepts of parent-child relationship. For one thing, parents have been confronted with situations in a changing social milieu which pose problems for which there are no ready solutions; for another, the behavior sciences have broadened our understanding of the individual's needs for personality development and emotional health.[22] The new recognition—that the child must have affection, security, and a mutually-recognized place in the family interaction, has made the traditional concepts of parenthood untenable. In their place has come the concept of "developmental parenthood," which means that the family is child-centered in its aims, and that the major efforts of parenthood are directed toward fostering the child's own personality development.[23]

It must be recognized that this new concept of parenthood is not as yet universally accepted in our society. There are sharp differences in the degree of acceptance between, as well as within, social classes.[24] It is this uneven acceptance that is our concern here. Since our concepts of parenthood stem in good measure from our own family experience, many couples approaching parenthood bring with them either the traditional concepts, which are no longer tenable, or find themselves confused and frustrated in their attempts to reconcile the old with the new. The challenge, then, is for the parents of the future to avail themselves of the newer knowledge of what child rearing demands.

Understanding Child Development

The old joke about the father standing at the delivery room door with an electric train, boxing gloves, and a catcher's mitt

[22] Cf. Alfred L. Baldwin, "Socialization and the Parent-Child Relationships," *Child Development* (1949).

[23] See Chapter 4.

[24] Cf. Evelyn M. Duvall, "Conceptions of Parenthood," *American Journal of Sociology*, 51: 193 ff. (1946).

carries by implication more truth than fancy. Parents sometimes have little idea of what to expect as the child grows and only vague impressions of what has occurred as the child has passed from one age to another. Adequate parenthood requires at least a general understanding of what the developmental stages are and mean, and of how they affect the parent-child relationship. We need not belabor this matter of child development for we have already outlined it in some detail in Chapter 4.[25] Adequate parenthood demands not only the understanding of the how and why of child development, but also it imposes certain fundamentals of behavior, which must be understood from the beginning. *One is that both husband and wife share equally—and constantly—in the job of being parents.* To assume that the baby "belongs to the mother, but that when he becomes an athletically inclined adolescent he is father's responsibility," is to do a grave disservice to that child. Certain responsibilities fall naturally to one or the other parent as the child grows, but this does not mean that each assumes his role only at those times, or that responsibility is always divided. The child's need for security can be satisfied only when both parents act concurrently; to offer him love and affection and care in a serial fashion serves only to deprive him of what he needs from both parents.

Another fundamental of parent behavior is that *they be consistent in their relationships with the child* and present a united front at all times. If he is to grow effectively, the child cannot be given freedom today and be "sat upon" tomorrow. Similarly, he cannot be disciplined by one parent, and have his own way with the other. Nor can one parent give orders only to have them countermanded by the other; to do so is to weaken the contribution each makes to the child and places in his hands a weapon with which he can avoid responsibility to both parents.

A third fundamental in parent behavior requires that parents *continue to live for each other.* The woman who "dispossesses" her

[25] The understanding of child development has a twofold function: one, to appreciate our own personality development in the family of orientation, and two, to appreciate our contribution as parents in the family of procreation.

husband from his place in her emotional life and focuses it upon her child may become a mother but ceases to be a wife, but this does occur where the many roles of the wife-mother are not clearly understood. Taylor has stated the need for continued focus of husband and wife upon each other in these words.

> It may help both young parents to realize that the mother's capacity to give the young child the quality of care and affection he needs depends primarily upon the quality of understanding and support she receives from her husband. If he feels rejected, he will find it difficult not to respond with hostility instead of affection; and if she feels isolated by his hostility, she cannot give the baby a sense of being supported on a vast sea of love essential to his wholesome growth. The emotional tone of the husband-wife relationship is the climate in which the child thrives or starves. Therefore husband and wife should continue to cherish and cultivate their own love relationship, both as the best source of fulfilling their primary need for love, and equally important as the essential strand determining the quality of all other family ties.[26]

PARENTHOOD AND MARITAL ADJUSTMENT

Is the couple with children likely to be better adjusted in their marriage than the childless couple? For an answer, which cannot be conclusive, we must turn to the findings of studies of marital adjustment. Terman found no evidence that the presence or absence of children was significantly associated with the marital adjustment of the couple;[27] Bernard found no correlation between the couple's being childless and their success in marriage;[28] Landis reported that the chance for happiness in marriage decreased as the number of children increased.[29] Burgess and Cottrell reported that couples who desired children—whether or not they had

[26] Katherine Whiteside Taylor, "The Opportunities of Parenthood," in Howard Becker and Reuben Hill, *Family, Marriage and Parenthood*, p. 461.

[27] Cf. L. M. Terman, *et al.*, *Psychological Factors in Marital Happiness*, *passim*.

[28] Cf. Jessie Bernard, "Factors in the Distribution of Success in Marriage," *American Journal of Sociology*, 40: 51 (1934).

[29] Cf. Judson T. Landis, "Length of Time Required to Achieve Adjustment in Marriage," *American Sociological Review*, XI: 672 f. (1946).

them—were happier in marriage than were those who did not desire children.[30] Locke, in contrasting happily married and divorced couples, found that the desire for children was much stronger among those who were childless and happily married than among the childless divorced.[31]

What these studies appear to high-light is not the fact that children create happiness in marriage, *but that people who do not desire children are not always good marital risks.*[32] This is not difficult to understand, since the mature personality has both the need and the desire to protect and to love; the very helplessness and need for love that characterize the child make his presence in the family a natural goal for the married couple. The mature personality needs, also, to continue to grow, to meet new situations, and to gain recognition. Opportunities for all these are offered by marriage but are offered tenfold in the family group. Finally, in Hill's words.

> Children provide parents with the opportunity, in a sense, to live their lives over again—something which most persons, including those who will not admit it, would like to do. Here in the relationship with children is the nearest approach to such an opportunity. Carried to the point where the parents impose on the children activities and pursuits not of the latter's own choice, the experience may be unhealthy for both generations, but conceived as a means of fostering the growth and development of the young, it can be a major satisfaction of parenthood.[33]

In the light of findings such as these, and especially in the light of Hill's statement, we must say that marriage does not require children in order that it be a success. They may, as we have seen earlier, inhibit success. However, it is the conviction of most people that—taking into account all of the factors discussed to this point—the married couple who are possessed of mature personalities, complementary goals, and sufficient resources to

---

[30] Cf. Burgess and Cottrell, *op. cit.*, pp. 258 ff.

[31] Cf. Harvey J. Locke, *Predicting Adjustment in Marriage*, pp. 158 ff.

[32] Cf. Willard Waller (revised by Hill), *The Family: A Dynamic Interpretation,* Chs. 18-20.

[33] *Ibid.*, p. 379.

provide adequately for children, find their lives enriched immeasurably through parenthood.

SUMMARY

In this chapter we have noted the increasingly voluntary nature of childbearing, and have indicated the psychological, economic, and other factors which directly affect the decisions regarding having children. We have discussed, too, the alternatives which couples unable to have children of their own must face, and have outlined briefly what modern parenthood demands.

In all this discussion, the emphasis has been upon the place of the child in the total values system of the couple, and upon the need to recognize that parenthood makes a variety of demands upon the couple which they must assess fully before having children. Having children is a very fruitful expression of and satisfaction of personality need, but the couple are challenged to view themselves and their potentialities realistically in this as well as in other areas of married life.

READINGS AND TOPICS FOR REPORTS

1. Imagine yourself to be a social worker. What would you say to a young couple who wanted to adopt a child in order to preserve a marriage which the husband considered to be unsatisfactory?
2. Interview a group of young married parents. What do they suggest as the major problems they face as parents? Then interview a comparable group of parents whose children are in the early years of adolescence. Do they see their responsibilities and problems as being markedly different from those of the first group?
3. What criteria would you suggest to a young couple who wished to determine whether or not they were suitable for parenthood? Would these differ from the criteria you would suggest regarding being ready for parenthood?
4. Interview a Roman Catholic priest and a "liberal" Protestant clergyman. How do they differ in their attitudes toward having

children? What is the basic difference offered by the two regarding the place of the child in the family?

ADVANCED READINGS

Applegate, M., *Everybody's Business: Our Children.*
Driekurs, R., *The Challenge of Parenthood.*
Ribble, M., *The Rights of Infants.*
Witmer, Helen, and R. Kotinsky, *Personality in the Making.*

17

Marriage and Extrafamily Relationships

N o MARRIAGE EXISTS only within itself—except that of the couple cast up on an otherwise deserted island. Every husband and wife have contacts outside the home—in business, in friendships, in the community. These are quite apart from any family and in-law contacts, and they are important in determining how the couple will meet their needs and gain their satisfactions in the marriage.

The increase in these extrafamily relationships is in part due to changes in the manner of getting the family living, in part to technological changes, and in part to the multiplication of functions—and hence of organizations to meet those functions—in our society. The members of the family once worked together in the common production of the livelihood—father, mother, and children all contributing. In the rural family, the jobs were interrelated and integrated; every member of the family had his or her part to play, and the tasks consumed the major portion of the time of all members old enough to work. In the urban family, the father worked in the factory or office, the mother in the home (and homemaking was a full-time occupation!) and the children had a multiplicity of chores in helping to keep the home going. With increased industrialization and the changing technology, the work week has been shortened—from sixty to fifty-four, then to forty-eight, and now—in many cases—to forty hours. In consequence, the breadwinner has time for things unknown in earlier generations. Homemaking, too, has changed—the decrease in the labor required for homemaking has given the wife-mother more hours to devote to nonhomemaking pursuits.[1] The children's chores are less numerous and time consuming, in most cases.[2]

In contrast, there are more demands—at least in the middle class—upon the individual's time from outside the home. Luncheon clubs, civic groups, organized drives for money for this and that, church social groups—all these make demands upon the middle-class husband. Parent-Teacher activities, clubs for civic improvement and civic righteousness—these and a hundred others demand time of his wife. Boy Scouts, Girl Scouts, 4-H, and Future Homemaker groups—to name only a few—all seek the attention and time of the younger generation.

The importance here is not in how easy life has become, but in the increased number of contacts the family members have outside the family.

FRIENDSHIP AND RECREATION

Friendships[3] ordinarily are of several kinds: Some are husband-centered, some wife-centered, still others arrived at through mutual contacts. In the relatively simple life of the early family, the first two of these were exceptional, for the family worked and

---

[1] For numbers of women, of course, these "extra" hours are now devoted to earning money outside the home. Cf. Ethel Goldwater, "Woman Place," *Commentary*, December, 1947, pp. 578 ff.

[2] They are, in fact, almost nonexistent in many urban families. It is not unusual for such parents to resort to "made work" in order to have the children participate in home activities.

[3] As used here the term denotes extrafamily relationships not involving relatives.

played together, and tended to relate to other families as units. Today, however, with the husband, wife, and children moving in quite distinct orbits for a good part of their day, these have come to be important. Men find satisfying contacts in their work, as do women in their activities outside the home. These may carry over into the joint social life of the couple, but they may also be a source of tension and even conflict. Thus:

> John and I get along with no problems except about our friends. We have some we've learned to know together, but I belong to a [postcollege] sorority and am very fond of the girls. . . . But when I try to bring them into our home, John just acts impossible! He says they are a bunch of gossipy old biddies, and that their husbands are worse! I never can be happy when I try to entertain them in our home. . . . He has some cronies at work—they play bridge every noon together. I've tried inviting them and their wives for an evening, but somehow it doesn't work out. I'm afraid I feel about them the way John does about my friends.

A situation such as this demands an adjustment if one member of the marriage is not to be disappointed in the other. Adjustment is largely a matter of learning to understand each other's needs and of being willing to make whatever moves are needed in meeting those needs. In this case, each was "let down" by the other, after having built high hopes that their personal friends could become "family friends." When this couple took the time to analyze the reasons for their rejection of each other's friends, they found that the differences lay in what each enjoyed in his own friends and rejected in his partner's. The values each brought to marriage included many very minute items, and each built his or her friendships in terms of meeting the needs associated with those items.

Exactly the same point may be made regarding recreation. What one values in relation to his use of spare time may differ sharply from that valued by the mate. (It is in this connection that dating has a high value, since it is recreation-centered and gives the prospective mates a chance to learn whether or not they hold the same values without requiring commitments.)

Having friends (which is one type of recreation) and other forms of recreation are of increasing importance—not only because of the need to "blot up" free time, but because our tension-creating culture makes it mandatory that we get release from the "confinings of our middle-class life." To recreate means to gain a sense of ease and relaxation that is the opposite of the tension demanded by an industrial society such as ours.[4] This is not the place to discuss what the couple shall engage in for their recreation, for that can be determined only by the couple themselves—in terms of their physical abilities, their values, and the extent of their needs.[5] *How* they engage in whatever it is they do is of considerable importance, and *what they hope to gain* from recreation is of equal importance. Playing golf may be hard work for the wife but provide a great release from tension for the husband. Playing bridge may be an intellectual challenge (of a sort) to the wife and a deadly bore to her mate. Does this mean, then, that the wife "suffers" through a game of golf and, as a *quid pro quo,*

then   en "endures" a game of bridge? Neither would
h this   an exchange, for it would not be recreation. We
t each   ne question about whether John or Eileen (in the
         earlier) should "endure" each other's friends.
         observation that marriage is not an all-consuming
         at—as was suggested earlier—each member of the
         vn personality, needs, and values, to hold at the
from   he enters into the "otherness" of love. Not to
tance   own identity in marriage is to become a slave to
m its   lation—and this is in no sense defensible.
dence   nd recreation, then, appear to be of two orders:
and   aged in as a person, and second, engaged in as a
been   ormer, the individual gives expression to his indi-
tions   e latter, to the "togetherness" that is love. However
have   ted and implemented is not our concern; John and
         e themselves one night a week free from the other—

means
jawing   on, *Recreation and the Total Personality.*
her."   Locke, *Predicting Adjustment in Marriage,* pp. 373 ff.

John in a poker party, Eileen in a "hen party." Or they may find some practical division of their time which allows "to each his own" but also provides the time for mutual recreations.

Certainly the couple who marry have values in common or else there has been extremely poor mate selection. These commonly-held values, where they relate to friends and leisure-time activities, have real functions for the interpersonal workings of the marriage. First, they provide a means of identifying with each other, which is a part of successful marriage. "*We* saw the Grand Canyon" means more than just two people having been in one place at one time; where the values and needs of the couple have been satisfied by such an activity, the whole emotional interaction of that couple is strengthened, and a new interdependence is added to those already present.[6] Such an addition to the interdependence of the couple ramifies through the whole of their existence, for if they have found a "togetherness" in recreation, it is easier to find a similar togetherness in meeting the daily tasks that make u[p] married life. The mutual use of friendship and leisure tim[e] can contribute to the "wholeness" of the marriage. It is wi[th this] in mind that the couple planning to marry need to search ou[t each] other's values and needs, and to plan accordingly.

COMMUNITY RELATIONSHIPS

Community relationships cannot readily be separated [from] social relationships in general, but they are of sufficient impo[rtance] to warrant mention here. No couple lives in isolation fr[om the] community. Not only is there increased economic interdepen[dence] but increasing social interdependence as well. The churc[h and] school—sole group activities in the rural past—have now [been] supplemented and/or supplanted by a vast array of organiz[ations] with specialized functions. While governmental agencies

[6] Recreation may have an opposite but equally beneficial effect, that is, as a [means] of relieving tensions. In one husband's words, "When I can't stand my wife's [——] any longer, I go out and saw wood like ——. It helps me to get along wit[h ——]"

assumed much of the responsibility for welfare, the frontiers of social action are in many instances pushed back by private agencies—either local or national in extent. Some of these are concerned with research and the financing of educational programs; others are frankly pressure groups; all make their impact upon the conscientious family, both in terms of money and of effort expended.

The governmental (public) agencies utilize tax funds and paid workers. Our concern here is with the private agencies which are usually guided by paid workers but manned in good part by volunteers (for example, the American Red Cross). Each year the demands of such agencies grow—and the agencies themselves proliferate at an astonishing rate—and the average family (especially in the middle class) becomes more involved in such activities. As a result, there is need for a realistic budgeting of both money and time by the family—especially while it is in the child-rearing years. Also, there is a possible source of interpersonal tension, and even conflict, here. One reason for this is the difference in sensitivity of husband and wife to community needs. This can affect the family in different ways. The husband is subjected, in the office or factory, to propaganda and pressures which are quite different from those to which his wife is exposed. "Payroll deductions" are increasingly in order in our society—the company deducts the pledged amount from the pay check in one or more "painless" installments, and there are often very real group pressures exerted upon the wage earner by his peers or superiors.[7] Giving, in such circumstances, can become unrealistic in terms of the family's total budget. Thus:

> Every drive is conducted right in our plant. The union is going to have to make them cut it out. They hand out cards and then each department tries to do better than the next one. . . . They make you ashamed to give a buck, so you give twice that or five times that. It's got so that Red Cross, Red Feather, the music drive—everything you're pressured to give to. . . . It's O.K., I want to do my part,

[7] This is a common criticism leveled at many of today's "Red Feather" campaigns.

but it throws the take-home out of order. . . . We have a budget, but these drives ruin it.

It is smart fund raising, of course, to use tactics such as these, and from the standpoint of the community agency it is effective. The couple (especially those in the early years of married life) needs to set a realistic limit upon what their income will allow them to give to such activities, and then to resist the pressures for larger gifts.[8] In some cases the pressures are more upon the wife than the husband. The wife makes contributions, either under equivalent pressures or because of a sympathetic understanding of the need, only to have her husband take exception. This whole matter of charitable giving is one which needs clearly to be understood and agreed upon.

This is not to suggest that the couple, however young, should not feel a responsibility for supporting worthwhile community projects. Quite the opposite! Our culture is based upon Judeo-Christian values which emphasize the larger responsibility of the individual, and it is not simply a need for conventionality or conformity that should cause us to give. The larger social responsibility is, rather, an extension of the responsibility we feel within the family, and should be seen as such. It is important, however, that we place all our responsibilities in proper relation to each other, and this the young couple may not do without conscious effort. Thus, in the words of a bride:

> The first time anybody solicited us was for the —— —— drive. We'd never talked about it, and Bill wasn't there, so I gave them five dollars. When Bill came home, he hit the ceiling. "Five dollars, one ninth of our weekly check"—we really had quite a "discussion." . . . I'll never do it again, though. Now we plan how much we can give in the whole year, and I parcel it out.

Time, too, must be budgeted, if the young family is to be free of tensions in this matter of community relationships. It is natural for community organizations, the P.T.A., the Red Cross, and so

---

[8] One advantage of the "Red Feather" or community chest campaigns is that it reduces the number (if not the size) of demands upon the family's budget.

on, to call upon those who serve well; therefore, service begets calls for more service. For the older family, where the wife has fewer responsibilities within the home, these calls for service need cause less concern. For the young wife, however, they can serve to create tension—and even conflict. (Such calls for service are most often directed to the wife, for this is "women's business" in many cases.) In one community study, more than 70 percent of the middle-class husbands expressed some feeling about their wives being "too active" in local community affairs.[9] In contrast only about 20 percent of the wives indicated such an attitude in regard to their husbands. The explanation appeared to lie in the fact that husbands' participation was so unusual that a rather special status was achieved by the family where it occurred (as in the case of the man who serves as president of the local P.T.A.); the wife's participation caused more resentment because it took her away from the home "for a large part of what little time [the husband] has to spend at home." A characteristic reaction follows.

> Here in [Regionville] we're organized to the hilt. My wife's a good worker and a good leader, but you can overdo it. . . . We don't see her more than about three nights a week. It's P.T.A., or some women's church meeting, or a drive for polio, or something else. . . . All I am at night is a baby sitter, not a husband. . . . I know these things have got to be done, but it doesn't help us any. Next year she's going to be a wife—not a community boss.

This is, certainly, an extreme situation, but it does illustrate our point—that the married couple's responsibility to its community must be balanced against that couple's responsibility to itself. Just as money must be budgeted, so must time be budgeted. Where values and personal needs are involved, there is again the need to recognize them, and to bring them into accord with the realities of the life the couple must live. In either case, however, the couple entering marriage need to see that this is an area in which adjustments may be called for, and that sympathetic understanding is demanded on the part of both husband and wife.

9 Cf. the writer's *The Health of Regionville.*

SUMMARY

Despite contemporary emphasis upon the highly individual nature of marriage, few marriages today can exist without outside contacts. Some of these are in the realm of personal friendships, while others are related to the organizations and other functioning groups in the larger community. Each of these necessary contacts, whether involving both husband and wife or not, requires time and often money. Each involves, too, a distribution of loyalties; each has its own part in structuring the whole dynamic relation of husband and wife.

The concern in this chapter is that the couple recognize the impact of these extrafamily relationships upon their own inter-personal relations, and that they be prepared to make such adjustments in terms of their own particular circumstances. Such adjustments are necessarily made in terms of personality needs, the values shared by the couple, and their over-all goals in life.

READINGS AND TOPICS FOR REPORTS

1. Make a study of the friendships of a number of young married couples. Have they tended to accept the earlier friendships of the husband, the wife, of both, or to have rejected all these after marriage? Have their friendships shifted from one group to another as they have moved from the adjustment stage into the childbearing and child-rearing stages of married life? How do they account for the changes you find?
2. Study the memberships in formal organizations held by a number of married couples. Were these established for special reasons (for example, for occupational or economic advantage)? Are these memberships considered to be necessary to the intrafamily relations of the couples? Are they considered to be detrimental to such relationships?

18

Marriage in a War-minded World

As this is written there is no evidence that our society will be free from the threat of war in the foreseeable future. The Selective Service Act remains in force, and young men have every expectation of spending some time in the armed forces. There have, therefore, been significant changes in the aspirations and expectations of both young men and young women, and these are directly related to marriage.

SOME SOCIAL EFFECTS OF MILITARY SERVICE

The fact that the average young man can expect to spend from six months to three years in the service of his country—even though it is not actually at war—is closely related to his attitudes and expectations regarding marriage. There is, inevitably, a concomitant affecting of the young woman's attitudes and expectations. In the middle class, the old pattern of selecting a

mate while in college or shortly thereafter, marrying after certain
material goals have been achieved, and "settling down" to married
life, has in some measure been abandoned. This is, in part at least,
the result of our society's having experienced a long-time war
within the memory of this generation.

War and the Present Attitudes Toward Marriage

World War II drew many men (and some women) out of their
usual social relationships and into the "artificial" social groups of
the armed forces. It created great culture change through demanding much mobility, and through drawing many women into the
industrial world. It changed, at least temporarily, the economic
and social status of many individuals and families. Also, it caused
many young men and women to shift their moral and spiritual
values toward a less conventional position. As Bossard has said:

> War is a stirring phenomenon. It stimulates the emotions. It
> shakes individuals out of the routines of their behavior and their
> thinking. It emphasizes new experiences and precipitates new
> judgments. Implied in all of this is the loosening of the hold of
> customary inhibitions. Traditional ways of doing and thinking give
> way to new desires; impulses long latent find opportunity for
> release. The social threshold of inhibition is lowered. The mores of
> the entire society pass into a stage of active transition. New forms
> of conduct come to be approved, based on a present that seems
> unreal and a future that is obviously uncertain.[1]

Such new values and forms of conduct, once established, are
never entirely abolished. It is in this sense that war makes its
greatest contributions to social change; it is these changes which
the present and future generations of youth inherit from their
older brothers and sisters and from their parents, and which
create perceptions, attitudes, and behavior patterns that are important for the couple who will marry today.

---

[1] James H. S. Bossard, "War and the Family," in Howard Becker and Reuben Hill
(eds.), *Family, Marriage and Parenthood*, p. 722. The student should read the whole
chapter.

MARRIAGE AND MILITARY SERVICE

In normal times, as we have suggested, marriage ordinarily occurs within a pattern of long-established expectations. Today, however, two general alternatives confront the couple who have come to view each other as potential mates. Shall they postpone marriage until the man's (hopefully brief) service in the armed forces has been completed? Shall they marry immediately, and have makeshift living arrangements for the wife until the husband is discharged? In the latter case, shall the wife work at home, or attempt to follow her husband—getting such jobs as are available? Unfortunately, there is again no one answer. Just as the success of marriage—when there was no war or peacetime draft—depended upon a number of interrelated factors, so does adjustment to either of these alternatives depend upon an array of factors. All that can be done is to indicate the important aspects of each.

The Postponed Versus the Hurried Marriage

We are not concerned here with the let's-marry-anyone-today-for-tomorrow-we-shall-die marriages that occurred all too frequently during World War II, nor with those in which there were only financial advantages to be gained.[2] People legitimately fall in love, and plan to marry, whether or not there is war or Selective Service, and this chapter is concerned only with that group. The basic decision in such cases is whether to hurry a process of mate selection already under way, or to lengthen that process. The proponents of delaying marriage until the man has served his "stint" in the armed forces offer several arguments, as do those who argue for marriage before military service begins.

One argument for postponement centers in the fact that this affords the couple a longer period for testing the strength of the relationship. If the marriage is put off and one or the other

---

[2] For example, the writer knew one woman who, during World War II, kept five servicemen "on the hook" and was the stated beneficiary for the National Service Life Insurance policy carried by each. She had no intention of marrying any of them, but did collect on one policy when her "fiancé" was killed in England.

changes his mind, this is all to the good—it proves that the marriage would not have lasted. If the marriage is postponed until the military service is completed, and then goes through, fine—this proves that the marriage is strong and will succeed. In contrast, opponents of this position believe that people who are in love should not be asked to postpone their marriage because the international situation is uncertain. "Half a loaf is better than none"; "it is better to have loved for a day than not to have loved at all," and so on. Only those who are mid-Victorian in their thinking can fail to appreciate the compelling power of love in today's marriages.

A second argument suggests that no one can live on a G.I.'s pay, and that to delay marriage while the man saves his pay and the girl works and saves will give the marriage a greater financial stability when it does occur. The opponents of this position suggest that people who live on a G.I.'s pay, together with what the wife may earn, are in no worse shape for not having waited. "A majority of wives continue to work, anyway, and you can save money just as well married as single."

A third argument for postponement suggests that waiting affords the couple more adequate time for planning a home, and gives them a chance to start in a home of their own—thereby lessening the chances of in-law troubles if the wife should have to live with either set of parents. The counterargument is that other people have married and lived with their in-laws, and that planning a home can go on whether or not the husband is in the service.

A fourth argument centers in the possibility of pregnancy. Proponents of delay believe that postponement prevents pregnancy, and that the husband should certainly be present while the wife is pregnant. Proponents of marriage believe that pregnancy can be prevented today, and that, while admitting the need of the wife for her husband during pregnancy, the couple's having each other at least for a short time is worth any such risk. It is unfair, say they, to ask any couple who are genuinely in love to submit to the prolonged frustration of being kept from sexual relations.

Finally, the opponents of marriage before the man enters service emphasize the fact that—whether or not there is war—military service is dangerous, and the girl who marries under such circumstances runs the risk of having a disabled husband after his discharge or of becoming a widow. The proponents of the hurried-up marriage say that if love is great enough (and it always is!) the girl would want the man however crippled he might be, and that every girl who marries accepts the chance of early widowhood—whether caused by military service or an automobile accident.

These are by no means all the arguments advanced by students and parents, but they are among those most frequently heard. Sometimes they are given rationally; sometimes to the accompaniment of tears. The fact is that both sides are partially right, and both are wrong to some degree. Putting off the marriage is no guarantee that the delay will test the couple's depth of feeling; too many other factors complicate the situation to make it this simple. The certainty that nothing that could happen to a man in time of war would kill a girl's love for him is a noble sentiment, but the nobility of the sentiment is no guarantee of its truth. People fall in love for strange reasons, and they can cease to love for equally strange (and unpredictable) reasons. One of the most unfortunate things about military service is that it does separate individuals, does cause them to think and feel differently about themselves and each other, does mature (and sometimes harden) them. This fact must always be kept very much in mind as the couple weigh the reasons for marrying or postponing marriage.

The attitudes of one's family are important in this connection. If parents oppose the idea of marriage, they are likely to be of less help if the couple marry. If they show a high degree of understanding and sympathy, they will probably do much to help during the period of enforced separation. The economic status of the families is important, too. It is one thing if the married daughter knows it will be easy for her parents to support her in their home should she become pregnant and not be able to support herself or live on her husband's allotment; it is something quite different if she must see herself as a possible financial burden to his or her parents.

It is important, too, to realize that no couple can lightly dismiss the possibility of pregnancy. Regardless of intentions, no method of preventing pregnancy is as yet completely sure, and pregnancy can therefore occur at the most unexpected—and ill-timed— moments. Also, a wife experiencing her first pregnancy is in a quite different situation as regards her need for support and understanding—which is the case in such marriages—than is the wife to whom the wonders and problems of this state have previously been revealed.

The hurried marriage can suffer from one important handicap not previously mentioned. There is inevitably a foreshortening of the processes of accommodation and identification discussed in earlier chapters, and this can make the difficulties of the "separated" marriage more difficult than it otherwise would have been. Growing in love requires—as we have said—both time and opportunity. The war service marriage shortens the former, and does nothing to provide the latter.

These are only suggestions of the difficulties which face the couple who must decide whether or not they shall marry in the face of military demands. Some of such marriages have been highly successful—and others bitter failures. In the last analysis, the decision can be made only: (1) *in terms of the personalities of the individuals concerned*, in terms of their adaptability and their resiliency under adverse circumstances, which such marriages are almost bound to encounter; (2) *in terms of their own expectations of marriage*, for if they want from marriage more than it can give under such circumstances, they are bound to be frustrated and disappointed; (3) *in terms of the degree of their love for each other*, for it requires much interpersonal identification to withstand the pressures and pulls of living in two different worlds—which is, in effect, what happens when one is in civilian and the other in military life.

Married Living for the Service-separated Couple

The couple who decide to marry after weighing all the factors involved face a variety of problems, many of which can have important effects upon their later years together. Some of these have been suggested above, but need further discussion here. One of the most important of these is that each individual during the period of separation must live—and therefore adjust and re-adjust—in a world separate and different from that of his mate. Only in exceptional cases can these separate experiences be shared, and then through the rather unsatisfactory media of letters and short visits. The husband and wife, in most cases, not only find it difficult to communicate their experiences, but—more important—find themselves without the support of the mate in attempting to make the adjustments that the war situation demands. A recent college graduate shows this in the following quotation from an interview.

> We were really alert to the problems we would face, but we didn't understand how complicated they could be. Bill tries to tell me in letters what his problems are—he hates the Army—and I try to help him by being understanding. But an APO address is a long way off, and even air mail doesn't help when he's in Germany and I'm here. I want very much to help him, as any wife does, but we're so far apart, I don't seem to be much good at it. . . . The bigger problems are here. I'm living with [his people], and I'm sure they love us both very much, but there are differences between us that Bill could help iron out if he was here. But, of course, if he was here I wouldn't be living with them. As it is, I try not to tell him about my little problems, because he couldn't understand unless he could *see* what I mean, and he can't see because he's too far away. Anyway, if I told him, it would just make him more unhappy about being in the Army—so what can I do?

This quotation high-lights the inability of husband and wife to provide each other with sympathy and support when separated by his being in military service, but it does not show another possible difficulty—that of differing rates of growth in personality and social experience. We have earlier indicated that personality development is a continuing process, and any experiences inevitably foster this development to some degree. Where the girl remains at home, doing the same things from day to day, while the man goes on to new experiences, new responsibilities, and probably to changed values, the identification they have previously had can be lost. The husband may return, under these circumstances, with aspirations that are totally incompatible with those of his wife, and they may have little upon which to build a continuing marriage.

The possibility of pregnancy was given above as one of the arguments often advanced against marriage before military service has been completed. When pregnancy does occur, the wife has to carry on alone in a situation that always needs the utmost cooperation and support from her husband. Letters and infrequent leaves are poor substitutes for the comforting understanding that she has a right to expect. Even parents and in-laws, helpful as they may be, are poor substitutes for her husband's presence and support. The emotional cost to the husband can be almost as great, since he is far away, under a rigid schedule, and often overwhelmed with a feeling of being completely helpless.

The *possibility* of pregnancy can be almost as much a source of tension as is the actual pregnancy. In those cases where pregnancy is to be avoided, there can be a period after each visit during which the fear that conception has taken place will dominate. Some couples have indicated that the pregnancy would have occasioned less tension than did the fear of it.[3]

Many couples who contemplate marriage before or while the man is in service believe that being apart is unnecessary—that the wife can accompany her husband and live in a town or city near his post. This could well be a reasonable substitute for living together at home, were it not for the circumstances under which military men live. The armed services move men (especially those who are not career soldiers) without regard for their marital

[3] Many Red Cross social case workers reported this to be an outstanding problem in service-related cases during World War II.

status. The use of a man's time is also determined without regard for any obligations he may feel toward his wife. The living accommodations available on the base or in the community are rarely what the couple would desire. Finally, most communities near military installations have become so accustomed to the presence of military personnel that no great effort is made to include them or their wives in community activities. A wife who followed her Air Force private-first-class husband from Illinois to an air base in Georgia had the following to say about this aspect of married life.

> I'm completely and absolutely fed up with this life—I'm going back to —— as soon as we can do it. I thought I'd be with George every night and week ends, but the Air Force doesn't give a darn about me. He works on the planes as a maintenance man, and they put him on any schedule they feel like. . . . Sometimes he's with me only two nights a week, and if it's his turn, he's on the base week ends, too. . . . The people in [town] act as though they don't care whether we are here or not. I tried going to church, but they don't welcome us. I'm "from the base"—that puts me in my place! And I don't care much for most of the wives who are here, either. I don't have a thing in common with most of them—except being lonely. . . . I'm going home and wait for his enlistment to end. At least at home I'll have some satisfaction, even if it's only letters from George, and being with my folks.

This young woman's account indicates some of the difficulties "husband-following" presents, but her problems are of relatively minor importance when compared with those of young wives who either take small children with them or bear children while living under such circumstances. Unless the young couple are prepared to face—and to accept—such eventualities, they may well question the wisdom of a wartime marriage in which one partner or both demands proximity of residence.

After Military Service

Even though the young couple may marry and successfully master the problems that arise during military service, they can

face additional problems when that period is over—some of them
unique. We have already mentioned the difficulties that can arise
out of differences in personality growth and social experience—
these can reach their greatest magnitude when the husband has
returned and the threads of active married living are picked up
again—or, in those cases where the marriage was followed directly
by departure for service—where the couple really begins married
living. In either case, readjustment or adjustment is demanded,
and the marriage must sustain itself under unusual circumstances.

Difficulties are to be encountered, probably, in inverse proportion to the amount of communication which has been had
during the husband's absence. Where communication has been
more adequate, each has been able to share somewhat in the
changes that have occurred in the other. New goals and expectations do not come as a complete surprise under these circumstances, and—where communication is adequate—the personalities
are likely to be able to adapt themselves to each other. But where
communication has been inadequate, each change comes as a
surprise, and if adaptability is not a strong characteristic of both,
tension and conflict may well arise. The real possibility of difficulties in this area should have been considered, however, before
the decision was made to marry.

Other problems faced by the couple may involve both family
and friends. The young man who enters military service as a
youth, even though he has married, comes out a man of worldly
wisdom—but not necessarily to his or his wife's families. Even
though his wife has grown with him, and accepts his new status
and the changes wrought in him by his experiences, his parents
may not have made equivalent adjustments in their relationships—
adjustments that would more likely have been made had everyone
been in more direct communication. This lag in the parents'
adjustment can reflect itself in problems for the couple:

> My brothers never had any trouble with our parents, but then,
> they didn't marry and ship off into the service as I did. . . . I lived
> at home until the day Marge and I were married, one week after

graduating from college. . . . Marge and I got along all right while I was away; she had a job in her home town and we saved money and were set to go when I got out. . . . But the "old man" can't see it that way—he keeps trying to treat me as a kid. I wanted to go into his business with him, but I'm a man now, and he can't treat me like one.

Other problems can confront the young couple after war separation, too. Relatives and friends have to be brought into proper relation to the couple's new married status; this is not always easy where the usual courtship, engagement, and early marital adjustments have been foreshortened or omitted. The implication is not that such adjustments cannot be made, but rather that the couple must recognize the difficulties they may encounter in this area.

"The returning soldier is a hero for ten days. After that, he's just an ordinary Joe, but with ten times the problems of other ordinary people." This was a student's way of indicating the difficulties the wartime marriage may face as a result of the husband's having an unusual status in the community. Our society is, on the whole, not kind to the returning soldier—or to his family. Separation allowances, bonuses, and inexpensive government insurance are hardly adequate compensations for having to start marriage anew under the special circumstances outlined here.

Finally, where a child is born in the father's absence, a problem confronts the couple upon his return. The child's successful development normally depends upon his relations from birth with both his mother and his father; where the father enters the child's experience at a later date, significant adjustments have to be made. The father has the problem of adjusting his affectional relations to both mother and child, of "fitting himself into the already established mother-child scheme," and of sharing in a working relationship, which has heretofore necessarily excluded him.

Little is available in the way of concrete help from research for the man and woman who must decide whether or not to marry. The only research that offers any real semblance of help is that by

Hill, in his painstaking study of the "successes and failures of 135 Iowa families in meeting the crises of war separation and peace-arranged reunion."[4] While this study was concerned with *families and with war conditions*, the findings probably state the case equally well for service marriages. These are (with slight editorial modification) as follows.

1. Those [marriages] in which the wife . . . is relatively irresponsible or excessively dependent will succeed best in adjusting to separation if kinfolk or substitutes are accessible and willing to assume the [husband's] managerial and decision-making roles during his absence.

2. A [marriage] that has inadequate internal resources can make a good adjustment to [separation] if it can draw on the resources of other families or agencies, whether it be on the basis of friendship, blood relationship, or simply a business or client relationship.

3. When one . . . member [of the marriage] has an inadequate personal adjustment, a crisis of dismemberment that deprives the maladjusted member of the . . . resources [of the other] may result in his further deterioration and spread to produce disorganization of the [marriage].

4. When maladjustment or disorganization has occurred in a [marriage] as a result of the failure of the social environment to meet certain deep-seated needs of one or [the other] individual . . . , a change in the direction of a more favorable social environment for [that] individual may set in motion a beneficent cycle which enables [him] to function more effectively . . . so that an improved level of adjustment is achieved [in the marriage].

5. [Marriages] that have been badly used by trial and circumstance but include in their definition of marriage the expressed or unexpressed assumption of permanence and successful persistence of the marriage relation succeed best in the face of the [separation].

6. Adequate resources are not by themselves sufficient to produce a good . . . adjustment to crisis [in marriage] unless accompanied by *savoir-faire*, the ability to utilize . . . resources effectively. Reversely, [marriages] meagerly endowed may nevertheless make expedient and successful adjustments to [separation] by the "know-how" of problem-solving, utilizing effectively the few resources at their disposal.

[4] Cf. Reuben Hill, *Families Under Stress.*

7. [Marriages] tend to succeed better than expected in [separation] in which one or both of the spouses has been delayed in maturing and/or is developmentally ripe for a maturational spurt which the [separation] precipitates.[5]

Even with suggestions such as these, it is impossible for anyone to tell a couple that they will or will not succeed if they marry while a call to military service is a possibility. The only answer that can be given is by the couple themselves, and that answer only after all the factors which affect both "normal" and "hurried" marriages are taken into account. If there are any doubts regarding any of the points made above, postponement seems indicated.

SUMMARY

The continuing threat of possible military service for young men in our country has had a considerable effect upon our attitudes regarding "service-connected marriages." In this chapter we have been concerned with the fact that the new attitudes which are emerging present us with questions regarding whether or not and why we shall or shall not marry if military service is a possibility. The differences between the "hurried up" and the hasty marriage have been outlined, and arguments given *pro* and *con* regarding the advisability of the former. The student who recognizes the realities of both sides of this question, and who faces the need for decision, must take into account the recurring thesis of this text—that decisions such as these can only be made in terms of the personality needs of the couple, of the values and goals the individuals hold regarding marriage, and of the practical problems they will face.

READINGS AND TOPICS FOR REPORTS

1. Read Herbert Kupper, *Back to Life*, and show how the problems outlined therein are related to pre-enlistment marriages of college people.

    [5] *Ibid.*, pp. 309 ff. Hill regards the findings given here more as hypotheses for further research than as definite conclusions. Their worth in the present discussion is apparent, however.

2. Interview a number of wives who married while in college and prior to their husbands' entering the armed services. What do they see as the major problems which confronted them? Are these in any major degree related to in-law relationships?

3. Interview a number of college deans and other administrative personnel to learn their opinions of preservice marriages. Are their opinions practical and based upon a realistic approach to the problems of college people? Do they offer any practical suggestions for such marriages when they do occur?

ADVANCED READINGS

Becker, Howard, and Reuben Hill, *Family, Marriage and Parenthood*, Ch. 24.
Hill, Reuben, *Families Under Stress*.
Waller, Willard, *The Veteran Comes Back*.

19

If Marriage Doesn't Work

At the risk of being accused of pessimism, we include a chapter on the marriage that fails. It is not pessimism but realism that causes this inclusion, for the unhappy fact is that about one out of every six marriages contracted today ends in divorce.[1] Only in the minds of a minority in the United States is divorce an impossibility. Members of the Church of the Latter-Day Saints (the Mormons) regard marriage as a never-ending relationship, lasting through eternity. The Roman Catholic Church allows marriage to be broken only by death, ecclesiastical fiat (annulment) or separation—in which latter case remarriage is impossible. A few other groups hold to this attitude, but for the majority there is an increasing acceptance of the idea that where there is no longer affection and common purpose in marriage, there is no longer the need to hold the couple to their marital agreement.[2]

---

[1] This ratio includes, of course, those marriages which are really only serial monogamy. Cf. *Time's* characteristic terse statement: "Married, he for the *n*th time; she for the *n*th."

[2] There is no intent in this statement to quarrel with those who hold a more traditional position regarding divorce, but to indicate the current trend of thought in our society.

Under such circumstances it is inevitable that some couples will seek divorce, if they have chosen each other unwisely or without due concern; it is equally inevitable that all of us are at one point or another called upon to understand (and perhaps to help) others whose marriages end in divorce.

THE MEANING OF DIVORCE

The fact of divorce per se is unimportant to those who believe that the unadjusted (and unadjustable) couple should be allowed to break their marriage. The significance of what lies behind the legal action is of tremendous importance—for where there is divorce (or separation or desertion) it means that two people have been unable to meet each others' needs, that they have chosen unwisely in the first place, or that they have failed to adapt to the demands of marriage (in a culture which views failure harshly). We need have little concern here for those who look upon marriage as "serial monogamy,"[3] for it is evident that they bring little to marriage and expect too much in return; our concern is mainly with those unhappy situations where one or both have cared mightily, and where the breaking of the marriage wreaks havoc upon what once held great promise.

THE CAUSES OF DIVORCE

It is useless to look to the formal reports of governmental agencies for the causes of divorce. In New York State, for example, every divorce is automatically listed on the ground of adultery, but such evidence is easily manufactured if the parties do not object to this, and such divorces are not often contested. In other states, the most "acceptable"—or "respectable"—cause is often reported. We must look, therefore, at what lies behind the reported cause for the real reasons for breaking a marriage in this fashion.

[3] Cf. Footnote 1.

Personality Needs and Divorce

From the first chapter on, this text has emphasized the need of marriage partners for personalities that complement and supplement each other and are adequate to themselves, and it has highlighted the need for psychological interinvolvement and identification. Research has increasingly shown that in cases of separation and divorce these requirements have been lacking.[4] We may well expect that personality differences are to be found in most instances of divorce. Where the individual chooses a mate in order to meet his need for dependence upon another, and then finds that there is no complementary ability to provide the necessary strength and dominance,[5] the marriage is almost certain to be unsatisfactory to the couple. Conversely, where the individual needs to dominate and the mate is unwilling or unable to be dominated, there can be little satisfaction in the marriage. Again, the individual may have sought not a mate but a parent substitute, and found himself instead to have a partner who wants no part in such a relationship—with resulting discord.

There is more, however, to getting along in marriage than is implied in the last paragraph. Marriage, as we have pointed out, consists in good measure of a search for the satisfaction of one's needs, and these are not confined to the independence-dependence continuum. One partner searches for the satisfaction of certain expectations in life, but the other may not be equipped psychologically to aid in this satisfaction. One attempts to live in terms of certain values, but the other may not be able to adapt himself to those values. One sees life as ruled by behavior patterns—which in a sense are values; the other may not be able to live successfully within such patterns. All this is another way of saying that the characteristics we have identified as inherent in maturity of the personality are—in their absence—the cause of divorce.

---

[4] Cf. Harvey J. Locke, *Predicting Adjustment in Marriage.* This is one of the areas in which research is seriously lacking.

[5] Such cases may fit Winch's concept of "complementary needs" (see Ch. 5).

But this does not explain why one couple who were badly chosen as mates continue to live together while a couple equally ill-matched resort to divorce. Part of the answer must be looked for elsewhere.

Social Contributions to Divorce

To this point research in the social causes of divorce has been concerned largely with the identification of certain "social characteristics" of the divorces.[6] Did the divorced couples have urban or rural backgrounds? Did each have or not have early religious training? Was the courtship brief or extended? Do people who marry in church have less divorces than those who marry with civil ceremonies? These and a multitude of other questions have been asked, and the answers tabulated and correlated. From such studies have come impressive interpretations of data, which have in at least one instance then been compared with similar interpretations of data secured from happily married couples.[7] These studies explain what is present in the life of a divorced couple, but they do not answer the question posed above as to why one couple seeks a divorce while another couple, no better adjusted, does not.[8] Only as students of the human family are able to isolate unhappy marriages which "stay put," identify the forces holding them together, and then contrast these with equivalent forces in marriages ending in divorce will this question receive a satisfactory answer. To date, certain impressionistic explanations are all that are available.

One of these explanations lies in the compulsive power of culture. If the culture considers certain ways of behaving as *right*, and strongly indoctrinates the individual with these as part of his values system, he will hew to a line of behavior consistent with those ways. We have indicated in Chapter 1 that our culture

[6] One problem that plagues the student of marriage in this connection is the inability to gain access to adequate case materials. Few people who seek divorces are willing to be "guinea pigs" for such research.

[7] Cf. Locke, *op. cit.*

[8] The problem noted in Footnote 6 applies equally in this connection.

places increasing emphasis upon individualism as a primary value, and that marriages are therefore increasingly made in terms of the couple's own definitions of their needs. But this trend is still uneven in both scope and character. (One evidence of this is the continuing disparity in what the states allow as grounds for divorce.) Where both individuals have been raised in a cultural setting in which divorce is taboo, and have not been subjected to the liberalizing influences of education, a rejection of divorce will continue. This is well seen in the following abstracts.

> My wife and I both know that we are unhappy together. We fight like cats and dogs, and just make each other miserable. . . . We've talked about getting a divorce, or at least a legal separation, many times, but each time there is something that holds us back. I guess it is the way we were raised. We are both Pennsylvania Dutch, and you know about *them.* All our lives we've been taught that marriage is something that lasts. Why, I don't think there was ever but one divorced woman in our town, and she was looked on as something out of this world. Nobody would have a thing to do with her; she finally had to leave town. My mother and father would no more have had anything to do with her than anything— she was a "scarlet woman." . . . When you've been brought up that way, you just can't turn around and get a divorce. There's something inside you, conscience or whatever, that says you don't do that. I'd always feel that I couldn't look myself in the face ever again if we got a divorce, or if I left her. . . . It's my *duty* to remain married.

This respondent never heard of the compulsive power of culture, but his, "It's my *duty* to remain married," is evidence that it exists in his life, just as it exists—in one form or another—in the lives of everyone. Some people, in other words, stay married in the face of any amount of discord, simply because divorce is not a part of their culturally-determined value system. (This includes, of course, those people whose religious beliefs prohibit the breaking of a marriage.) But this is an explanation of why people *do not* obtain divorces rather than an indication of any social causes of divorce.

There is probably no real social contribution to divorce other than the creation of a subcultural milieu in which *the couple's inability to find satisfaction of their needs allows them to accept the idea of divorce.* The characteristics of the couple, uncovered in the research referred to above, are, in the final analysis, not of primary importance. What is important is that the couple's needs—whether deeply psychological or psychosocial—have not been met in the marriage and there are now cultural prescriptions for them which include divorce as the way out of a bad situation. Where these needs are not met, and the religious and other values of the couple prescribe marriage, that marriage will continue.

This poses a challenging question: Will divorce as a means of solving the problems of the unhappy marriage be used increasingly? The answer seems to be in the affirmative, but needs qualification. As the institutions continue to change and human knowledge grows and is more widely diffused, there will probably be less acceptance of the rigorous holding to marriage that has characterized the past and a greater willingness to regard divorce as a means for correcting human mistakes in mate selection. Whether or not divorce will increase equally among all social groups in the community is open to question; Kingsley Davis suggests that there is a saturation point for any population, and that this point is at least in sight.[9] There is no doubt, however, that there are substantial population groups in this country that are only now liberalizing their views on divorce, and that an increased acceptance by these groups may well further increase the use of divorce for the purposes suggested.

This emphasizes, however, the need for helping youth to develop satisfactory and adequate personalities, for educating them in the fundamentals of mate selection and marriage adjustment, and for providing suitable facilities for aiding "sick" marriages. If these needs are satisfied, divorce will not grow to be a characteristic way of solving problems in marriage; but if they are not satisfied, our society can expect the divorce rate to continue to rise.

[9] Cf. Kingsley Davis, "Statistical Perspective on Marriage and Divorce," *Annals of the American Academy of Political and Social Science*, 272: 9 ff. (1950).

THE MOVEMENT TOWARD DIVORCE

We cannot think of divorce as something which becomes a *fait accompli* without prior difficulty. It is impossible to imagine any genuine marriage which was not discord-free at its inception.[10] The movement toward divorce, which Waller termed "the process of alienation," should be understood. Waller posited six stages in the movement toward divorce: (1) some disturbance in the erotic life of the pair, with accompanying affectional disturbances; (2) the mention of the possibility of divorce; (3) the breaking of the "fiction of solidarity"; (4) the decision to divorce; (5) the crisis of separation; and (6) the final severance. While these can be accepted as separate stages, there is no indication that in all cases they necessarily occur in this order.[11] These can be illustrated with two cases studied by the writer.

In the case of couple *A*, both were urban dwellers and well educated, both had grown up with no pronounced attitudes against divorce, and both saw marriage as a relationship in which good personal relationships were of the greatest importance. Their difficulties arose out of strong differences in personality, values, and social habits. The husband was an extroverted businessman whose chief interests lay in making money, playing bridge, and golfing; his wife was a quiet, withdrawn person whose interests were largely confined to her home, her children, and certain intellectual activities. Their friends knew for a long time that they were not happy together and had freely predicted that the marriage would not last. The decision to seek a divorce was mutual; they separated only after elaborate arrangements had been made for an adequate disposition of property and income. The crisis of separation was delayed until a few weeks before the filing of the divorce action. The arrangement was rational and (in the word of a mutual friend) "coldblooded."

In the case of couple *B*, the picture was quite different. Both had rural and highly religious backgrounds; there had been almost no divorces among the people they had known; divorce was considered

---

[10] Cf. Ch. 11.

[11] Nor is this to be construed as a continuous movement toward divorce. In most situations involving divorce, the couple have made one or more efforts to regain their earlier adjustment, only to "backslide" as the aggravation returned and grew. Cf. Willard Waller, *The Family: A Dynamic Interpretation*, pp. 54 ff.

by both to be an evidence of personal inadequacy and moral
digression. Mr. B's need in a mate was for a mother-substitute, but
Mrs. B was quite unable to fulfill such a need. The "fiction of
solidarity" was broken only after many months and was followed
by a separation; each believed that if they lived apart for a time
their emotional differences might be reconciled. The possibility of
divorce was not mentioned, nor even considered, until they had
been apart for nearly a year, and then only after they had both met
people with whom they believed they might find happiness. This
possibility was followed rapidly by a rather "desperate" decision
to go against all their past beliefs, and the divorce followed quickly.

This brief account of the movement toward divorce illustrates
a number of important points (see Figure 22). The differences
between couples A and B in the order of "stages of alienation" are
important. The B's, primarily for *cultural* reasons, held much
longer to a hope that the marriage might be saved, and avoided
any recognition of the possibility of divorce. The A's, in contrast,
readily admitted that divorce might be a way out, and broke the
fiction of solidarity at a very early date. The A's decided well
ahead that a divorce was their only solution, planned for the
separation over a period of many months, and lived together
"practically in a state of separation" for more than a year.[12] The
striking differences in the way couples can handle the problem of
a divorce are thus demonstrated.

One good reason for including this discussion of the movement
toward divorce is to point out the chance for the employment of
corrective measures. While there is no absolute claim that in
either case the differences between husband and wife could have
been resolved, there is some reason to believe that here—as in
many cases of separation or divorce—the problems could have
been discussed with a professional marriage counselor, psychiatrist, or other trained person, and the break prevented. This is
especially true where the time intervals are similar to those in the
case of the B's, where so many months went by before the couple

12 The student should realize that the conduct of the A's, if known to the court,
would have been a clear indication of collusion, and would have invalidated any
divorce action.

TIME IN MONTHS	COUPLE A	COUPLE B
0	(1) First erotic-affectional disturbance	(1) First erotic-affectional disturbance
3	(2) Mention of possibility of divorce	
4	(3) Breaking the "fiction of solidarity"	
27		(3) Breaking the "fiction of solidarity"
33	(4) The decision to divorce	
38		(5) The crisis of separation
40	(5) The crisis of separation	
42		(2) Mention of the possibility of divorce
44		(4) The decision to divorce
48	(6) The divorce	(6) The divorce

Figure 23. A "timetable" of the events leading to divorce, as discussed in the accompanying example.

was willing to break the fiction of solidarity; professional advice might similarly have helped the *A*'s in the long period between the breaking of solidarity and the actual decision to divorce. Many other factors enter in, of course, but the emphasis here is upon the fact that divorces do not ordinarily occur immediately after the first erotic-affectional disturbances and that there is usually time to secure assistance before the situation is beyond remedy.

THE EFFECTS OF DIVORCE

It was indicated earlier that marriage requires the forsaking of one set of habits and the assumption of another. Divorce or separation imposes a similar requirement, although the "off with the old and on with the new" is not quite of the same order.[13] The earlier change was one filled with potentialities; the state of single

[13] Cf. Willard Waller, *The Old Love and the New: Divorce and Readjustment.*

(and empty) blessedness was forsaken for a relationship which promised much in the way of physical and social satisfactions. That transition had the sanction and blessing of one's family, friends, and society; it was the culmination of a process long desired and greatly anticipated. The change from the married to the divorced state is rarely accompanied by paeons. One has, inevitably, the sense of having failed. While the break has been sanctioned by the state, and even by one's family and friends, there is no occasion for rejoicing. It is the culmination of a foregoing process, and one that has most often been filled with bitterness, recriminations, and the sense of frustration. The future promises little or nothing.

This is, of course, not always the case. The individual who divorces in order that he or she may marry another with whom love is already shared is in a less difficult position, but this is not often the case. Even if it were, the old marriage is not abandoned without some residual effects. No one, in fact, however glad he or she may be to be rid of the marriage, goes through the experience without some emotional costs.

One of the effects of breaking the marriage through separation or divorce is to require the formation of new habit patterns.[14] The habits of marriage are in some measure sloughed off in the pre-divorce days as the couple progressively relinquish their more intimate relationships. There is, therefore, a partial adjustment, a piecemeal acceptance of the new ways of thinking and doing.[15] All this adds to the difficulty, especially for the partner who is still in love and does not want to end the marriage. Such a person is not only faced with the necessity of giving up what he or she has had, but in this period also has constant reminders that what once was is to be no more. The following quotation illustrates this point.

> The worst part of [breaking the marriage] was knowing that I had agreed to a divorce, even though I didn't want it, so far ahead.

[14] The vital contribution of habit patterns in providing *stability* in life should be kept in mind throughout this discussion.

[15] Any of these, of course, require significant changes in the habit patterns of the individual.

> It took almost three months for the case to come up in court. In all that time I was still married—but I wasn't, too. . . . Everything that I did as Mrs. *F* —— was for the last time. . . . I was always finding myself struggling not to do things that Jack and I had done together, because every time I did, it was almost more than I could take. . . . And yet, I *did* want the divorce because if Jack didn't want me I didn't want to hold him.

Even though the predivorce activity serves as something of a dress rehearsal for what is to come, the finality of the break (with the absolute necessity for new patterns) usually comes only after the actual separation. At this point the dilemma is at its height, because new habits must be established or old (premarital) ones readopted. The former is difficult, since behavior requires both time and reward to become habitual; the latter is equally difficult, since time has in a sense passed by, and it is not easy to reactivate old relationships. The woman, for example, who for five years has been accustomed to spending her evenings playing bridge, listening to the radio, or reading with (or at least in the company of) her husband finds it difficult to learn to do these things alone or with new associates, and finds it equally difficult to go back to the associates and ways of her girlhood.

The dilemma is made no easier by the fact that as yet there are no generally accepted and culturally approved ways by which the divorced person is helped to adjust. In the case of death, the widowed person is allowed a period of mourning, and is then generally brought back gradually to the usual activities, albeit without the mate. As yet, no comparable folkways have been established for the divorcee. Are such persons expected to go through a comparable period of retirement, or are they expected to "land on their feet" and go on as though nothing untoward had happened? A recently divorced woman had this to say:

> You don't know what to do. Do you act as though nothing had happened, or try to avoid anyone who knew you before? You can't do either one, and nobody helps you very much. . . . I finally decided that I'd just be as factual as I could about the whole thing—we couldn't get along, so we divorced! But it was the worst part of

the whole thing for me—the weeks before I could make up my mind how to act.

Part of the habitual behavior in marriage centers upon the sex drive, especially after the passions of the first months of marriage have subsided. Denial of the usual outlet for the sexual drive demands a degree of repression, and very often a conscious sublimation. Changing the sex habits is probably one of the most difficult and certainly one of the most readily identified of all the adjustments that have to be made. As one divorcee expressed it, "It isn't a matter of refocusing; it is a matter of defocusing."

The reforming of habits must not be interpreted in too narrow a fashion. Habits involve not only physical acts, but affectional relationships as well. The fact that the normal individual must give as well as receive affection means that, as the mate (the object upon which that affection has been centered) withdraws, a new love object is required. Whether this means returning to a former attachment, forming a new affectional relation, or developing a strong degree of self-love is a matter of insight, preference, and opportunity. In the first of these, this means returning to an earlier love, which is not always easy; in the second, it means entering upon the search for another mate, which may seem hazardous after the past experience; in the last, it means that the individual becomes self-centered and often ill-adjusted.

Finally, the social-psychological effect of divorce is partially to destroy one's concept of his own self and to require the rebuilding of that self. As Cooley has indicated, the self has three elements; the imagination of one's appearance to the other person; the imagination of the other person's judgment of that appearance; and a self-feeling, as of pride, chagrin, or guilt; these constitute what he called the "looking-glass self."[16] No one, whether aggressor or aggrieved, can go through the experience of breaking a marriage without having this "looking-glass" self cracked or even shattered. Through the whole of the premarital and preschism stages of the relationship, each has grown to recognize himself,

[16] Cf. C. H. Cooley, *Social Organization*, Chs. 30-33.

and to behave in terms of what he believes the other to see. With the break comes the partial destruction of that self, and the necessity for reconstructing it later in terms of new associates and new interaction patterns. But memory can be an unpleasant resident of the mind. Try as hard as one will to forget, there is always a residuum of this earlier self remaining, and this residuum acts as a brake on the adjustments demanded of the individual at a later date.[17]

THE REACTION TO DIVORCE

Waller's conceptualizations of what happens to those who resort to divorce have been substantially confirmed in a study of contested divorces which the writer is continuing.[18] To date we have been able to identify three differing mental states which are discussed here for the light they throw on how the individual accepts his or her new freedom.

The first reaction, as was suggested above, is that of *depression*. There is a realization that the separation is now final, and the action irretrievable except through remarriage. The individual has a new status, and one not always or entirely acceptable to others. Individuals report themselves as having avoided social contacts in this stage, and "every day is Blue Monday." Life is not really worth living, and a sense of personal unworthiness and failure prevails. (This stage appears to occur in both the aggrieved and the aggressor, although to a lesser degree in the latter. It is probably occasioned in the latter by a sense of failure mentioned earlier—which is so important to the American middle class.) The severity of the depression and the length of time it occurs depends, apparently, upon (1) the degree of the earlier interpersonal involvement, (2) the attitudes and behavior of family and friends, and (3) the amount of guilt associated with the act of divorce.

[17] The individual is, in such cases, attempting (in effect) to live in two "worlds" at once.

[18] Cf. Willard Waller, *The Old Love and the New: Divorce and Readjustment.*

This feeling of depression is uniformly followed by one of *euphoria*. Here there is a pronounced feeling of optimism and well-being. This shows itself in what Hill has termed "a great increase in egocentricity." He illustrates this increase in the following words.

> In this period, people who have never before lost perspective upon their own abilities deem themselves capable of everything and bring to expression the most grandiose purposes. A woman in her forties who has never done anything in the literary or scientific world is quite certain that in a short time she is going to become a famous scholar or a great literary figure, and is quite frank in the expression of her belief. Another woman, who has never been able to earn more than a few dollars a month, suddenly becomes convinced that in a few years she will be making six to ten thousand dollars a year. A man revives all the long-lost dreams of his boyhood and believes that it is a matter of only a few years until he becomes a famous lawyer or a great general. Or a man makes an alimony settlement far beyond his means, feeling that he will easily liquidate this obligation in a not distant future.[19]

This euphoric state is seen to find expression in these and a variety of other ways. One of the more important of the latter is in the spending of money unwisely. For example,

> I don't know what got into me, but I felt so good after a while that I spent money right and left. I only had my alimony ($125 a month) and $300 in the savings bank, but I spent that $300 like water. . . . I had dinner out every night, and entertained my friends such as I had, all of the time—spent money like I never had before in all of my twenty-six years. . . . Something just came over me, that's the only way I can explain it. It was just like being happy because a tooth had quit hurting.

This quotation illustrates a further difference between the euphoric and the depression stages. The earlier effort to avoid social contacts is replaced with a fever of social activity. Thus far there has been no evidence to show that this heightened social activity is an effort to find a second mate. This euphoric stage may be

[19] Used by permission from Willard Waller (revised by Hill), *The Family: A Dynamic Interpretation*, p. 516.

attributed, as Hill suggests, to the enhancement-of-self activity, or seen as a compensatory fantasy which finds outlet in physical activity and possessing things.[20] The writer prefers, however, to see this reaction, as Hill probably would agree, as resulting in good part from the release divorcees feel at having been freed from an unpleasant relationship. Thus:

> When I look back, I think [the euphoric] state was just a final relief at getting it over with. The trouble had been getting worse and worse, until something just had to give. The "blues" I felt first, I think, came from not knowing quite how my people would act toward me now that I was a divorcee. Once that was over, and I didn't feel I had to hide, I just felt so good I went to the opposite end—and had a good time.

The "final relief at getting it over with" and knowing "how people would act" appears to offer a reasonable explanation for this second stage.

Having experienced the wide variations of depression and euphoria, the individual somehow "comes to earth," and evidently enters the stage of *rehabilitation*. This is the time when one learns to live again; much depends, in this stage, upon what the individual perceives to be the situation of the divorcé (or divorcee) in society, and upon the self he is able to envisage in that situation. If, out of his cultural heritage and his group interaction, the individual defines the situation of the divorcé as one of lessened status and enforced social isolation, resuming his place in the orderly relationships of society will be difficult. If, too, his conception of his own self has been devalued (through the divorce experience) to the point where his self-depreciation inhibits social participation, his rehabilitation will be very difficult. Where, in contrast, the divorcé's situation is not defined in such negative terms, and where devaluation of the self has not been too great (perhaps because interpersonal strife has not been of too intense or damaging a nature), this process can be relatively easy.

[20] Cf. Waller (revised by Hill), *ibid.*, p. 518.

But it is not quite this simple! Even though the individual may have within himself attitudes that facilitate rehabilitation, other forces may work to counteract an adjustment. Group-shared attitudes may interpose barriers to social acceptance; where there are no "extra" men or women in the community, the divorced person finds social participation difficult. Where there is no interest in remarriage or where age makes remarriage difficult, the successful re-establishment of social relations is often hampered. It is not an exaggeration to say that the lot of the divorced person in this stage of his whole reaction is often an unhappy one. This is seen, for example, in the following abstracts from a series of interviews.

> I'm going to leave this town. It's my home, and all of my people are here, but I can't take it any longer. . . . [I] feel all right now—I was depressed but I got over it—but there's no use trying to live (the divorce) down. If I go out with a man for an innocent evening at a movie, I'm "chasing" the men. I'm an odd duck. My friends entertain couples, and I haven't a man and they aren't going to throw any man into my clutches. . . . It's just not worth while; I'll go somewhere where being a divorced woman isn't the same as being damned. . . . No woman can possibly live that down in this town.

SHALL A COUPLE RESORT TO DIVORCE?

This is a personal question and, like all others raised in connection with the marriage relationship, can be answered only by the couple involved. The assumption in posing this question is that the marriage "is on the rocks" and that the couple must decide whether or not they are to continue their marriage. In an effort to help the student arrive at a philosophy applicable to this question, other questions must be raised and answered.

The earlier discussion of causes need not be repeated here, but whether or not a divorce is sought depends upon the nature of those causes. If they involve deep-seated psychological maladjustments or inadequate personality development, the situation is obviously different from one in which there is a nagging wife, or selfish mother-in-law attempts to take her son from his wife. In the latter case, given help in recognizing and admitting the problem, the couple can probably avert divorce by eliminating in some way (as by change of residence) the in-law influence. (Such a moving away can hardly be construed in such cases as cowardice or running away from trouble.) The same is true for a variety of other social and cultural factors. In the case of personality factors, is professional assistance available, is it acceptable to the individual who needs it, and is it financially possible to obtain it? The condition that can be remedied only through long and costly psychoanalytical procedures can obviously not be corrected unless adequate funds are available, and unless the individual lives in certain areas in the United States. All this implies, of course, that the individuals are willing to correct whatever conditions have helped to break the relationship. In cases where there is no willingness even to look at the causes, or to face the possibility of reconciliation, such inquiries become academic, and the question has a quite different dimension.

In any event, the decision requires that each member look squarely at the needs which have not been met, at the expectations that have not been realized, at the values which have not been brought into adjustment. If these cannot be met, realized, and adjusted, there seems—for those who can accept the idea of divorce—little reason to continue the marriage.

The Cost of Divorce

Divorce is by no means inexpensive, but the financial costs are of little importance in the total picture. Here the concern must be with the social and psychological costs. If the divorce is sought in a community having strong proscriptions against the breaking of any marriage, for whatever reason, the result will be to ostracize the aggressor and even the aggrieved and, therefore, make difficult their future readjustment. Jobs have been lost because "the boss" did not believe in divorce; respectable women have been rendered friendless and driven to neurotic breakdowns because the community refused to see the need for ending a hopeless personal relationship. In some cases, then, it may be better to live in an icy apartness than to face denunciation and rejection by the larger social group.

Equally important is the need to evaluate the probable psychological costs. The original intensity of the involvement of each with the other, the extent to which a break will traumatize that involvement, and the potential ability of each to heal his wounds and to rebuild his life are all important considerations. They are especially important to the couple, because the outsider cannot easily help evaluate these as he can the more overt social and cultural factors.

How long, too, has the marriage lasted? The longer the period of involvement, the more likely are the couple to have adjusted to each other's ways and to have become fixed in those ways, the more identified their values have become, and the more settled their paired position in the community. To break a marriage within the first two or three years is one thing; to allow it to persist for fifteen or twenty years and then to propose a break is quite another. Here again, the total cost of a divorce in the latter case may be greater than the cost of living together in a strained relationship.

And what about children? Where children are in the picture, the decision to divorce is manifestly different, for the family—at least in the American middle class—is child-centered. As Truxal has said,

> Children whose world is oriented about their immediate parents, with all the resultant emotional intensities, see that world collapse about their ears when their mother and father come to the parting of the ways. The declining importance of many erstwhile family functions emphasizes the emotional and affectional, with the result that marital permanence is more difficult since it is based upon the more ephemeral elements of love and affection. When and if the break comes, the children are affected to an intensified degree, since they have been the recipients of the hopes, ambitions, and frustra-

tions of the parents—in addition to the affection normally directed to them as children.[21]

Divorce, then, results in insecurity for the child, and it is this insecurity which leads, in Plant's words, to a "loss of morale, a figurative hanging of the head. As [the child of divorced parents] grows older, he may cover this with bitter driving punishment of others, or guard and possess [his own mate] and children with an ever-hungry zeal . . . or encapsulate all this part of life, defending it with a thick shell that defies memory or intrusion."[22]

There may, however, be a positive value to the child in that:

> Parental discord frequently presents to the child all the real problems of not being wanted, of being rejected, that are present in actual desertion. Moreover, there is the increased irritation that comes from "forever having things stirred up." This means, often, that the actual step of divorce or desertion is a point of relief for the child.[23]

When seen in this light, the question of the suitability of divorce where children are concerned assumes a new light. If the marriage is to continue with the child "forever having things stirred up," it is obvious that it does a disservice not only to the parents but to the child as well. If there is any marked relation between happiness in childhood and marital adjustment, then causing a child to continue to live in an unhappy home is to contribute to his own unhappy marriage at a later date.[24] This obviously requires that the whole question be decided with the child's interests kept very much in mind.

The decision, then, as to whether or not to seek a divorce or, in contrast, whether or not to contest such an action, must be seen not as any one simple answer to an uncomplicated question. It, like all other decisions in mate selection and marriage, can be

[21] Used by permission from Andrew G. Truxal and F. E. Merrill, *The Family in American Culture*, pp. 213 ff.

[22] Cf. James F. Plant, *The Envelope: A Study of the Impact of the World Upon the Child*, p. 21.

[23] *Ibid.*, p. 23.

[24] Cf. Chapter 4.

arrived at only by examining and weighing many interrelated factors. Only as individuals thus examine and weigh all factors have they a chance to remedy past mistakes and to make an adequate adjustment in what is at best an unfortunate situation.

SUMMARY

A realistic view of marriage today requires that we consider the possibility—if not the probability—of divorce. In this chapter we have outlined the personal rather than the legal aspects of the whole problem of dissolving a marriage that has failed to meet its expectations and where divorce appears to be inevitable. The important place of the child in discussions *pro* and *con* of the possibility of divorce has been emphasized. It must also be emphasized that it is fatuous to say that *any* marriage can be made to work. Given basic differences in personality needs, in values and goals, some marriages can never be brought into accord. (This, as we have pointed out earlier, is essentially a matter of failure, most often in the mate selection process.) The need for objectivity and insight regarding the needs of the couple (and of the children when present) is of paramount importance, and should be kept in mind.

READINGS AND TOPICS FOR REPORTS

1. Interview a number of lawyers who accept divorce and separation cases. What are their opinions regarding the real versus the expressed reasons for their clients seeking divorces? How well are they able to identify the several stages of reaction discussed in this chapter? Do they have consistent policies regarding efforts to reconcile the husband and wife? What are their attitudes regarding the custody of children in case of divorce?
2. Interview a number of social workers who deal with the problems of children of divorced or separated parents. What do they see as the important effects of divorce or separation upon children?

3. Read Edmund Bergler, *Divorce Won't Help*, and present arguments to refute the position taken by that author.
4. Read William J. Goode, "Problems in Postdivorce Adjustment," *American Sociological Review*, 14:726 ff. (1949), and present an analysis of possible ways in which these problems could be met.

ADVANCED READINGS

Baber, Ray, *Marriage and the Family* (2d ed.), Chs. 13, 14.

Kane, John, *Marriage and the Family: A Catholic Approach*, Ch. 12.

Mudd, Emily H., *The Practice of Marriage Counseling*, Ch. 1.

Winch, Robert, and Robert McGinnis, *Selected Studies in Marriage and the Family*, Ch. 18.

Growing Old in Marriage

THAT A CHAPTER with a title such as this should be included in a textbook intended for those who are only at the threshold of marriage may seem odd. It is included for two reasons: First, what happens in the latter years of marriage is directly related to what happens in the mate selection period and in the early years of marriage; and second, most young people have need to understand some of the problems of the latter years of marriage because of their own dealings with their parents.[1]

It is pertinent to recognize, in this connection, that the life expectancy has increased tremendously in the last several decades. One hundred years ago, the average life expectancy was approximately forty years; today it is about sixty-seven years. The average couple, has, therefore, a considerable number of years to live after the children have gone from the home—which gives this subject very practical importance.

Old age is, of course, a relative matter. It is not unusual for the well-preserved father in his early forties to have a son or daughter

---

[1] The importance of this topic is also increased by the tendency for the older-generation individual to be excluded from the homes of the children.

ask about conditions "in olden times," nor are there many things more aggravating. Old age is a relative matter in another and more important way, however, The fact that age sixty-five is usually the point at which retirement occurs indicates that it is customarily considered to be the point at which old age begins. This is a matter of culture, rather than of physiology. Most retirement plans "put a person on the shelf" at that age; most insurance companies and other economic groups appear to assign a certain magic to that year of life. The fact that many individuals are intellectually and socially useful for many years beyond that point, while others have passed the prime of life well before it, indicates that old age is a matter of cell deterioration rather than of calendar-year accumulations.

SOME PROBLEMS

The problems associated with the later years of married life are many and are in one sense similar to those accompanying adolescence. A major problem of the adolescent lies in the contradictions thrust upon him; the later years of marriage bear equal contradictions, although of a different order. The adolescent strives for adulthood in a society that poorly defines his place; the couple in their later years reach back for the life they have known, but find themselves pushed on toward a place in life that is equally ill-defined. The result for many if not most couples is "confusion compounded."

Problems Related to Health

One of the important hazards of the later years of marriage is that associated with health. The human machine begins to deteriorate as the individual reaches the half-century mark; as yet, the processes associated with this deterioration (aging) are not completely identified. Until such time as they are more clearly understood, and until remedies or alleviations have been established for many of the diseases (rheumatism, arthritis, cardiac conditions, arteriosclerosis, and so on) associated with physical aging, the later years of marriage will always be confronted with special problems.[2] One of these is related to the climacteric (the cessation of reproductivity activity). This phenomenon exhibits itself differently in the male and the female. It is widely recognized in the latter, since it involves a cessation of menstruation (the menopause); a comparable process occurs in the male but is not so generally recognized or understood. Fundamentally the process is the same—the male and female sex glands gradually cease the endocrine functions they have performed since puberty, and the balance among the other endocrine glands (the pituitary, thyroid, parathyroids, adrenals, and pancreas) is disturbed for a time. Eventually a new balance among all of these is established, but at a new level, and the climacteric ends.

During this period, however, the situation is sometimes acute—especially for the female. The physical symptoms may be unpleasant; frequently there are emotional and nervous disturbances. For some women these are of brief duration and of slight importance; for others they extend over a period of years and are severe in their effect. In recent years supportive glandular therapy has been developed to the point where the menopause is no longer a major threat to the health of women.[3]

Whatever the degree of disturbance, this phenomenon needs to be understood by all members of the family. The psychic disturbances can be of such a nature that family living is markedly disturbed, and the effects—if the cause is not recognized—can be serious. In some cases, the wife may be irritable in regard to happenings which formerly would have been overlooked or adjusted to; these "spells" may come without warning and be explosive in nature. They may be preceded or followed by periods of acute depression. Whether predictable or not, the psychic effects

[2] One evidence of society's concern in this connection is the development of a special field of medicine called geriatrics. National organizations, both public and private, are now focusing much attention upon this topic.

[3] Treatment for severe disorders in this period of life should be sought from the best-trained specialists available, rather than from the general practitioner.

are symptomatic of the basic problem, and indicate that some form of therapy is advisable. Also, they indicate the need for sympathetic understanding on the part of both husband and children. In contrast, however, some women have little or no reaction of such a nature as to cause even great physical discomfort, and there are no psychic upheavals.[4]

In the male the climacteric usually occurs somewhat later, and is rarely dramatic in its effects. There is a general decline in physical vigor, but it appears that family interaction is less likely to be affected. How much of the change in both male and female can be charged to an internal conflict over the fact of aging, and how much to actual physical change are matters yet to be established by research. Certainly physical changes do occur, and the help of a competent physician should be sought if problems arise in this connection; this is one of the situations in which an annual physical checkup can be especially useful.

Problems Related to Sexual Behavior

Insufficient attention has been paid to the matter of sexual behavior in the later years of marriage. One of the folk ideas often encountered focuses upon the "fact" that people who have passed their forties have—or should have—little interest in sex, and that sexual activity after the menopause is somehow "indecent." While sexual interest is most often diminished, there is no evidence of its cessation. The fact that the couple no longer need to be concerned about conception is very often a source of satisfaction, and gives a renewed value to the sex act. The psychological values inherent in sexual experience, which have already been discussed in Chapter 12, can well take a major position in the values of the couple. While the frequency and intensity of earlier sexual activity may not be equalled, the nature of the sexual relationship may be such as actually to bind the couple more closely than in the years

---

[4] In a series of 165 cases studied by the writer in an out-patient gynecological clinic, more than 40 percent of the couples reported behavior related to the climacteric to be such as to have caused major tension or conflicts in the home.

when there were underlying concerns about conception and pregnancy.

Problems Related to Dependency

The economic institutions of our society have shown an increasing inclination to release the older worker and to refuse to employ people past forty on the grounds that "older people produce less, that they are more prone to accidents, and that they are less adaptable" to the demands of modern industry.[5] Whether or not such reasoning is justified—and there is reason to question it—the fact remains that many older people are deprived of satisfying jobs, or for that matter, of any jobs. Since industrial wages have not always been adequate to allow saving for the later unproductive years, many people have been placed at a great disadvantage. (Pension plans have in general been too recent in their development to provide adequate security for most older workers of this generation, and the social-security system is too new to have given many couples a return adequate to their needs.) At the same time, younger people have been faced with increasing difficulty in attempting to meet their parents' economic needs. Increased mobility (which separates parents and children), changing patterns of housing (which makes the inclusion of older people in the home an impossibility in many cases), and a rising standard of living have created difficulties for the young in this regard. The development of institutionalized forms of extramural support for the aging (particularly Old Age Assistance programs) has in many instances provided a rationale for the young who seek to avoid the responsibility for their parents' care.[6]

All these factors have contributed to the dilemma of many couples in their later years. Added to these is the fact that suitable housing facilities are rarely available for the older family in our communities. The aging couple may have Old Age Assistance

---

5 Cf. Beulah Amidon, "Jobs After Forty," *Public Affairs Pamphlet* No. 35.

6 In many cases such young people tend to view public welfare grants as a "right" of the retired worker.

grants which enable them to *exist*, but there are not many housing units suited to their needs. An Old Age Assistance recipient indicated the plight of many older people in these words.

> We're both too old to take care of a house, but there isn't any place we can go except to an old folks' home or to the poorhouse. We can get along on our "pensions" but the place to live is the big thing. If there was just somebody who'd build little apartments so they wouldn't cost more than we can afford, and who'd take care of the big jobs—we'd be all right. But nobody thinks of us older people when they build places to live. They build these hundred-dollar-a-month places, and not for fifteen dollars. We don't need anything fancy—just some place to keep us covered and warm.

Whether or not private capital can build small apartments to rent at the rate suggested here is debatable. It may well be that government subsidy is the only way in which this problem can be met for many couples, just as the federal social security program is the only way in which their financial problems can be met.[7]

The over-all problem of dependency in the later years of marriage involves a number of solutions. The first, a federal security program, has already been mentioned, in which outright grants (Old Age Assistance) or "earned pensions" (Old Age and Survivors' Insurance) meet at least a part of the couple's or individual's needs. The second involves the couple themselves—their planning for the later years and budgeting the family income in such a way that an invested surplus becomes available when needed. This obviously can only be wishful thinking for large numbers of low-income families, who can live within their incomes only by depriving themselves of many necessities. The third involves the children's accepting at least partial responsibility for their parents' care when they are no longer able to support themselves financially or physically. This, too, poses problems, especially among low-income families. No one solution of the problem is applicable in

---

[7] At least one city (Rochester, N. Y.) has definitely planned public housing projects to meet the needs of such couples.

all cases, but certainly any of these must be carried out in such a way that the dignity and worth of the aging person is preserved.[8]

Problems Related to Retirement

The enforced abandonment of regular activities is a serious matter for many older people. The man whose whole life has been geared to a regular eight-to-five work routine and who suddenly finds himself with no use for that amount of time can face serious adjustment problems. The wife whose life has been filled with the multiple tasks of caring for her family, only to have that family reduced to her husband and herself, can be faced with similar problems.[9]

It must be remembered that the Calvinistic doctrine of "the holiness of work" still influences many people. To be idle is to be sinful; therefore there are sometimes tremendous feelings of guilt over being idle, even when there are ample funds and work is not necessary. Moreover, work does have psychological and social values, as Lemkau has shown in these words:

> For some men the productive activity of work is their only creative outlet. It channels not only their intellect and their social drive, but also what artistic, creative urges they may have. Furthermore, their work may be an outlet for a need to show their power—power over men if they are supervisory personnel, over things if they are not at that level. For many the work relationships give a status, a position in the eyes of others, that is a source of satisfaction. The union relationship may be of great importance to the individual as an outlet for his feelings of social or community responsibility. A large part of the man's intellectual and emotional life may be all in one basket, his job.[10]

Depriving a man (or woman) of values such as these means that other values must be substituted if he or she is not simply to

---

[8] For example, nutritionists have encountered difficulty in getting older people to accept certain diets because these place the individual in a special (and presumably inferior) category.

[9] This is essentially a matter of redefining or transferring roles (see Chapter 10).

[10] Used by permission from Paul V. Lemkau, *Mental Hygiene in Public Health*, p. 311.

vegetate in old age. New interests, new "time users," must be developed if the individual is to have some equivalent for work. Here again our society has been shortsighted in not making available opportunities for such substitutions and in not helping individuals to develop new interests in the years prior to their retirement.[11]

The married couple has, under these circumstances, a responsibility for developing interests that will carry over into their later childless years, but such a responsibility can—and will—be assumed only as the need is understood. The couple entering marriage may very well plan their family activities in such a way as to lead them in later years into fruitful activities that meet their needs. For example, the woodworking shop (intended to be used for keeping the family's home in good repair) can become a useful implement for the fulfilling of later psychological needs; any activity that interests the individual or couple can be built up during the child-rearing years to the point where it becomes a vital part of the life experience of later years.[12]

Relationship Problems

The need for parents to release their children from emotional dependence—and of children to free themselves from such dependence—has been discussed earlier. As each child leaves the home, the emotional habits built upon many years of living together must be broken and new ones established. For the child, this is not ordinarily so difficult, since new orientations based upon love contribute to the attrition of the old ties. For the parents, however, there are fewer positive substitutions. "The nest is empty, and the heart is lonely." This is probably more often the case with the mother than the father, since her interests have been home- and child-oriented to a greater extent.

---

[11] Some efforts to meet these needs are to be found in the small workshops being developed today in community centers.

[12] It is in this respect that *early* anticipation of the problems of later life is most valuable.

The married couple is challenged, then, to prepare to meet this problem. It is a preparation that must begin with the coming of the first child and continue until the last child has gone from the home. It requires a number of continuing recognitions: (1) that generations do grow apart in their thinking as a result of constant social change; (2) that children must go out from the home and build families of their own as part of the whole process of human growth; (3) that children must not be expected to regard their own parents as the major focal points of affection once they have established families of their own; and (4) that adequate relationships can be maintained between families of successive generations. It is unfortunate that the last of these is not always clearly recognized.[13] Under the pressures of modern living, many couples in their later years adopt an "all or nothing" policy in regard to their children's own families. Either they will have a major relationship—perhaps even involving living with the new family— or they will adopt a complete "hands off" policy. Neither is called for if both generations are emotionally mature. Parents can be helpful, and relationships can be continued to the benefit of both the old and the new families, but this involves viewing the whole life process in proper perspective. It requires the recognition that relationships do not *require* interference and that the new family can be freed from parental control without an accompanying "icy apartness." To secure such a balance requires effort, of course, and a constant recognition of the dignity and worth of all the individuals involved. It is one of the important problems faced by the young family, and one which is best understood from the very beginning.

The Problem of Accepting New Roles

The later years of married life require the abandoning of some of the earlier roles and the modification of others; they also permit the assumption of new roles, which can be equally satis-

[13] This may well be one of the basic elements in the in-law problems discussed in Chapter 15.

fying. One of the remarks often heard among women whose children are adolescent goes something like this: "I'll just have to get something to do now that my children are growing up and no longer need me." The mother who makes this type of remark often fails to see the contributions she can make to her children; but in the case of the older woman whose children have gone from home, such a remark may be entirely justified. To what, indeed, shall she turn? No longer does she function as the child bearer and child rearer; her talents as a homemaker are no longer as fully exploited. What new roles can she assume? If the husband and wife can think through the possibilities of new roles, their adjustment to "the empty life" can be as satisfying—if not more so, in some cases—as were their earlier relationships.

The grandparent role. One of the unique roles, not always fully appreciated—and certainly one not always properly exercised—is that of the grandparent. Too often the grandparent is merely a potential baby sitter, or perhaps the emergency helper "when the going gets tough." In contrast, the grandparent can have a unique place in the life of the young family. Lacking the need to be directive or a disciplinarian, he or she can very often provide a warmth of affection and companionship to the grandchild which may fill an important need in the lives of both. The circumscribed social life of the child can be expanded and deepened through his contacts (via the grandparents) with the broader world of both the past and the present. "What were things like in the old days?" is a question the older generation is uniquely equipped to answer. Lacking many of the economic and social pressures that confront the parent, grandparents may well become surrogates in fulfilling many of these ordinary needs of the third generation. In the writer's study of three-generation families,[14] all three generations expressed their satisfaction with the grandparent role thus understood. The older generation appreciated it because it gave them a sense of status, "wantedness," and satisfaction; the second generation because their own tasks as parents were thus

[14] To be reported in *The Changing Family: A Study of Three Generations.*

made easier and the child's needs better met; the younger generation because they felt a freedom and warmth of relationship which contributed much to their own development.

Such a contribution requires, of course, a mature personality, but given this (plus the recognition of the opportunities to be of use in this way) the grandparent role becomes a satisfying one. A grandmother expressed this satisfaction in these words.

> I dreaded the time when all of my children would be grown up and away from home. Actually, I found that I needn't have dreaded it at all. . . . I have a most wonderful time with my grandchildren; I tell them of all the things—well, not all—I experienced as a girl, and of the things their granddaddy and I did together. I tell them about things that happened to their own parents when they were small. . . . I don't have always to be being sure that they do things right; I think I can be more natural with them in some ways than my daughter and her husband can be. . . . I look forward to the times when I can be with them, and I'm sure they look forward to the times when I can be with them. . . . It's wonderful, being a grandmother, but I never realized until lately that I had a real place in their lives.

The companion role.   The emotionally mature person is the one who is adaptable and who continues to grow through his new contacts and experiences. The emotionally mature person, then, does not see life ending at forty, fifty, or sixty, but recognizes that while life will be different, it need not have ended except for the awaiting of death. Our culture affords us many stereotypes of the "folded-hands behavior" of the aging person. It is therefore assumed by many that "the nest will be empty"—which in itself is a forlorn and ghastly description—and that the purpose of life has ended. That such ideas are the product of a time when "work for the sake of work was holy," and when there were very few years of married life to look forward to after the child had gone from the home seems not to have been sufficiently recognized. Renewed companionship and the revitalizing of the interpersonal contacts which were characteristic of the courtship and adjustment stages (but which were de-emphasized during the years when the children had to be the *central* focus of life) are possible in the later years of married life to an extent never before envisaged. This is seen in the following quotations from an interview given to one of our research workers in a recent study.

> We [at fifty-six and fifty-four respectively] are just beginning to get to know each other. Papa has been so busy working and I've been so busy raising our three children—that was work, too—that we didn't know what we would find when [the children] were gone. . . . Well, it's wonderful! We just have the best time together. All the things we couldn't do together before we're beginning to do now. . . . We haven't very much money but his pension is steady and we know what we can count on, and we make the most of it. . . . We just feel as though we're really *knowing* each other all over again. He isn't such a bad fellow, after all—that's a joke, young lady! . . . We're even beginning to do other things, too. The children gave their papa a tool shop for Christmas, and he's making things for people's gardens. Finds he's quite a shop man, too, and has a wonderful time running his little business—he calls it. He always worked for somebody else before—now he's the boss himself.

This quotation, taken from the records of a study of small-town life,[15] illustrates the couple's rediscovery of each other in the companionship role; it also illustrates how individuals who approach realistically the possibilities of the later years of marriage may newly develop what Parsons has called the autonomous roles—those which the individual develops independently. "Papa," in this illustration, was becoming, in a very small way a businessman, and while his "business" was of no great importance financially, it afforded him psychological satisfaction and social contacts which were of genuine worth in giving meaning to the aging years. Wives, too, have opportunities for developing such autonomous roles. The older woman may work for the church and for community "causes" to an extent previously impossible because of her homemaking responsibilities.

[15] Cf. the writer's *The Health of Regionville*.

Successful Aging Requires New Expectations of Life

Inherent in the preceding discussion is the need of the couple to develop goals for the later years of married living. These are, in many instances, the postponements of earlier goals, and certainly need not be of great magnitude. As Lemkau has pointed out, "The nature of aging itself prepares the person to be satisfied with less variety than in the earlier, lustier years of life." The small goals that earlier had to be put aside can serve—but goals they must be. Young husbands and wives are often heard to say that "I wish I could do (so-and-so), but we have the children to take care of, and there isn't time or money." Such goals do have to be put aside because of parenthood, but the end of "active parenthood" is no longer identical with the end of active life. These necessarily postponed goals can become the foci of future goals toward which to move. It is the static couple who suffer from old age—not those who live toward something. If we are able to recognize the dynamic values of living toward something new—of striving to continue the growth processes in life—we can expect to achieve satisfactions in the later childless years.

Nor need these goals always be confined entirely within the old limits of family or personal experience. The most significant activities for any one person or couple may lie within fields that have not yet been encountered. An elderly man—a carpenter with limited social contacts—illustrated this in these words.

> They got me to go to the —— Settlement; said they wanted somebody who could show a bunch of boys how to use some carpenter tools. I didn't want to go, didn't know anything about settlements or boys' gangs, and didn't think I could do anything that would help them. . . . I sure got a surprise. I've had a wonderful time with those kids. They're making a lot of things for their homes, and we're really getting along good together. . . . I was about to fold up when they got me down there; now I think I'm good for another ten years. . . . My wife says I'm almost human to live with again.

The settlement worker, who was responsible for enlisting this man's help in their group work program, made this comment.

> It's almost unbelievable what finding a new interest, and one with which he was entirely unfamiliar, has done for Frank. When he came to us he was an old man; today [after three years as a volunteer] his step is firm; his eyes sparkle; he really has something for which he can live. His wife comes with him at various times, and she has told me that his finding new interests has done wonders for *both* their lives.

This is a homely example, but it illustrates the way in which the individual who will avail himself of the opportunity to go outside his own established patterns—who will seek new horizons, new activities—can better the later years of life and of family living.

We hardly need indicate the importance of mate selection in this connection. Successful adjustment in the later years of marriage demands exactly the same of the couple—maturity of personality, the compatibility of traits and interests, the identity of needs and expectations, and the intent to have marriage succeed—as does any other stage of marriage. The added importance here—if it can be so considered—lies in the fact that physical and social aging and the release from earlier familial responsibilities give the couple "unused time" and energies to be utilized.

SUMMARY

The fact that life expectancy has increased markedly in recent decades for Americans means that most young couples marrying today will live for many years after their children have grown and departed from the home. Preparation for that period of life and for the realization of its potentialities demands forethought and careful planning. It may mean planning for adequate retirement funds, where Social Security or other pension plans are inadequate, or for some other aspect of the couple's later life together. In any event, it means that viewing married life as a whole, rather than as a series of separate and unrelated steps, becomes essential in the couple's thinking and planning.

READINGS AND TOPICS FOR REPORTS

1. Interview a number of couples whose children have established homes of their own. What do they list as the most important problems they face as "elder citizens?"
2. Interview a number of social workers who deal with the problems of older people. What do they see as the major marital problems of this group? Then analyze the services offered to see if an effort is made to meet these problems?
3. Interview a number of widowed men and women who live apart from their children. What problems do they identify with having to end their lives in this fashion? Do these men and women see any way in which they could more adequately have prepared themselves for this period of life?

ADVANCED READINGS

Cavan, Ruth S., *et al.*, *Personal Adjustment in Old Age.*
Lawton, George, *Aging Successfully.*
——, *New Goals for Old Age.*
Stern, E., and M. Ross, *You and Your Aging Parents.*

21

In Summation

The preceding chapters have dealt with the many factors which affect mate selection and with the achieving of a basic adjustment in marriage. In conclusion, we may well summarize what we have indicated—by implication, at least—as being important. This summary can be offered in the form of seven postulates. They are not totally inclusive, nor are they totally exclusive, and involved in the recognition of the truth of each is a basic understanding of the marriage relationship. But whether inclusive or not, they constitute a "platform" for success in modern marriage—as this text perceives it.

Success in marriage in our present-day society is directly dependent upon the couple concerned. It is achieved not because marriage is socially prescribed or economically advantageous, but because a man and a woman choose to live their lives together, to share the successes and the hazards of human existence, and "to reap what they sow."

Success in marriage in our present-day society is dependent upon the couple's being conscious of what they have to offer, and what they need for personality fulfillment. The emerging nature of marriage as a personal relationship—with a vastly decreased emphasis upon its social and economic aspects—means that the couple will succeed only to the extent that they fulfill each other's needs for affection, security, and the sense of being a person of individual worth.

Success in marriage in our present-day society is directly dependent upon the couple's sharing aspirations and goals which are compatible with their abilities and the conditions under which they must live. What the couple has to give and needs to get in marriage is not divorcable from what the couple wants and will strive for. But not everything we hope for is attainable in a world such as ours, which leads to a fourth proposition.

Success in marriage in our present-day society demands an ability to face tragedy and failure. Tragedy is an inevitable accompaniment of living; "failure is the playmate of success." To expect that a marriage will involve neither tragedy nor failure is to expect the impossible. Only as the couple view these as part of the whole life process—as integral in marriage interaction—can success be hoped for. Such a view requires, however, a further postulate.

Success in marriage in our present-day society demands that the couple recognize their individual roles in the drama that is marriage, that they accept these, and that they recognize and accept the roles of the other. For it is only as they recognize their several contributions to the whole of the marriage that the couple can expect to have the marriage work.

Success in marriage in our present-day society demands further, that unity be consciously striven for. Unity, as someone has said, is not uniformity, and seeking the latter involves the abolishing of personal differences, personal worth, personal values. These, however, are basically part of personality, and it is for the achievement of personality that modern marriage is uniquely designed.

Finally, success in marriage in our present-day society requires arrival at decisions through collective concern. Only as each contributes his or her share in the decision-making process, to the extent that human personalities are nourished by such participation, can the couple expect to reach the goals which are inherent in modern marriage.

Difficult? Of course, but it is a truism that anything worth having is worth working for. Impossible of attainment? Hardly, for in the written records of our society only the failures achieve the headlines. It is easy to be impressed with the divorces of our day—for they fill the headlines. In contrast, the multitude of successful marriages—those which follow these postulates, whether consciously or not—do not even find mention in the fine print of our recorded civilization. But succeed they do—as their satisfying lives give mute testimony—and in their experience lies the promise for marriage today.

Bibliography

TEXTBOOK CORRELATED READINGS

In the following table are listed the chapters in current textbooks which appeal to the author of this textbook as the most suitable for complementary readings. These books are as follows:

Baber, Ray E., *Marriage and the Family*. New York: McGraw-Hill Book Co., Inc., 2d ed., 1953.

Becker, Howard, and Reuben Hill (eds.), *Family, Marriage and Parenthood*. Boston: D. C. Heath and Co., 2d ed., 1955.

Bowman, Henry A., *Marriage for Moderns*. New York: McGraw-Hill Book Co., Inc., 3d ed., 1954.

Peterson, James A., *Education for Marriage*. New York: Charles Scribner's Sons, 1956.

Waller, Willard (revised by Reuben Hill), *The Family: A Dynamic Interpretation*. New York: The Dryden Press, 1951.

Winch, Robert, *The Modern Family*. New York: Henry Holt & Co., Inc., 1952.

Chapter in this text	Baber	Becker and Hill	Bowman	Peterson	Waller	Winch
1	1, 2	1		1		
2	3					
3		14				
4		6		2, 3, 4	3, 4, 5	8, 9, 10
5		8	7, 8	6, 7	11	15
6		7		5	9	16
7	4, 5				7	12, 16
8	4, 5	9		10	12	16
9			9			
10	6, 7		10, 11	12, 13	10	
11		12		20	14, 15	
12		10	14, 15	15, 16		
13	12	13	13	18		
14	20			17		
15						
16	8, 9	16		14	18, 19, 20	7
17						
18		24		9		
19	13, 14	23	16		23, 24	
20						
21						

SUPPLEMENTARY READINGS

It is impracticable to attempt a complete bibliography of all pertinent books and articles on marriage. The following are considered to be most suitable for use with this text. Since in each case more than one passage or chapter in a book may deal with a given topic, annotations or specific passages are not given. The student should be encouraged to be selective in his reading in these works.

Anderson, J. E., *The Psychology of Development and Personal Adjustment.* New York: Henry Holt and Co., 1949.

Anshen, Ruth, *The Family, Its Function and Destiny.* New York: Harper and Brothers, 1949.

Bergler, Edmund, *Divorce Won't Help.* New York: Harper and Brothers, 1948.

———, *Unhappy Marriage and Divorce.* New York: International Universities Press, 1946.

Blood, Robert O., "Consequences of Permissiveness for Parents of Young Children." *Marriage and Family Living,* 15: 209 ff. (1953).

———, "A Retest of Waller's Rating Complex." *Marriage and Family Living.* 17: 41 ff. (1955).

Bossard, James H. S., *Parent and Child.* Philadelphia: University of Pennsylvania Press, 1953.

———, and Eleanor S. Bol, *Ritual in Family Living.* Philadelphia: University of Pennsylvania Press, 1950.

Burgess, E. W., and Leonard S. Cottrell, *Predicting Success or Failure in Marriage.* New York: Prentice-Hall, Inc., 1939.

———, and Harvey J. Locke, *The Family,* 2d ed. New York: American Book Co., 1953.

———, and Paul Wallin, *Engagement and Marriage.* Philadelphia: J. B. Lippincott Co., 1953.

Carroll, Herbert, *Mental Hygiene, The Dynamics of Adjustment,* 2nd. ed., New York: Prentice-Hall, Inc., 1953.

Cavan, Ruth, *The American Family,* New York: Thomas Y. Crowell Co., 1953.

Christensen, Harold T., *Marriage Analysis.* New York: The Ronald Press Co., 1950.

Cuber, John F., "Changing Courtship Customs," *The Annals of the American Academy of Political and Social Science.* 229: 31 ff. (1943).

Cyrus, D., "What's Wrong with the Family." *Atlantic Monthly.* 178: 67 ff. (1946).

Dickinson, R. L., *Technique of Conception Control.* Baltimore: The Williams and Wilkins Co., 1950.

Dreikurs, Rudolph, *The Challenge of Marriage.* New York: Duell, Sloane and Pearce, 1946.

Drucher, A. J., *et al.* "Some Background Factors in Socio-Sexual Modernism," *Marriage and Family Living,* 14: 334 ff. (1952).

Duvall, Evelyn M., *Inlaws: Pro and Con.* New York: Association Press, 1954.

Elder, Rachel Ann, "Traditional and Developmental Conceptions of Fatherhood." *Marriage and Family Living,* 11: 98 ff. (1949).

Ernst, Morris L. and David Loth, *For Better or Worse.* New York: Harper and Brothers, 1951.

Fishbein, Morris and E. W. Burgess (eds). *Successful Marriage.* New York: Doubleday and Co., 1955.

Foote, Nelson, "Love", *Psychiatry.* 16: 245 ff. (1953).

Fromme, Allan, *The Psychologist Looks at Sex and Marriage.* New York: Prentice-Hall, Inc., 1950.

Glicke, Paul C., "The Life Cycle of the Family," *Marriage and Family Living.* 17: 3 ff. (1955).

Goodrich, F. W., *Natural Childbirth.* New York: Prentice-Hall, Inc., 1950.

Guttmacher, Alan, *The Story of Human Birth.* New York: Pelican Press, 1947.

Hill, Reuben, *Families Under Stress.* New York: Harper and Brothers, 1949.

Hollingshead, August B., "Cultural Factors in Selection of Marriage Mates," *American Sociological Review,* 15: 619 ff. (1950).

————, "Marital Status and Wedding Behavior," *Marriage and Family Living.* 14: 308 ff. (1952).

Jacobson, A. H., "Conflict of Attitudes Toward Marital Roles," *American Sociological Review,* 17: 146 ff. (1952).

Kane, John J., *Marriage and the Family: A Catholic Approach.* New York: The Dryden Press, Inc., 1952.

Kolb, William L., "Family Sociology, Marriage Education, and the Romantic Complex," *Social Forces,* 29: 65 ff. (1950).

Komarovsky, Mirra, *The Unemployed Man and His Family.* New York: The Dryden Press, Inc., 1939.

————, "Functional Analysis of Sex Roles," *American Sociological Review,* 15: 508 ff. (1950).

Landis, Judson and Mary G. Landis, *Building a Successful Marriage*. New York: Prentice-Hall, Inc., 1953.

Landis, Paul, *Making the Most of Marriage*. New York: Appleton-Century-Crofts, Inc., 1955.

Levy, David M., *Maternal Overprotection*. New York: Columbia University Press, 1943.

Levy, John, and Ruth Monroe, *The Happy Family*. New York: Alfred A. Knopf, Inc., 1938.

Locke, Harvey J., *Predicting Adjustment in Marriage*. New York: Henry Holt and Co., 1951.

Mead, Margaret, *Male and Female*. New York: William Morrow and Co., 1949.

Mudd, Emily H., *The Practice of Marriage Counseling*. New York: Association Press, 1951.

Nye, Ivan, "Adolescent-Parent Adjustment," *Marriage and Family Living*. 14: 327 ff. (1952).

Pilpel, Harriet, and Theodore Zavin, *Your Marriage and the Law*. New York: Rinehart and Co., 1952.

Read, Grantley, *Childbirth Without Fear*. New York: Harper and Brothers, 1944.

Ribble, Margaret, *The Rights of Infants*. New York: Columbia University Press, 1943.

Scheinfeld, Amram, *Women and Men*, New York: Harcourt, Brace and Co., 1944.

———, *The New You and Heredity*. Philadelphia: J. B. Lippincott Co., 1950.

Stone, Abraham and Hannah M. Stone, *A Marriage Manual*. New York: Simon and Schuster, 1952.

Terman, Lewis M., *Psychological Factors in Marital Happiness*. New York: McGraw-Hill Book Co., Inc., 1938.

Thomas, John L., "The Factor of Religion in the Selection of Marriage Mates," *American Sociological Review*, 15: 487 ff. (1951).

Truxall, Andrew G. and Frances E. Merrill, *The Family in American Culture*. New York: Prentice-Hall, Inc., 1947.

Weiman, Regina, *The Family Lives Its Religion*. New York: Harper and Brothers, 1941.

Winch, Robert and Robert McGinnis, *Selected Studies in Marriage and the Family*, New York: Henry Holt and Co., 1953.

Motion Picture Films

This list includes only the films which appear to the author best to meet the needs of a course using this textbook. Many other films are available, and are listed in the *Educational Film Guide* (H. W. Wilson Co., New York). A directory of film libraries which lend or rent these films, *Directory of 2002 16 mm. Film Libraries*, is available from the Superintendent of Documents, Government Printing Office, Washington 25, D. C.

HEREDITY AND PRENATAL DEVELOPMENT (McGraw-Hill). The role of the chromosomes in determining human characteristics; prenatal development. Chapters 3, 12 (20 minutes).

OVER-DEPENDENCY (McGraw-Hill). A portrayal of how overdependency can affect a marriage, and of the steps needed in overcoming its effects. Chapter 4. (32 minutes). (Other suitable films in the same series are FEELING OF HOSTILITY (26 minutes) and FEELING OF REJECTION (23 minutes).)

WHO'S RIGHT (McGraw-Hill). The importance of psychological characteristics in achieving success in marriage. Chapter 4 (17 minutes).

CHOOSING FOR HAPPINESS (McGraw-Hill). The importance of understanding the needs of human personalities in choosing a mate. Chapters 5, 6, 7 (15 minutes).

IT TAKES ALL KINDS (McGraw-Hill). The importance of complementary personality characteristics in choosing a mate. Chapters 5, 6, 7 (20 minutes).

THE MEANING OF THE ENGAGEMENT (Coronet). The importance of the engagement period in readying the couple for marriage. Chapters 7, 8 (13 minutes).

A FAMILY AFFAIR (New York University). The importance of roles in determining family behavior. Chapter 10 (20 minutes).

JEALOUSY (McGraw-Hill). Some of the ways in which failure to adapt to the roles in marriage can affect the relationship. Chapters 10, 11 (14 minutes).

THE FAMILY (United World Films). The importance of role recognition and understanding in contributing to marital interaction. Chapters 10, 11 (20 minutes).

IN TIME OF TROUBLE (McGraw-Hill). The use of a marriage counselor in meeting a marital problem. Shows how a husband reacts, by increased drinking, to his wife's domination in the marriage. Chapter 11 (15 minutes).

336

THIS CHARMING COUPLE (McGraw-Hill). Some sources of difficulty in achieving marital happiness. Chapter 11 (19 minutes).

CHILDBIRTH (Medical Films). An unemotional portrayal of the physical aspects of the birth process. Chapter 12 (15 minutes).

HUMAN REPRODUCTION (McGraw-Hill). A review of human reproduction anatomy and physiology. Chapter 12 (20 minutes).

YOUR FAMILY BUDGET (Coronet). The importance of planned spending for the family. Chapter 13 (10 minutes).

WOMAN AGAINST WOMAN (New York University). A portrayal of the problems which confront those who must adjust after divorce. Chapter 19 (20 minutes).

THE STEPS OF AGE (International Film Bureau). A portrayal of important problems in the life of a couple who did not prepare for the later years of married life. Chapter 20 (23 minutes).

SOURCES OF FILMS

Coronet Instructional Films
65 East Water Street, Chicago, Illinois

International Film Bureau
6 North Michigan Avenue, Chicago, Illinois

McGraw-Hill Book Co., Inc., Text-Film Department
330 West 42nd Street, New York, New York

Medical Films, Inc.
116 Natona Street, San Francisco, California

New York University Film Library
26 Washington Square, New York, New York

United World Films, Inc.
1445 Park Avenue, New York, New York

Index of Names

Index of Subjects